The Abingdon Guide to Funding Ministry

An Innovative Sourcebook for Church Leaders

Volume 3

EDITORS

Donald W. Joiner
Norma Wimberly

ABINGDON PRESS
NASHVILLE

THE ABINGDON GUIDE TO FUNDING MINISTRY:
AN INNOVATIVE SOURCEBOOK FOR CHURCH LEADERS
VOLUME 3

Copyright © 1997 by Abingdon Press

ISBN 0-687-05718-3
ISSN 0181-4957

The "Pontius' Puddle" cartoons are by Joel Kauffmann

Cartoons by Joseph Brown appear on pages 127, 132, 142, 146, and 156

This book is printed on recycled, acid-free paper.

Unless otherwise noted, Scripture quotations are from the New Revised Standard Version Bible, Copyright 1989 by the Division of Christian Education of the National Council of the Churches of Christ in the USA. Used by permission.

Those noted NKJ are from the New King James Version. Copyright © 1979, 1980, 1982, Thomas Nelson Inc., Publishers. Used by permission.

Those noted NIV are from the *Holy Bible, New International Version,* Copyright © 1973, 1978, 1984 International Bible Society. Used by permission of Zondervan Publishing House. All rights reserved.

Those noted RSV are from the Revised Standard Version of the Bible, copyright 1946, 1952, 1971 by the Division of Christian Education of the National Council of the Churches of Christ in the USA. Used by permission.

Those noted KJV are from the King James Version of the Bible.

97 98 99 00 01 02 03 04 05 06—10 9 8 7 6 5 4 3 2 1

MANUFACTURED IN THE UNITED STATES OF AMERICA

 Book Review

 Budget tool

 Bulletin

 Calendar

 Checklist

 Commitment Campaign

 Devotional

 Drama

 Handout

 Meditation

 Money Talk

 Newsletter

 Planned Giving

 Planning Tool

 Sermon Help

 Small Group Study

 Tax Clinic

 Teaching Help

 Legal Clinic

CONTENTS

INTRODUCTION

You're standin' there on the corner
With your Bible and pamphlets in hand;
Ever since you've been saved from the darkness,
You want to share the Word all you can.
But it's good to see what you're doin'
As that hungry man passes you by;
You lay everything down, run to catch him,
And give him your sack lunch with love in your eyes.

Chorus:
Oh, Believers, so many souls have been hurt;
And it's always well to remember
Actions speak louder than words.
So, take all the light you've been given,
Let it shine for the whole world to see,
'Cause you might be the only gospel
Somebody ever will read,
The only gospel somebody will read.

Volume 3 of THE ABINGDON GUIDE TO FUNDING MINISTRY focuses on proclaiming the joy of giving. In Volumes I and II, the focus was "developing a perspective on giving," and "teaching the joy of giving," respectively. If you are already familiar with the previous volumes, the concepts of proclaiming, preaching, and/or witnessing are a fairly logical step into action. For new readers, you are invited to examine your current attitudes, motives, and actions related to giving. Your lives already proclaim your relationships with God and giving! What are you expressing? All individuals and congregations are urged to start right where you are. Join Don and me as we continue to explore our hearts, minds, actions, and spirits in the area of personal and congregational witness.

Several years ago, "Miss Margaret," a friend whom my husband and I treasure, declared that, "You may be the only [Bible] somebody will ever read." For me, as a stewardship consultant, and for my husband, a songwriter and pastor, those words were a call to yet another examination of who we say we are, to whom we say we belong, and of what we actually do each moment of our lives. Lee (my husband) was able to embody Miss Margaret's directive in song. I have used her ideas as a personal inventory of my plans and actions—often to my great sadness and chagrin.

Words are often necessary for full communication. Proclaiming. Preaching. Witnessing. We assume the verbal. Miss Margaret begs us to remember the action. As parents, teachers, preachers, leaders, we accept the axiom that "actions speak louder than words." However, do we honestly assess our words and our actions, believing that we may be "the only gospel somebody will read"?

* When we "proclaim," are we willing to proclaim publicly?
* When we "preach," do we advocate earnestly? Do we urge others to hear, believe, and act?
* When we "witness," can we honestly attest to our personal experiences? Do we furnish "proof" of the glory of God, of the joy of giving?

Few of us will argue the existence of modern taboos surrounding "money talk." Salaries, the prices of houses, clothes, gadgets and cars, investments, and charitable giving rarely dominate conversations with friends (unless we know we can brag!). It is indeed the exception when a group of church members or leaders openly struggle

> "The heart that gives gathers."

with the faith-filled issue of proclaiming the gospel of generosity! To this date, I have yet to see a calendar, personal or congregational, that reflects reckless, risky, intentional witnessing. Yet, many of us realize that our checkbooks and our calendars are a fair reflection of who we are and where our loyalties lie.

Do we manifest "an inward and spiritual grace" in what we say and do? Are we "doers of the word," not just hearers and possibly sayers?

> Oh, there are so many people among us
> Who walk through this life all alone,
> Who never experience kindness
> From someone else on their way home.
> You'll recall after all, it is written,
> "Show His love in all that you do."
> Who knows, somebody may come to the light
> All because of what they see in you.

Chorus:
> Oh, Believers, so many souls have been hurt,
> And it's always well to remember
> Actions speak louder than words.
> So, take all the light you've been given,
> Let it shine for the whole world to see,
> 'Cause you might be the only gospel
> Somebody ever will read,
> The only gospel somebody will read.

"The Only Gospel Somebody Will Read," written by Lee Domann. Used by permission, Careers-BMG Music Publishing, Inc. (Gospel Division) (BMI)

A Vision

Our vision of funding ministry is like a painting that appears blurry from a distance, but assumes clarity as we approach it step by step. Our vision is that pastors and church leaders will begin, or continue to develop, a perspective on giving, that they will teach giving consistently and effectively, and will proclaim the joy of giving.

"When it comes to giving, some stop at nothing."

To achieve that vision, to step ever closer to the picture, we present this "almanac for good stewards," with stories of giving and suggestions, sermons, tips, tools, worksheets, and much more for developing generous disciples. The aim in this volume of *The Abingdon Guide to Funding Ministry* is to provide a resource to encourage pastors and leaders to examine and cultivate our willingness to proclaim the joy of giving.

This publication on finance is informational and motivational. We want it to help leaders look not only at themselves, but beyond current programs, for tangible results.

We assume a diverse readership, and we know that reliable and faithful Christians disagree about money as often as they do about doctrine. Some of you have significant experience in financial stewardship and are hungry for new ideas. Others have little or no history of exploration in this discipline, and we hope to delight you with usable tools and practical suggestions. As we assemble the parts of this "almanac," we imagine a diversity of age, denomination, theology, geography, church size, and "comfort zone" with the topic.

We believe that growth in giving is an ongoing, lifelong process. The *Guide* is compiled to suggest, as well as to direct each of us to the next steps of the journey. The next step may be clear for some of you. For others, it may include a question, a doubt, more searching. In some instances, the next step may offer a choice. What is God leading you to do?

How This Guide Will Help You

1. It will reveal ways to motivate people to give more generously.
2. It will offer tips for eliminating waste.
3. It will broaden your perspective on fund development possibilities.
4. It will provide the latest information on legal challenges.
5. It will suggest ways to attain better accountability. And much more . . .

In Volume 3, we are concentrating on "proclaiming the joy of giving." (Volume 1 focused on developing a perspective on giving. Volume 2 had as its theme "teaching the joy of generosity.")

A COVENANT WITH THE READERS

We hope to help people look at the critical issues of their relationship with God, their relationship with money, and find faithful ways to practice generosity and healthy church finance. We believe that developing Christian givers is a process, rather than a quick-fix program, that it takes daily practice and is a journey, rather than a destination.

Donald W. Joiner is a director of local church funding for the General Board of Discipleship of The United Methodist Church. He also directs the Planned Giving Resource Center for that agency. He is an ordained clergyman from the Detroit Conference of The United Methodist Church.

Norma Wimberly is a stewardship teacher, writer, and editor. She has served on the stewardship staff of the General Board of Discipleship of The United Methodist Church and as Executive Director of the United Methodist Foundation of the Nashville (Tennessee) Area. Ms. Wimberly and her husband, the Reverend Lee Domann, own The East Row Group, based in Nashville, Tennessee.

The Abingdon Guide to Funding Ministry is committed to:

1. Open dialogue with you. Each of us is a learner and a teacher. We will listen. We will impart. We desire to be co-searchers.

   What are some of your questions, concerns, insights?

   What topics would you like to have addressed?

   What experience, strength, and hope can we share?

2. Providing a leading edge of direction and information on church finance in North America.

3. Being inclusive—theologically and denominationally.

4. Being accessible. We want to hear from you.

> Norma Wimberly
> Donald W. Joiner
> *Abingdon Guide to Funding Ministry*
> c/o Abingdon Press
> P.O. Box 801
> 201 Eighth Avenue South
> Nashville TN 37202-0801

PART ONE

HELPING CHURCH LEADERS TALK ABOUT MONEY

Introduction

NORMA WIMBERLY

One of life's longest journeys is the one from the head to the heart. When I began my time in stewardship ministry, I acquired a great deal of head knowledge about this faith discipline. Soon, I was quite comfortable creating stewardship education resources and leading workshops on "holistic stewardship." Those who knew me well heard my repeated declaration that "stewardship is more than just money." Financial issues could be dealt with easily if people simply understood that all of life is stewardship. The one issue I refused to address was my heart—my deep discomfort with any conversation about money.

As grace would have it, I underwent a conversion: I saw my fears, named them, put them in God's hands, and KNEW that my lack of trust in money matters was a lack of trust in God. I still confront this struggle, less painfully and not quite as often. However, the "incongruity between our thoughts and our actions" continues to haunt us and our congregations.

The phrase in the preceding sentence was gleaned from Tim Ek's article, "Stewardship and Spiritual Health." All of us can benefit from Tim's reminders and insights. Also in this section of THE GUIDE, Bishop Edsel Ammons illuminates many of our faith gaps in "Stewardship as Discipleship." He believes that any statement about stewardship is "a statement about God." Do we witness, preach, proclaim—or do we apologize?

Robert Hempfling's story of "The Knight of the Empty Bucket" has often served as a map between my head and my heart. Brian Bauknight brings his unique, lighthearted approach to talking about money in the lead article in Part One.

Bible study, word study, small group discussion, reading, reflection, and prayer—let us be willing to use all of the tools that can help us talk about money, talk about God.

 **MONEY TALK**

Knowing What's Good for You

BRIAN K. BAUKNIGHT

A large company in the southwest employed several thousand people. The management attempted to put into place a new pension plan. But the plan could not take effect unless the company guaranteed 100 percent participation of employees.

One man refused to go along. Everyone else thought the plan was wonderful. Important benefits were covered. It was exactly what they needed. Nevertheless, this one man refused to budge. He dug in his heels and refused to sign up.

Finally, the president of the company called the man into his office. "Look! Here is a copy of the pension plan and here is a pen. Now sign it right now or you are fired!"

The man picked up the pen and signed. The president was dumbfounded. "I don't understand this," he said. "You have been so outspoken in your opposition to the plan. Why did you refuse to sign until now?"

"It's very simple, sir," came the reply. "You're the first person to explain it so clearly."

Jesus explained some things very clearly. For example, he was very clear about money and posses-

15

sions. In a variety of ways, he indicated that money was to be used wisely and faithfully, or it could destroy us.

That message is the essence of quoted words of Jesus in Acts 20:35: "For he himself said, 'It is more blessed to give than to receive.'" These words were apparently remembered from the sayings of Jesus. Here, Paul incorporated them into a sermon to the leaders of the Ephesian church. The overall message of Paul covers several topics. The final closure of the message comes with the words of Jesus, "It is more blessed to give than to receive."

Such wisdom must have been especially important for the leadership of the early church in Ephesus. Note that Paul was addressing leaders here, not the mainstream population. The words are also highly relevant to us.

The Secular Word for Our Time

The secular word for our time is loud and clear: Collect! Accumulate! Build a good stockpile of possessions! Perhaps you have seen the bumper sticker that illuminates this message: "He who dies with the most toys wins." Someone gave me a variation on that sticker: "He who dies with the most toys still dies!"

Possessions themselves are not evil. But they can be terribly distracting.

The pressure is on: accumulate enough! Accumulate enough to make life secure. Accumulate enough so that retirement will be comfortable. Accumulate enough so you can leave a nice inheritance for your children. Accumulate enough to assure a hedge against rampant inflation. Accumulate enough to allow travel at least twice each year.

Jesus' words cut through it all: "It is better to give than to receive."

The pressure is on: Maintain your preoccupation with capital gains. Make sure you are seeing good profit margins in your investments. Note that neither capital gains nor profit margins are wrong. Only the preoccupation is wrong!

Finally, the pressure is on for the worst trend of all—to succumb to the lure of chance. Gambling fever grips this nation. Everything from the hysterical hype

of the Publisher's Clearing House to front-page, prime-time publicity. State-sponsored gambling has become a national pastime.

Jesus says, "It is better to give than to receive." Some simple, basic truths reside in these words.

Giving Is a Way of Life

Giving is the way of life intended by God. We have strong witness to the fact that giving is essential to the very nature of God.

Someone recently reminded me of an irony in the parable of the prodigal son (Luke 15:11-32). Recall the outline of the story. The younger of two sons requests his inheritance from his father. The father agrees—a notion itself that must have shocked the hearers of Jesus' story. The son leaves home and squanders his money. He lives luxuriously and lavishly until the money is exhausted. In poverty, he tends some pigs for a while—the ultimate degradation for a Jewish man. Finally he "comes to his senses" and realizes that even as a hired hand in his father's house, he will be better off.

He returns home with a prepared speech for his father. But his father sees him coming. The father runs to meet him, embraces him, puts the family ring back on his finger, and shoes on his feet. The father then kills the fatted calf in honor of the son's return.

The son in that story is called "prodigal." The word means "recklessly extravagant." However, is this not also the case of the "prodigal" father? Is not the father recklessly extravagant as well?

And is this not the true nature of God?

We are created in the "image of God" (Gen. 1:27), which means that a life most fully lived is a life lived for giving!

I recently came across this quotation:

> In our culture, it is clear that we most often *deny* our money. . . . Dealing with money is basically a *spiritual* challenge requiring the miracle action and gift of God's love to bring about necessary changes.
> —JOHN HAUGHEY, SJ

Giving to live is, in fact, the only way to live fully. When each of us shares what has been given to us, we gain a new life. If each of us hangs on to what we have, it will never be enough.[1]

I once watched an NBA playoff game between the Orlando Magic and the Boston Celtics. I was particularly intrigued to watch the Magic's bright young star, Shaquille O'Neal. His talent is breathtaking. O'Neal then was 23 years old, just five years out of high school. Yet by age 25, he would receive nearly $25 million in various forms of compensation.

More important, O'Neal has the rapt attention of a whole generation of kids. He has a strong influence upon their development. Thus far, most of that influence is for good. O'Neal does not drink alcoholic beverages. He purchases twenty tickets for underprivileged kids for each Orlando Magic home game. He volunteers at homeless shelters in the Orlando area. And he helps feed hungry kids at Thanksgiving and Christmas.

He must face enormous temptations daily. If he could exercise and model a life of giving, he could have a global impact upon thousands, even millions.[2]

Stewardship and Spiritual Health

A recent, rather cynical editorial defined prosperity as "buying things we do not want with money we do not have to impress people we do not like." While no one takes such definitions too seriously, there is enough truth in the statement to deserve attention. Sadly, we have all felt tempted to live this principle out in areas of our lives. We can all remember times when we invested our valuable resources in the wrong thing, for the wrong reasons. If the church hopes to make a difference in the lives of its people, this incongruity between our beliefs and our actions must be addressed.

Giving in All Situations

Every situation can turn our thoughts toward giving. That is what Jesus is saying in our text.

When the downtown office building in Oklahoma City was bombed, giving began to pour in—sometimes more than the Red Cross knew how to use. But giving was an appropriate response.

In April of 1995, I attended the 50th anniversary Holocaust Observance—a moving and memorable service of worship. That night we remembered a small group of Huguenot Protestant Christians in southern France who sheltered some Jewish families from the Nazi search parties. Their efforts were described by one survivor as a "conspiracy of goodness and giving."

Life is meant to be a conspiracy of goodness and giving.

Even in prison camps like Auschwitz, giving was expressed. Menachem Rosensaft, director of the Holocaust Museum in Washington, said recently, "God was with the prisoners. God was in their compassion for one another. God was in the jokes they told, in the songs they sang to relieve the misery of a fellow human being."

It is far better, nobler, deeply fulfilling to give than to receive.

Giving is even exhibited in the gambling Mecca of our own country. A new Roman Catholic Church has been built right on the Las Vegas strip. Worshipers are encouraged to put winning gambling chips in the offering, if they so choose. Once in a while, they even get a $500 chip.

One of the priests of that parish then dons street clothes and goes to the casinos. There he cashes in the chips for the church's use. His colleagues in ministry have cleverly dubbed him the Chip Monk.

You have undoubtedly heard or read of the slogan making the rounds of this nation: "Practice random acts of kindness and senseless acts of beauty." A colleague of mine recently celebrated "Random Acts of Kindness Week" among the staff of his church.

He writes, "On two different occasions, I received a card—one on Valentine's Day, and the other on my birthday. Both were signed: 'RAK Warrior.' I cannot begin to tell you what an impact that made on me."[3]

We need to grow "RAK Warriors" in every household, every congregation, every community. It is the Christian way of life.

Giving is a lifestyle for all situations. We give because it is the only thing to do.

In every offering, at every giving opportunity, in every need situation, in every special circumstances, Jesus reminds us: It is *always* better to give than to receive!

One Special Note

It is important to note that Paul is not preaching for a particular financial offering in this text. Jesus is not talking about the Sunday offering here. He is talking about a lifestyle, about the essence of being, about a way of living. *Jesus is talking about knowing what's good for you!*

A few days ago I received a solicitation letter and a return envelope from the local hospice. I was moved by the inscription on the outside of the offering envelope: "A celebration of life to the very last moment."

I thought to myself, the true celebration of life is a life of giving to the very last moment! What a way to live! Even, what a way to die!

It is so much better to give than to receive.

NOTES:

1. Douglas M. Lawson, *The Abingdon Guide to Funding Ministry,* Vol. 1, p. 11.
2. Some of these details are from SpiritVenture Ministries, Inc., *Sweet's Soul Cafe,* April 1995, p. 7.
3. From Rodney Wilmoth, senior minister at Hennepen Avenue United Methodist Church, Minneapolis, Minn., a sermon preached on February 19, 1995; "RAK" stands for Random Acts of Kindness.

 MONEY TALK

Stewardship and Spiritual Health

TIMOTHY C. EK

A recent rather cynical editorial defined prosperity as "buying things we do not want with money we do not have to impress people we do not like." While no one takes such definitions too seriously, there is enough truth in the statement to deserve attention. Sadly, all of us have felt tempted to live this principle out in areas of our lives. We can all remember times when we invested our valuable resources in the wrong things, for the wrong reasons. If the church hopes to make a difference in the lives of its people, this incongruity between our beliefs and our actions must be addressed.

Lack of resources in general, and lack of money in specific, are not so much financial issues as spiritual issues for the church of Jesus Christ. Jesus emphasized that there is an important relationship between being a disciple and living with integrity. He repeatedly warned that unless a Christian is careful, it is easy to be absorbed in the material blessings of life. They can crowd out the central place of lordship that Jesus desires in our lives. The spiritual health of disciples requires proper training and perspective, to equip them to live their lives with integrity and priority.

Here are five statements that help to clarify the relationship between stewardship and spiritual health:

1. Our money does not necessarily make us happy or healthy.

A study in *Christianity Today* indicated that conflict surrounding money or sex accounts for 99 percent of the crimes committed in the United States. This study further disclosed that crimes involving money outnumber sexual offenses 4 to 1! In another study, psychiatrist Aaron Beck conducted a ten-year evaluation of patients hospitalized with suicidal intentions. They discovered that handling the pressures of large financial resources was one of the fifteen major risk factors contributing to a suicidal frame of mind. Their assessment was that the risk of suicide increases with the amount of financial resources. Even though we live in one of the wealthiest countries in the world, money is not necessarily making us happier or healthier.

2. Jesus recognized that giving is a barometer of our spiritual health.

Money is a very central issue in our society. Richard Halvorson has said, "Money is an exact index to a man's true character." Jesus noted that evidence of Zacchaeus' salvation came as he made a decision to return a significant portion of his wealth to the people from whom he had stolen it. In his conversation with the rich young ruler, Jesus challenged him to sell all he had and give to the poor—resulting in the young ruler leaving Jesus and continuing his life as it had been. He was too attached to his attachments. One proof of real spiritual change is an altered perspective on the way we handle money and possessions.

The discipline of giving becomes a measure of faithfulness—or, as John Westerhoff has noted, "What we give of our money is the closest sign of what we give of our lives."

3. The church must teach about giving because it is linked to our growth as Christ's disciples.

Martin Luther once remarked that people need three conversions: conversion of their hearts, their minds, and their pocketbooks. He also indicated that the church can preach the gospel of Jesus Christ, but if it does not affect the areas in which humankind struggles most, the gospel has not really been preached.

In Ephesians 4:11-14, Paul describes the purpose of the church. He reminds his readers that God has placed individuals with different gifts in the church to work together, preparing and equipping God's people for the work of ministry. In that way, the Body of Christ may be built up and experience "unity of the faith and of the knowledge of the Son of God and become mature, attaining to the measure of the full stature of Christ." Dealing with issues related to the pocketbook is essential if the church is to equip contemporary disciples for the work of ministry in our kind of world.

The church is the only organization in the world that exists for the sake of people who are not yet members of it! It consists of people God has called out of the world to equip, then send into the world to carry on the ministry that Jesus started when he was here in the flesh. The church is to equip the disciple to grow and become a whole-life steward.

4. The church must recognize that a life of stewardship is both taught and caught.

There is much evidence that right thinking does not necessarily produce right living. All too often, we observe Christians whose walk does not match their talk. How can the church be more effective in helping Christian disciples integrate their beliefs and actions—particularly in this critical area of stewardship?

Jesus was the world's most effective disciple-maker. How did he respond to this challenge? For three years, he invested most of his time in the lives of twelve men. The disciples had the opportunity to hear Jesus teach and engage in dialogue as they walked from place to place. They also saw Jesus lay

> ## "What fills the heart overflows the mouth."
> *—MARTIN LUTHER*
> *(1483–1546)*

hands on people and minister directly. They had the opportunity to witness how the truths he taught were being applied in real-life situations. This is the model the church must study with regard to disciple-making and whole-life steward building.

Leaders must recognize the importance of role models in teaching by example. Pastors and lay leaders are key models for the church family. Strong sermons need to be backed by the message being incarnated in the life and work of the minister. Today, we find that short-term mission trips are increasingly popular for Christian groups. The effect of these trips is often life-changing for those who participate, because they become engaged in fulfilling Christ's mission. Christ's mission becomes more than just talk. Hearts are touched and captured as people see needs firsthand and recognize that God has given them resources that can make a difference.

While sermons can and should be an important ingredient in teaching stewardship in the church, this teaching must be followed up by "hands-on" help that will enable families to learn how to budget, how to tithe, and how to see stewardship as more than just an appeal for funds. We need methods whereby new life in Christ—the life of whole-life stewardship—can be taught and caught!

5. Understanding and practicing biblical stewardship leads to spiritual wholeness and links us with God's mission.

A healthy church produces healthy people. Health obviously involves more than the absence of disease. Real health involves the growing realization that we are people of worth, with God-given gifts that can contribute to the betterment of the world and the building of Christ's kingdom.

A healthy church enables individuals to know they are eternally loved by the God of the universe—that he has made them in his image so that they also can give the gift of love. God created us in such a way that our need to love can be most fully satisfied as we love; that our need to feel worthwhile can best be satisfied when we live as persons of worth, making contributions that are consistent with God's purpose for our lives.

Such a whole-life response does not happen overnight. It takes time and God's touch to create a community of Christians who recognize their purpose—their calling—as whole-life stewards.

Throughout the centuries, God's people have been called out of the world to be changed and challenged to godly living. Christian disciples are then deployed back into the world to participate in God's mission as his agents of change—to demonstrate to a watching world the spiritual health of whole-life stewardship.

 MONEY TALK

Stewardship As Discipleship

BISHOP EDSEL A. AMMONS

I never fail to be impressed by what may appear to be Saint Paul's ambivalence concerning human wisdom. In one instance, he seems to chide the young Christians for their infatuation with Greek sophistication: "For since, in the wisdom of God, the world did not know God through wisdom, God decided, through the foolishness of our proclamation, to save those who believe" (I Cor. 1:21). At the same time, he implies the urgent need for understanding and intuition that is born not of human initiative but endowed by the Spirit, which alone enables discernment of spiritual things. Again and again he admonishes the church to claim for itself the "mind of Christ." What may on first glance seem to be ambivalence is not ambivalence at all. It is Paul's way of declaring the essential truth that the church's perspective, or view of things, is markedly different from that of the non-Christian secularist. Paul's Christianity breaks the boundaries of human comprehension, however extraordinary, and sees the world in the light of truth that is of the nature of the Holy.

The difference is one of perspective—how life is viewed. For Paul, it makes all the difference in the world, the difference not just between Apollos and Paul but, in our day, between life and nuclear death, between dangerous conformity and the new attitudes and values that are demanded by a sane society and a sustainable future. What Paul keeps inferring is the need for a transformation of perspective, a "renewal of mind" (Rom. 12:2). The reference is not to the intellect, as some separate faculty, but to the whole self in its knowing and perceiving. Implied is the need to see things in a world that is not in conformity with previous perception. A new perception, in Paul's view,

affects the whole self: One becomes a different person with a transformed outlook on life.

We really cannot talk about Christian stewardship to any meaningful extent without talking about perspective. Indeed, we have tried to do just that, and it has resulted, in almost every case, in marginal changes of attitude and behavior: church membership continues to be lukewarm if not nominal; Christian discipleship is hardly more than a reflection of the culture; and patterns of giving are motivated more by the desire to possess than to share. There are, of course, dramatic exceptions, but the tragedy is identified precisely with the fact that they are the exceptions. There is the nagging reality that marginality is the prevailing characteristic across our church and that the low per-capita record of pledging and giving brings the whole matter into bold and embarrassing focus.

A lot of effort has been put forth in the hope of improving upon that history and generating one that is more in keeping with the character of the church and its calling in ministry. I have benefited in a very special way from the very intriguing work of the biblical scholar, Bruce Birch. Over the last several years, Dr. Birch has suggested that a fundamental refocusing of theological perspective must happen if the church is to find the will and the resources for a determined and creative witness in our complex and demanding era of history. The need, he affirms, is to shift from a theology of crisis, which depicts the human situation as a predicament of travail, a precipice existence acquainted with despair and hopelessness from which God must deliver us, to a theology of creation, with images of life that are rooted in the experience of

"Giving is the thermometer of our love."
—UNKNOWN

God's blessings rather than God's deliverance, awareness of the glorious and harmonious order for which we have been created, rather than the terror-racked cosmos from which we must be rescued. In creation theology, according to Birch, "attention is diverted from the hope for God's redemptive intervention to the effort to discover the just order which God intended as the arena of human existence." This perspective concerns itself not with escape from emergencies but with the responsible functioning of day to day affairs. As in John 10:10, creation theology rejoices in the imagery of Shalom, the wholeness and abundance that God offers to all persons in the very act of creation itself, which is a present possibility and not some eventual fulfillment.

Here is the perspective that separates stewardship concerns from money crises, to which they are often identified (and from which we yearn to be delivered) and gives it grounding in the intent and will of the Creator. Stewardship is not a seasonal interest restricted to budget considerations. It cuts across the width and breadth of the entire faith spectrum. It is not an intrusion into the real business of the church but is of the very essence of Christian discipleship itself. "Be transformed by the renewal of the mind" or claim your inheritance in Christ by a change of perspective. That is the essence of the Apostle's word to us. Let us look briefly at what this implies.

Such a perspective means that a statement about stewardship is, in effect, a statement about God. To consider the breadth of its meaning, we must be willing to talk about God. It compels, in Birch's terms, disclosure of our deepest beliefs about the creation and its vast and threatened resources, about the work of a divine power for the purpose of relationship and a caring regard for the cosmos. The important change of perspective, in other words, moves our discourse to another level of awareness and conviction. In the spirit of a Hebrew proverb, we sense that God "has made everything for its purpose" (Prov. 16:4) and unto we ourselves. We move from pride to praise.

That is a monumental shift of insight. But with it, the issue of stewardship is viewed with little more than casual concern or as an unwelcome intrusion into the

appropriate agenda of the church's life and ministry. Self-sufficiency, independence, and a whole history of cultural conditioning related to these concepts form the framework of much of our thought about ourselves as persons, and have significantly influenced the life of our major social institutions, including the church. Thus, stewardship identifies with human initiative and goodwill, rather than with God's will and divine grace. Our dedication to stewardship will lack enthusiasm and end in failure, unless viewed as our response to something more compelling than our own generous nature or our aspiration toward a record of high achievement. Stewardship will mean more, will become deeply rooted conviction, when conceived in much the same way as we think of evangelism—namely, as a way of thinking and talking about God, of witnessing to the encompassing nature of our own faith in the God of all creation. More precisely, when understood in proper perspective, stewardship is recognized as another expression of evangelism, and we are moved beyond reliance on personal intuition or prideful self-interest as sufficient motivation. Stewardship becomes commitment beyond budget obligations when, like the priestly office of the Pentateuch, we declare: "In the beginning, God . . ." (Gen. 1:1).

Again, stewardship is a statement on the nature of creation. It is also the way in which the church thinks about the nature of community and its characteristics. Christian stewardship is acknowledgment of the meaning of our life together. It declares that a collection of individuals who live in casual and distant relationship is not community. It insists that authentic community is anticipation of Shalom, the heavenly city, characterized by its inclusiveness, its caring, its generous spirit, its hunger for justice and for peace. Stewardship is a view of community that will not let us be satisfied with anything that encourages separation or selfishness. It is community as Luke imagines it to be, in his story of the birth of the church in the Acts of the Apostles—a new people marked by what Earnest Troelsch has called "the communism of love," the resolve to affirm and care for all alike. We cannot understand stewardship in a more mundane and less expansive manner, or in terms, for instance, that are local, parochial, and

> "He who allows his day to pass by without practicing generosity and enjoying life's pleasures is like a blacksmith's bellows—he breathes but does not live."
> —SANSKRIT PROVERB

pedestrian. Whenever we have done so, we have failed to understand the meaning of community closest to where we live—namely, the community we call the church.

But, like Paul, we have done the very thing we would wish not to do. We have considered community—even the church—in ways that have barred its distinctiveness and beauty, reduced its meaning to the vagaries of ownership and possession, which are a corruption of the nature of the special people who have been fashioned by God through water and the Word. In place of a sense of our life together in shared affection and support, we have thought of the church as "local church," defined by geography and the character of the people themselves, and even the specific of architecture. I will not deny, of course, that the church also does exist in concrete embodiment in a group of persons and their context. Each of us wishing not to be spiritual parasites must identify with the "local" manifestation of the communion of the saints. But while it may be the place where community begins, the community that loves and serves Christ is always more than a local gathering of people, is never content to "lay up for itself treasures on earth," to offer and give anything less than a consecrated life demands.

Another evidence of the corruption of the meaning of the community of faith as the people whose ministry of service and suffering extends to the ends of the earth, is the description of ourselves as denomination. To be sure, there are creative aspects of denominational life. And within the Christian community, the "wholeness" of the church—given symbolic significance in the concept of stewardship—can be maintained through a variety of denominational forms. However, when a denomination claims, as some often do, to be the exclusive road to the Shalom of God, then denominationalism becomes an evil. Paul's horror struck question to the Corinthians, "Is Christ divided?" is a relevant question today to people who would reduce the blessed community to little more than factions.

> ## The language of stewardship is the way we talk about Jesus Christ.

It is because we so easily adopt these corrupting definitions of community that it is important to remember that the language of stewardship is the way we talk about Jesus Christ. His singularly unique life is the source of the uniqueness of the new community we know as the church. The fullness of creation, the Shalom envisioned by faith, and love that gives unto the uttermost—these speak to us of Christ. Faith insists that he has made it all possible, that it rests on him and not on the whims of men and women. The life of the new community, the character of its caring, its imperfect but important work, is Christ's work. "The church's one foundation is Jesus Christ her Lord; . . . With his own (life) he bought her, and for her life he died." We cannot talk about stewardship, the wholistic work of the church, if we are unable or unwilling to talk about him. We truly can say that because of the way he lived and gave his life, the church, which used his body and the sign of the new humanity, also lives. Whenever we talk about stewardship, or about how the church gives itself and employs its resources, we are compelled to talk about Jesus Christ.

Finally, a mature perspective enlarges the meaning of stewardship by moving us beyond budget and finance to an awareness of what it has to do with the way we live as individual Christians. We do a pretty good job of rationalizing the meaning of stewardship as it relates to God and creation or to Christian community, the church, and Jesus Christ. We have a harder time relating it to the specifics of personal responsibility and private behavior. But that is the overwhelming mandate of this hour: how to embody intentions, how to bring denominations into step with disposition.

I think we have trouble getting belief and behavior into sync or into relationship, in the same way we have trouble really understanding divine grace and Jesus' expiatory death. We have learned that you get what you deserve or earn, that you get only your "fair share," that one good deed deserves a similar deed in return, or, conversely, "an eye for an eye and a tooth for a tooth." Philosophically, this is called the law of proportionality and has been, for a long while, the basis of the argument that some wars are justifiable. Much congregational stewardship effort fails because this is the way Christian discipleship is understood: Our people are asked to do or give "their share" of the defined need. And most agree to do that, interpreting fairness as a tithe of some percentage thereof. But stewardship, in proper perspective, cannot be understood that way. It has to be understood in the light of divine grace and the expiatory sacrifice of Jesus. Stewardship is a statement, then, about love's disproportionality, about consequences in excess of causality, about giving more than is deserved, about doing more than is asked. Stewardship is grounded in the life of Jesus, who "thought it not beneath him to strip off his royalty and take on the life of a servant," for the sake of the community and the promised Shalom of God.

Stewardship efforts in many places will do little to get our people turned on or excited and eager to make it happen by the appeal to "do your share." (About the only thing we turn on are the pocket calculators.) Stewardship is another way of defining discipleship. It touches not only our checkbooks but the management of every part of our personal existence. We must think of its claim upon us as a claim upon the whole of our lives, not just upon a manageable percentage of our lives. We cannot talk about it without talking about ourselves. Nor will we take it seriously if we think of it as something we would rather not do, or as an unavoidable chore to be given scant attention, or as a peripheral concern in the busy calendar of a congregation. Stewardship is essential to faith and to the life of a church. It holds up the central truth of the church's gospel—that all of us are debtors who are chosen by God, not because of our deserving, but simply because God loves us, in spite of our brokenness, betrayal, arrogance, and sin. Can you see, then, that stewardship, like the preaching of the gospel, can separate us not just from our money, but more important, can deliver us from pride to repentance and the promised newness of life that flows from God's mercy? Here is one of the most significant and practical ways of putting flesh on the Good News that we proclaim—by enabling the embodiment of it in our own life and behavior.

I am confident that by now you have sensed that I do not consider funding and stewardship to be synonymous terms. As I inferred earlier, stewardship is our way of giving clear and significant embodiment to discipleship. Funding, on the other hand, is one way in which we express our stewardship. This is not to suggest that funding is unimportant. In fact, if we consider it in the context of Christian stewardship, it will serve to identify for us some important issues to which we must give careful consideration. Several of those issues have been identified by Ezra Earl Jones, General Secretary of the General Board of Discipleship, The United Methodist Church. He lists them in the form of questions:

1. Are we inviting people to give *to* the church or *through* the church?
2. Are we focusing upon the "joy of giving" as Christian disciples, or upon the accumulation of funds for causes determined by the larger church?
3. Are we developing motivations for giving around "obligations of church membership," or around the working of God's grace in the lives of people? Do we put the primary focus on the obligation of a tithe, or on giving out of the abundance we have received?

A new perspective, grounded in the language and morality of the faith, frees us from the tyranny of our need to have dominion over everything, in order to surrender ourselves to the claim of God upon the whole of creation, including ourselves and our resources, and to press on toward the high calling in Jesus Christ, that new community which acts in love and service for one another, and for which our pilgrimage here is but preparation, when all things will be in subjection unto him.

MONEY TALK

A Clash of Symbols: The Transforming Power of the Christian Offering

DAN R. DICK

A murmur spread through the congregation as the prelude was being played. One by one, worshipers were becoming aware of the old, battered work boot sitting on the right side of the altar. The contrast was startling—the lighted candles, the silk altar dressings, the golden cross, the open Bible, and the ragged, dirty boot. Some people registered shock, others chuckled.

The pastors were oblivious to its presence, and the acolyte gave it hardly a glance. Throughout the service, people's attention kept being drawn to the boot on the altar.

Following the sermon, the offering was taken, and as the pastor turned toward the altar to ask God's blessing upon the collected gifts and tithes, he paused, staring at the boot. Carefully, he set the offering plates on the altar, and, picking up the boot, gently set it atop the currency and envelopes, and invited the congregation to pray: "Oh, gracious God, what we bring to you this day is more than money, for at this time we offer you our very lives . . . ."

To this day, no one is sure who left the old boot on the altar of the High Street United Methodist Church in Muncie, Indiana, but many people still talk about it. The story has become legend, and it is forever stamped upon the hearts and minds of the worshiping congregation from that Sunday morning in 1978. A seemingly insignificant event has had the power to capture the imagination of literally hundreds of people across almost two decades. It is a powerful illustration of how we understand, and misunderstand, the offering act in the context of Christian worship.

Primarily, this story confronts us with a clash of symbols—a paradoxical picture of the cared and the profane thrust together. The boot on the altar created a startling incongruity that forced observers to focus on "What is the offering really all about?" In churches where the fundamental purpose of the offering is to raise money to pay the bills and fund the programs of the church, this is all the offering ever can be.

People seeking to understand Christian discipleship are shortchanged when the main emphasis on giving is paying the church bills. It segregates giving and sharing from the total life of the believer/seeker. It indicates that in some way, the giving of money is of lesser importance than the giving of prayers or singing of hymns. It gives the sense that receiving the collection is an embarrassment, but a necessary evil, nonetheless. This is truly unfortunate. The message that is sent is patently false. The giving of gifts, offerings, and tithes is a noble and powerful expression of our faith in Jesus Christ and our willingness to serve and be obedient to God. For the majority of people who very seriously consider the gift they will bring to God, presenting the offering as a "commercial time out" is an insult.

> Giving is the highest expression of potency. In the very act of giving, I experience my strength, my wealth, my power. This experience of heightened vitality and potency fills me with joy. I experience myself as overflowing, spending, alive, hence as joyous. Giving is more joyous than receiving, not because it is a deprivation, but because in the act of giving lies the expression of aliveness.
>
> —*ERICH FROMM*

The second act of the offertory play is the sacrificial act. It is one thing to make a gift to God, but it is a completely different thing to make a sacrificial gift to God. In the Old Testament, we receive the concept of the tithe as an acceptable gift to God. Tithe means a tenth-part, and the practice of the Hebrew people was to present not only a tenth-part of their resources to God, but the *first* tenth-part—the best of all they had. To give a tenth of your whole living was to place yourself in dependency to God. To give the best (or the "first fruits") to God was a monumental act of faith. The concept of the tithe was a powerful and deeply meaningful act for the chosen people of God, because it constantly reminded them of their need for the Lord. As is often the case, however, through the centuries a concept that once brought life and liberation to the people who practiced it has been turned into a limiting legalism that causes stress and discord in the contemporary community. How does the concept of a tithe relate to the church of the twenty-first century?

William Mitchell, a British historian and anthropologist of the early twentieth century, claims that the concept of the tithe was originally a military concept borrowed by the Hebrew people from ancient Persian culture. In military terms, soldiers could continue in battle until they had been "tith-ed," at which point they were considered mortally wounded. Soldiers could stand and fight by their own fortitude to the point at which they were 90 percent whole, but once they were injured beyond a tenth-part, they were at the mercy of their opponents. In other words, a significant shift from independence to dependence occurred once a tithe was exacted. For the early Hebrew culture, the 10 percent figure was not the key to the tithe; the fundamental issue was the shift to dependence upon God. Ten percent was not representative of an amount of wealth, but of who was in charge. As long as a person controlled 91 percent of his resources, he had no need of God. To give the tenth-part was a voluntary, willful acknowledgment of the fundamental need for God. This "gift" was necessary to move the chosen people into a dependent relationship with their God.

Therein lies the significance for Christian worshipers in our day. What constitutes a "tithe" offering for us? For many people, 10 percent may in fact be more than sacrificial. However, for a substantial number of others, even 25 percent of their wealth might not constitute a sacrificial gift. The point is simply that the second act of the offertory drama is an opportunity to place ourselves under the Lordship of Jesus Christ. It is a way for us to physically (the giving act) and graphically (the symbolic act) acknowledge our dependence on God. The willingness to humble ourselves, to be obedient and subservient to God, is a mark of Christian maturity; it is therefore something that we must grow into. In many Methodist services, there is a time to invite participants into Christian discipleship, but when are people invited into faithful stewardship? The offering becomes both a way to educate believers about what it means to be servants to the Lord, and to invite them to become good stewards.

The third act of the offertory drama is the symbolic act. In the words of the hymn "What Gift Can We Bring?" the first line is, "What gift can we bring, what present, what token?" This is a beautiful entrée into the concept of offering as symbolic act.

In contemporary usage, the word *token* has the connotation of lack of value or substance. We accuse people of tokenism when we feel that they are patronizing us or merely bending to pressure, rather than behaving with integrity. A token gesture is an act that requires little or no sacrifice. In its original conception, the term "token" derived from the Greek word *deiknynai,* which means "to show fully"—the meta-meaning of who we really are, what we really mean, and what we truly believe. The gift that we present to the altar is our token—our statement of who we are in relation to God, what we understand that relationship to mean, and how that relationship shapes our way of living in this world. Symbolically, we express our life in Christ each time we place our gift in the offering plate.

This understanding of the offertory drama presents a crisis, in the positive sense. Out of this crisis comes a window of opportunity. If, indeed, the offertory drama operates at the three levels of the giving act, the sacrificial act, and the symbolic act, then the offering time should be occasion for more than simply putting envelopes and currency in a plate. Perhaps the sacrilege of the opening illustration was not that the

boot was placed on the altar of the church, but that many of the gifts were placed on the altar with no more thought or concern than might be given an old boot.

A young woman recounts a painful story from her childhood. When she was five years old, she remembered her pastor preaching a sermon about giving of your true self to God. The reason she remembers the sermon is because she went to her Sunday school class and drew a picture of herself and Jesus, and wrote across the bottom, "I love you God." Following Sunday school, she marched back to the sanctuary, climbed the steps of the chancel, then climbed up on the altar and reached to tape her picture to the cross. The pastor happened to look in at that moment and bellowed at the top of his voice, "Get off of there, you sinful child." The pastor dragged her from the sanctuary, took her to his study, and lectured her on respect and the meaning of blasphemy and sacrilege. When her parents took her home, they lectured her on "how we thought we brought you up better than that" and "how will we face the pastor after this?" She tore her picture into little bits and threw it away. She stopped going to church when she was a teenager, and didn't return until her thirties. The reason she offered was this: The church wasn't interested in what she had to offer.

When the focus of the morning offering is centered so completely on money, what hidden messages are delivered that other gifts are of lesser value? How do we disrespect the nonfinancial contributions that people make to the fellowship of Jesus Christ when we provide no avenues for expression during our times of worship together? Now more than ever, we need to reconsider the offertory drama in our churches and open up the possibilities for expression, allowing for all three acts to be performed.

At a small United Methodist Church in southern Vermont, a young woman pastor has created a living altar in the church. At the front of the church, a fountain bubbles, a continual reminder of the baptismal nature of our faith. Flowers are not given weekly to adorn the sanctuary, but grow right on and beside the altar, symbolizing the nurturing and fertile nature of the church. From a decaying log, a spray of violets grow, symbolizing the new life that springs forth from death in the power of the resurrection. Candles are nestled amongst the greenery, sending forth the light of Christ and illuminating this "token" of the richness, fullness, and beauty of life. These pieces have been given and lovingly arranged by the members of the church. They have been allowed to perform all three acts in the offertory play.

A youth assembly in Northern Indiana brings to the church "symbolic gifts"—toys, stuffed animals, figurines, poems, songs, jewelry, pictures, and a host of other mementos that have special significance in their lives. They place them on the altar and a prayer is said. During the service, the youth are given the opportunity to share the story of their gifts, the sentimental meaning of their offering. They unfold their life stories and their faith witness. At the conclusion of the service, the young people take their gifts and give them to other members of the congregation. The adults leave with a piece of the young people's lives shared with them as sacred trust. Connections are made, and the Body of Christ departs stronger than when it arrived.

A young unemployed woman in Colorado babysits for all the church events, works in the soup kitchen twice a week, mails out the church newsletter, and donates baked goods to all the church events. She once felt guilty that she had nothing to put in the offering plate, but a caring financial secretary in the church took note of the young woman and offered her grace. When quarterly giving reports are sent from the church, a statement is received by the young woman: "value of services offered to the church," with a dollar amount that estimates how much the church would have to pay someone to do what this young woman does. Each week she proudly places a card in the collection plate that reports how many hours of service she commits to the church for the week to come. Never in her life has she felt so valued and cared for.

The primary task of each congregation is to reach out and receive seeking men and women, relate them to God in significant ways, nurture and train them in the disciplines of the faith, and send them forth into the world to live as committed stewards and disciples. Much of what the church has to offer to equip people for life in Christ is symbolic. The cross, the Eucharist,

> "Gratitude is the memory of the heart."
>
> *UNKNOWN*

baptism, the candles, the hymnody—so many of the beloved and mystical experiences of the church lead people into a deeper relationship with God in Jesus Christ. So should the offering. The offering time is made sacred by the work of the Spirit to touch and transform lives. Every effort should be made to allow this work of the Spirit to flow freely. The offering should be planned with the same care and attention as the sermon, the worship flow, the prayers, and the invitations to discipleship. Three questions should be asked of each offertory drama:

1. Is it a play in three acts? (Allowing for giving, sacrifice, and symbolism)
2. Is it a celebration? (Characterized by gratitude, joy, and hope)
3. Does it connect people's hearts to the Good News?

Throughout his earthly ministry, Jesus challenged the symbolic nature of the Jewish faith. He washed the disciples' feet, he turned water into wine, he ate with sinners, associated with women, ate with unwashed hands, and made common bread and wine into holy icons. Palestine thundered with the clash and crash of symbols, and the echoes are still heard. Jesus continually replaced the old with the new; the outdated and outworn symbols of a previous day gave way to new, powerful, transforming symbols of the kingdom of God. The power of those symbols is beyond human comprehension. We still celebrate that power.

The offering time in the service of worship has incredible potential power. The way we manage and employ that power is a serious stewardship issue for the church. Through careful and intentional planning, the transforming power of the offering can be unleashed in our congregations. We can begin the process by not thinking of the offering time in terms of intrusion into the flow of worship, but as a key component in the larger system of fulfilling the primary task of the congregation. Through the offering, we can reach, teach, invite, and send. Through the offering, we can connect disciples to Jesus Christ.

 **DEVOTIONAL**

The Three Meanings of Giving

KEN CARTER

My friend Don Joiner once noted that giving is not as simple as we might first imagine. At least three factors contribute to the act of giving—and each needs to be understood. *Why* a person gives is an issue of spirituality: relationship to God. *Where* a person gives—whether to a church or a cause or an organization—is related to matters of communication, interpretation, and education. *How much* a person gives is often the result of the methods we use to encourage giving.

One: Why We Give

We give offerings and tithes because our lives have been touched by an experience with God. At some point along the way, we have come under the conviction that God has created us, that God has acted to save us, that God dwells within us. This conviction moves us to acknowledge Jesus Christ as our Savior and our Lord. As Savior, we are aware of the blessings that are ours through a relationship with Christ. As Lord, we are equally conscious of the truth that all that we have and all that we are has been claimed by Jesus.

Giving must have a solidly spiritual foundation. Our motivations to give rest upon our convictions and experiences of God's transforming grace. In II Corinthians 8, Paul speaks to the church at Corinth about an offering for the church in Jerusalem. He begins his appeal with these words: *You know the grace of God.*

Two False Assumptions

The grace of God, to which we respond in giving, is fundamental to Christian stewardship. But our awareness of this truth can lead to two false assumptions. First, we can assume that persons in our congregations have received God's grace, and are motivated to respond. The reality in many congregations is that persons need to be healed, discipled, comforted, challenged, or led forward into a deeper Christian experience. Second, we can assume that if a person's heart is in the right place, he or she will give. In fact, giving to churches is also shaped by two other dynamics—our *communication* and our *methods*.

Two: Where We Give

Congregations are filled with generous men and women. They give out of the spiritual conviction that Christians are motivated by God's example of self-giving in Jesus Christ. Their gifts are outward and visible signs—sacraments—of an inward and visible grace.

We should not *assume,* however, that convictions about God's grace and human response lead people to give to and through our congregations. *Why* they give is a spiritual issue; *where* they give is a communications issue.

Part of communication is telling the story of what God is doing through the mission of our church. I am often a part of groups that plead in a continuing refrain—that we need to find new ways to tell the story more effectively. Here are some insights into more effective communication:

1. We should not assume that our members are aware of our ministries in the world.
2. We should attempt to connect major human events with the responses made possible by our financial gifts.
3. We can learn something about communication from Jesus, who spoke in parables and used visual images: mustard seeds, fig trees, a treasure hidden in a field. A simple idea or picture is often sufficient to tell the story in a profound way.

Communication is essential to effective stewardship.
- Does communication from the pulpit and from the laity about stewardship seem liberating and empowering, or guilt-producing and moralizing?
- Who in your congregation has a story to tell about how the church's ministry has affected their lives?
- Should that story be told in worship?
- Through the newsletter?

How Much?

Why we give to God is a spiritual issue. *Where* we give our resources is determined by our communication. A third dynamic is also important: *how much* we give.

Congregations can be spiritually alive and still fall short of their financial goals. Churches can tell the story in a variety of ways, using different voices, and the end result of their stewardship is not the anticipated outcome. Why? The answer might be found in the methods we are using in stewardship education.

No baseball pitcher will throw the same pitch—say a fastball—time after time after time. The batter will see it coming very quickly and will learn how to dispose of it. Our ministry in the area of stewardship very easily lapses into a similar pattern: we make the same appeals in the same ways, at the same time of year, over and over again. And then we are puzzled by the lack of response.

Most stewardship leaders suggest a *variety* of approaches. Packet programs are wonderful the first few times, but after a few years there is a declining response. The same reality might very well emerge through overexposure to programs like "Consecration Sunday." No stewardship design can be implemented year after year without diminishing returns.

A simple three-year cycle, if planned and implemented well, is similar to a pitcher who throws first a fastball, then a curve, then a change-up. Methods do make a difference in the sum of gifts that people give to God through their congregations. And when combined with a solid spiritual emphasis and effective communication, God blesses a church with sufficient financial resources to carry out its ministry in the world.

In Year One, use a program like "Consecration Sunday" or "Celebrate Giving," which focuses on worship, celebration and our need to give, rather than the church's need to receive. During that year, launch some kind of stewardship/visitation that is *unrelated* to financial giving.

In Year Two, plan the campaign around relational groups in the church: let the stewardship happen in the choir, in circles, and in Sunday school classes.

In Year Three, use a congregational visitation program. This will be more effective if visitation/shepherding has already taken place (and no one can say "they only visit to ask for money!").

 MEDITATION

Congregational Prayer

BETSY SCHWARZENTRAUB

Our God and Father, we thank you that we have been daily recipients of your great bounty: We do not ask you to increase our blessings, but to make us worthy of the least of your gifts. Enable us to rejoice in the privilege of honoring you with our substance and the first fruits of our increases. Keep us from wasting your blessings in the pursuit of worldly pleasures.

Give us wisdom to heed your injunction not to lay up treasure on earth, but to set aside a heavenly treasure that nothing can destroy.

Help us make our financial resources serve the causes of Christ, so that the mission and ministry of his glorious Church can be strengthened and fulfilled through our giving.

 TEACHING HELP

Perspectives on Luke 12

NORMA WIMBERLY

In reading, reflecting upon, and discussing the Scriptures, it is best to follow the pattern of Jesus. Jesus dealt with a variety of situations in his teaching and leading ministry by saying, "It is written . . . ."

This was also the pattern of the early church leaders, who "devoted themselves to the Apostles' teachings." In I Peter 3:15, we are directed to "be prepared to give an answer to everyone who asks you to give the son for the hope that you have" (NIV). Continue the gift of this tradition by going again and again to the Scriptures. Read, reflect, talk with one another, and allow the living Word to speak.

Focusing on Scripture is one way to form and reform community. A community is formed around shared experiences and the opportunity (and willingness) for intimacy. When experiences and intimacies are both given and received, learning takes place. Not everyone interprets the faith experience with the Scripture in quite the same way. What one person feels, sees, hears, and thinks may not be the same as another feels, sees, hears, and thinks. So learning also takes place when we are honest and open-minded with one another—when we learn from one another and come to resolution and conclusion together.

Suggestions for Bible Discussions

Bible discussions may or may not be in formal study settings. Leadership may reside with the pastor, but just as often, may be assumed by a dedicated and enthusiastic layperson. These three approaches to reading, reflection, and discussion do not require special academic training, but only a willingness to take responsibility for guidance. Each group session will take approximately one hour. If the group is informal and relaxed, the discussion could be expanded. (There are additional questions and discussion suggestions at the end of each section.) If a more rigorous schedule needs to be maintained, the use of small groups within the larger group might be considered during times of discussion.

Each of the suggested formats uses a simple approach to group reflection on the Scripture. With some modification, they also can be used for individual meditation time. The first approach, used with Luke 12:3-21, is the R E A D (Read, Explain, Apply, Do) approach. With Luke 12:22-32, the group is asked to *begin* with *personal experiences* and stories, read the passage, and start to intersect the two perspectives. The third design, used with Luke 12:35-47, *begins* with each person *reading* the Gospel message, then remembering one's past, and examining the ways the Word is being spoken today. The three perspectives are three different kinds of Word. Through explanations, history, and the life of Jesus, God is with us and leading us in the Way.

The Parable of the Rich Fool

Luke 12:13-21

I. *Tell* the story of the "rich fool" in your own words.

II. Ask each person to *read* the passage silently.

III. The parable: Some *explanatory* notes

Stewardship is often synonymous with material possessions. Many of us are very like the man whose central concern was getting his fair share of the family money. In the North American culture, the messages are frequently something like this: the bigger, the better; more is better than some; there's never enough. (Ask the group to add their own clichés.) Faithful stewardship, however, is about giving, about responding to God, in every area of life, with open-hearted generosity and caring.

The "man in the crowd" and the rich man were not able to examine their relationships or their priorities of accumulation. Jesus implies both condemnation and grace. He admonishes his hearers to watch out, to guard against comparisons and greed. A person's true life is not made up of things owned. The rich man is not condemned for being forgetful. His very soul was dependent upon material possessions. His future was wrapped up in his goods. (He was bankrupt with the Lord!)

The issue in the conversation and parable is accountability.

IV. *Apply:* Bridging the gap between the story and now
   A. In pairs, discuss the elements of the story that touch your life—in the past, today.
   B. In small groups, determine some of the elements of the story that seem to touch the lives of those in your family, congregation, and community.

V. *Do:* If I take this story to heart, I might be led to:
   A. Share with a partner some of the things that come to mind. Name the attitudes and actions you see and experience every day that either reflect or negate the truths of the story.
   B. Make a personal covenant to do one thing differently today because of these insights.

VI. Additional questions and comments for discussion
   A. What does it mean to be rich toward God?
   B. If Jesus commented on your view of wealth today, what do you think he would say?
   C. Where are your riches? (Name two)
   D. What are your three top priorities in life right now, in the areas of money, time, and relationships?
   E. How would you like to be remembered?
   F. Where would you leave your riches?
   G. The concept of "good" financial stewardship is integral to the life of discipleship. Why?
   H. God gives more to us for the purpose of increasing what we might do for God.

Do Not Worry

Luke 12:22-34

I. Small group discussion
   A. How do you hear God's voice, God's leading in your life today? Be as specific as possible.
   B. Is worry or anxiety a factor in the way you arrange your days, make decisions, relate to others? Describe, or give an example.
   C. Name one concrete way you might be able to eliminate worry in your life.

II. The teaching of Jesus
   A. Read the passage aloud. (Ask the members of the group to close their eyes.)
   B. Ask them to read the passage silently.

III. As persons on the spiritual journey
   A. The simple life is the believer's inner relationship to God finding expression in his or her outward relationship to things and events. In pairs, begin to take a personal inventory regarding the complexity or simplicity of your past living style. What, if any, affect do you believe this has on the way you are in relationship with God through Jesus Christ today?
   B. Based on your conversation, name specific ways you can use knowledge of your own history and begin to do things differently to reflect your commitment to spiritual growth and freedom from worry.

IV. A group covenant of promise
   A. Ask each person in the group to commit to one way to model "Instead, be concerned with God's kingdom, and all these things will be provided."
   B. Reread the passage. Close your time together with silent prayer. Emphasize gratitude for our memories—to be able to see how things were and to envision how they can improve with Christ.

V. Additional questions and comments for discussion
   A. What are some of the differences between what the world says and what the Scriptures say about money and possessions?
   B. From this passage, list your perception of some qualities of a faithful steward—one in healthy relationship with God and with money.
   C. Are there any changes (inner/outward) that you might make in order to live more faithfully? How would you take action?

NOTE: The following four activities may be best suited for "homework" or a time of personal meditation.
   D. Name some of the situations that have caused you to worry most in the past. What about today?
   E. On a scale of 1 to 10, what is your worry quotient right now? Why?
   F. Create a brief telegram defining worry; defining gift.
   G. Make a list of a "day's worth of gifts" you do not earn (time, patience, talents, air, images of beauty, a smile, a loving community, etc.).

Watchfulness

Luke 12:35-47

I. The Gospel story, the Good News!
   A. Ask each person to read the passage silently.
   B. In small groups, discuss these questions:
      1. If you had lived your life during the past twenty-four hours while focusing on this passage, what might you have done differently?
      2. Is this one of those messages that seems to be an example of "good news, bad news"? Each person may hear a different message.

Talk about this. Be specific, as you reexamine the passage.

II. More Good News!

A. Ask all to listen as the passage is read aloud.

B. Reflect on and discuss these statements:

- Faith, not fear, is the driving force, the motivation of faithful stewardship.

- To be ready is not an invitation to fear, but a reminder to be constant in faith and in relationship to God. It is to be awake to Jesus Christ.

- Jesus will not make our choices for us, but reminds us of how quickly the results of our decisions are apparent.

C. Individually, try to recollect an event in your life when you were not watchful. What were the results? When you were watchful? What were the results?

III. A next step

A. Make personal, individual notes for a "spiritual fitness" program. What are some of the things you can do to become more spiritually fit—faithful, watchful, intentional in thought and action?

B. If persons are comfortable, share some of these notes with a partner or with the group.

IV. Additional questions and comments for discussion

A. The faithful steward is the one (or ones) put in charge of all the possessions of the master. Responsibility of that magnitude demands a great deal of the steward. Begin to imagine an ordinary day in the life of a steward in the time of Jesus' ministry. Describe it. Add your own details.

B. In the culture of North America, what are some of the invitations to good stewardship? What are some of the barriers or constraints? List them. Why do they exist?

C. What qualities of living is Jesus stressing to his disciples? What will they receive?

D. What does "reward" mean in this passage, in a broad context or perspective?

E. Is Jesus saying yes or no to Peter's questions?

F. How does Jesus summarize the passage in verse 48?

G. What particularly has God entrusted to you? How are you taking care of this responsibility?

H. If you knew that in 30 days, you would be held accountable for your life, what would you do to get ready?

I. Draft a letter to a friend, telling them your perspective on the "good news" of watchfulness and faith.

NOTE: If you are part of a group that wants to engage in Bible reading, reflection, and discussion on a regular basis, it is suggested that a regular format be developed. While the approach to particular passages may vary from time to time, it is advisable to have parameters that are dependable.

One design you may wish to use includes these elements:

1. An opening prayer, either by the leader or shared among the participants.

2. A hymn.

3. Some brief remarks by the leader, describing the particular approach for that session.

4. The time of reading, reflection, and discussion, perhaps using one of the designs suggested in this article.

5. Additional discussion or possible commitments to action determined by the group dynamics.

6. Any announcements or information of other sessions.

7. A closing prayer.

31

 HANDOUT

A Word Study

GREGORY G. M. INGRAM

The word *stewardship* occurs in the Bible four times, *steward* thirteen times, and *stewards* five times. Luke uses *stewardship* three times *(Luke 16:2, 3, 4)*, and applies it to the office of administrator of the property of another. Paul employs it once *(I Cor. 9:17)*, using it to indicate the responsibility that God has entrusted to him—preaching the gospel to the world.

The most common meaning of the word *steward* in the Old Testament is "the man who is over." This is close to its most frequent meaning in the New Testament: "an overseer, one to whom something has been entrusted, a house-manager." Throughout the English version of the Bible, therefore, this word conveys practically the same idea as the relationship between God and man—that God is our Master, his interests are paramount, and we operate for him as his managers, overseers, or representatives.

The larger meaning and broader implications of Christian stewardship are confirmed by a study of the term itself. The first word in the term is "Christian," used here as an adjective. It means "relating to" Christ, belonging to Christ, or Christlike. *Stewardship that is Christian is Christlike stewardship.* Christ is its norm; his life is its chart; his teachings are its compass. His mind is final; the principles and ideals which he enunciated are ultimate.

The second word in the term is "stewardship." "Steward" comes from the Anglo-Saxon *stigweard,* which in turn is derived from *stigu,* a sty, of the pigsty, or the protector of cattle. From this humble origin, the word rose in dignity until it came to mean the person in charge of the affairs of the household of another; the keeper of an estate, as "steward of the manor"; or the holder of a position of public trust, as the Lord High Steward of England.

All words ending in "ship" imply a definite relation between two persons or things. In the case of "stewardship" this definite relation is between two persons—man and God. At bottom, therefore, the relation between man and God may be interpreted in terms of stewardship.

According to the historical meaning of the word, therefore, the steward had authority and responsibility delegated to him by his master or lord, and he enjoyed fellowship with his master in proportion to his faithfulness or unfaithfulness in the discharge of the trust committed to his hand. This historical meaning must be brought over and applied to the Christian steward. He, too, has authority and responsibility as well as fellowship with his Lord and Master. God has given his children the privilege and the responsibility of participating with God in his purpose.

TEST YOUR KNOWLEDGE

1. Write a short defining statement of what Stewardship means to you.

2. Tithing is giving _____ percent of one's earnings.

   Stewardship giving is _____.

3. What is a Steward? _____

4. Where are the following Scriptures found?

   a. Bring ye all the Tithes into the Storehouse _____

   b. Upon the first day of the week, let everyone lay by him a store as God has prospered him _____

   c. The Earth is the Lord's and the Fullness thereof _____

PLANNING TOOL

Biblical Study: Stewardship of Money

Matthew 25:14-30

VIRGIL CRUZ, BARBARA TESORERO, RANDY WILCHER

Not every parable of Jesus will immediately cheer the reader or convey a feeling of security. One example is the well-known parable of the talents. Even a quick perusal of its final words: "throw him into the outer darkness, where there will be weeping and gnashing of teeth," is enough to trigger a chill. However, the parable does have valuable lessons for our study of stewardship, especially the stewardship of money.

A businessman/master, prior to leaving on a journey, signed over units of his property to three employees/servants: five talents, two talents, and one talent respectively. These were considerable amounts in first-century Palestine, where it is estimated that a talent was the equivalent of a laborer's wages for fifteen years! It is emphasized that the amount each employee received was in proportion to ability.

The master returned after a very long delay. The servant who had been entrusted with the largest amount had doubled his holdings through shrewd business dealing. The master at once lavished on him high praise and a promotion, involving significantly increased responsibilities.

The second servant, whose working capital had been two talents, likewise could report a 100 percent gain. He received an identical commendation: "Well done, good and trustworthy slave; you have been trustworthy in a few things, I will put you in charge of many things; enter into the joy of your master." The master had ample reason to rejoice, for the value of his estate had been appreciably increased, and his trust in both employees clearly justified.

The dramatic high point of the story rests with the third servant. In stark contrast to what had gone before, this last individual has absolutely no profit to deliver, largely because of fear brought on by his appraisal of the master: "I knew that you were a harsh man, reaping where you did not sow, and gathering where you did not scatter seed; so I was afraid, and I went and hid your talent in the ground. Here you have what is yours." Paralyzed by fear, the servant did not seek to fully utilize the talent.

This is one of a series of parables in Matthew 24 and 25 which, in the opinion of many scholars, deal with the second coming of Jesus Christ. This parable presents guidance for living, while waiting for Christ's return. We are told that these parables and the kingdom of God have certain principles in common (cf. 25:1, 14); therefore we can expect to receive insight that will increase our understanding of the reign of God.

First, it is given that God's explicit plans for the church involve entrusting to individuals gifts to be used for the benefit of the whole community of faith and beyond (cf. I Tim. 6:17-19). The focus of the parable is on material resources, especially money. What we learn about its use provides responsible guidance for good stewardship of all the gifts entrusted to us.

The parable also reinforces the conclusion that God has given to the church the responsibility of serving as God's agents. Empowered by the Holy Spirit, the church carries out the mission begun by Jesus Christ. To indicate how God depends upon the church for work and witness, we might also say, "God has no hands but our hands to do God's work today."

Another implication of the parable is that believers must not shrink from risk-taking as they follow God's mandate. It is not the size of the accomplishment that is important, but the fact that something has been attempted in good faith for God. If nothing is ventured, whether due to laziness, wickedness, or both (cf. 25:26), the result is great sadness.

The examples of the two faithful servants should encourage believers to risk investing money and other gifts to support the work of the church, whether to restore vitality to the church's activities or to lend crucial support to new and creative ventures with the promise of meeting needs. Such gifts advance God's kingdom and give joy to God.

The fact remains that God is displeased and grieved when confronted with the irresponsibility and inaction of believers. We cannot discount the stark warning of the parable, with its images of punishment and even rejection.

How many contemporary problems in the life and work of the church can be traced to bad theology? In the parable, the neglectful servant's problems were primarily the result of misreading the master's character.

Suppose the master deserved the reputation of being harsh, unfair, and someone to be feared. Surely the other two servants also would have been immobilized by fear. Further, an unfair master would not have been capable of rejoicing with them and rewarding them for their success. It seems that the fault lies with the third servant. Although he claims, "I knew that you were a harsh man," one must inquire as to the reliability of that knowledge. He certainly did not ask his two colleagues for collaboration. The master's verdict, "You wicked and lazy slave!" most likely contains the clue.

We must face the hard truth that, for similar reasons, people in the church often fail to be good stewards of money and other gifts. Some resent the effort required to serve God and the church with their gifts. Others are bound by covetousness and find it impossible to release any considerable amount of their material resources, other than for personal ends, even if they can well afford to do so. And still others suffer for lack of reliable information or responsible theology. The lament is widespread that many church members no longer possess a living, vital understanding of Christianity.

One may ask how the early church understood this parable. In particular, who would have been seen as the neglectful servant? No doubt any person held captive by selfishness would qualify. Also targeted were those who took refuge in false humility, claiming that they had no gifts to share, or becoming excessively concerned about the possibility of failure. The believers who used the excuse that their resources were too small would have been reminded of the widow who did what she could with what she had (Mark 12:42-44). When talent was understood figuratively and seen as an indication of how we should practice stewardship with all gifts, some may have thought of the scribes who were entrusted with much knowledge, but did not always pass it on to others (Luke 11:52).

With little effort, we can apply all these examples to our own situation. We may add to the list those congregations that have become so inwardly oriented that they actually fear newcomers, making any kind of sharing with "outsiders" next to impossible. All congregations have a call to go, risk, and serve (Matt. 28:18-20), and must struggle with the temptation to become an exclusive club for those with the right skin color and economic status. Small churches may succumb to defeatism and self-pity, forgetting their first love and turning from that vision which inspires and empowers risk-taking for God and God's needy world.

In spite of the seriousness with which one properly hears this parable, the welcome song announcing mercy and renewal, forgiveness and restoration, should not be overlooked.

In the first place, it was mercy which prompted Jesus to warn his followers by means of this story. The parable is actually a call to repentance and an invitation to start over. Second, in the picture of the master, there are intimations of the surpassing justice of God, and the overwhelming concern of God that all should be found worthy of what has been entrusted to them. Rest assured, the desire of God's heart is to affirm each of us with these words, "Well done, good and trustworthy slave; . . . enter into the joy of your master."

 HANDOUT

Top Ten Reasons People Give for Not Tithing

MARY ANN JOHNSON

10. I can't support this church all by myself!
9. If everyone in my congregation started tithing—our congregation would be able to do things I'm not sure I want them to do!
8. I can't afford it because I bought a new car (boat, house, built a new barn).
7. The Lord giveth and the Lord taketh away—if the Lord wants it, let the Lord take it!
6. If I gave as much as I should, I would be audited by the IRS!
5. I would feel so bad if I couldn't keep my promise (pledge).
4. My kids would never believe that I was that generous.
3. If I support the church, my mother will expect me to support her too!
2. I should be the one who receives—I want to get something from the church.
1. *As often as I come to church, I would have to give a whole paycheck each time!*

 # MEDITATION

The Knight of the Empty Bucket

ROBERT J. HEMPFLING

Everybody likes a good story. Especially one that teaches important truths. Maybe that is the reason Jesus told so many. He knew that a good story could stimulate thoughts and dreams. Here's one:

Once upon a time, there was a young man who was a Knight of the Ancient Order. He joined crusades, rescued young damsels, fought terrible dragons, and all the rest. One day as he was riding his horse in the country, he remembered that it was Good Friday, a day of confession.

Being a pious Christian knight, he knew he had to make confession. Where was he to find a priest? As luck would have it, he came upon a cave, and there crouching by its entrance, was a hermit monk.

"Will you hear my confession, Father?"

"Why, yes, my son," came the reply.

Unfortunately, the knight could think of nothing to confess. He racked his brain and finally came up with three things he thought he had done wrong.

So he confessed, "Father, I have shown mercy to an enemy soldier who had lost his sword, and Father, I have missed an opportunity to gain more wealth by joining in a raid on a neighboring city. Further, Father, I failed to invest my gold with a particular friend who would have made me a richer man."

Needless to say, the priest was taken aback by such a confession. He wanted to prescribe an appropriate penance, but what would it be? First, he suggested that the knight give some of his wealth to build a new church in a nearby village. But the knight said he could never do that, since he didn't have nearly enough wealth for himself.

Then the priest suggested that he give some time to help the lepers in a neighboring colony. But the knight said he was a very busy man and couldn't possibly do that.

Finally, in exasperation, the old monk handed him an empty bucket and said, "Here, this will be your penance; take this bucket and bring me a drink of water!"

The knight responded happily, "This is easy. Is this all I have to do to receive absolution?" The old priest nodded, gravely.

Immediately, the knight ran to a nearby stream and dipped the bucket into the water. But when he drew it out, the bucket was empty. Strange, he thought, and did it again. Still, the bucket was empty.

The knight went back to the priest and told him that there seemed to be something wrong with the bucket. He would soon come back with the water.

So, the knight went off, traveling throughout the land, hunting for a place to fill the bucket. He visited lakes, wells, rivers, and seashores, but the bucket remained empty. So engrossed did he become with this project, that he came to be known as the Knight of the Empty Bucket.

One day, the knight came upon an old man and a boy who had been hurt in a wagon accident. Both were bleeding and in need of help. He stopped, leaped from his horse and began cleaning their wounds. Soon he could see that he needed more water to do a thorough job and to satisfy their thirst. So, jumping up, he grabbed the bucket and rushed down to a nearby stream. Dipping the bucket quickly in the water, he was halfway up the hill before he realized what had happened. The bucket was full!

To me, that is a stewardship story because stewardship can only be understood in the midst of the doing. Maybe that's why stewardship has seldom been taught successfully in seminaries. Maybe that's why it never seems to fit into church school curriculum.

It is amusing to dream up modern confessions similar to the ones offered by the knight. Here is one possibility. "I did something wrong."

 SERMON HELP

The Promise of the Covenant

THE REVEREND NORMAN V. OSBORNE

PROMISE 1

A very strong case can be made for the interchange of the two words *promise* and *covenant*. In one sense, the entire structure and strength of this faith of ours is predicated on a promise. A promise was made to Noah, symbolized by the rainbow, that God would never again deluge the earth with water. God promised Abraham that he would be a father of nations. Moses and the nation of Israel were recipients of the promise at Mt. Sinai, indicated by the Torah, or Law. This understanding is not intrinsic to the Old Testament but carries over into the New. The greatest promise of all is that characterized by the sacrament of the Holy Communion, a promise sealed by the body and blood of Christ in a new relationship, a new understanding, a new direction and life.

A closer look at the life and teachings of Jesus reveals that he made a series of promises. He promised us a place. "In my Father's house are many mansions." He promised us his presence: "I will not leave you comfortless." He promised us his power: power to make us adequate for both the good times and the bad. He promised us his peace. He promised us life: "I have come that you might have life and have it more abundantly." Such promises give this faith the essence that makes it unique in the religious world.

We, in other words, are a people of the promise; it is that which makes us what we are. Our understanding of life and confidence for living is rooted and grounded in the promises of God. It is the source of our joys and the reservoir of our hopes.

PROMISE 2

However, I am often troubled by the fact that many have only a one-dimensional view of the promise. Often we claim and proclaim the promises of the Lord without serious reflection upon the fact that we also are claimed by the promise. In truth, a covenant, a promise, is reciprocal; without the sense of reciprocity, a promise lacks integrity. As God has made a promise to me, I in turn, if I am to enter into the joys of this faith and experience its power, also must be willing to make a promise. I must be willing to enter into this relationship without hesitation or reservation. I must enter with my total being, with all that I have spiritually, socially, ethically, and financially. It is not a matter of my giving in accordance with some standard that I have devised, or shaping the rules in accordance with some "comfortable" and "complacent" fashion; rather, it is a matter of subscribing to a higher claim that puts a demand upon me.

Frederick Meeks made this abundantly clear when he wrote: "Our only salvation is to be sure that the righteousness we seek is God's righteousness, shaped by his love and tempered by his mercy, and that we are not substituting for it our own human righteousness, made to the specifications for our own desires."

PROMISE 3

In acknowledging the promises of God that shape us and, in turn, making the promise, there is a claim made upon us. To be Christian is to be "Christlike," to assume and embody the character of Christ in all we do and say.

It is acknowledged, further, that God's love for us is essentially a gift. We must be clear on one point: God does not only love; his nature is love. Everything he does has its ultimate reason in his love. Therefore, God's giving is inevitable. The question may be asked: "Why does God love a cheerful giver?" Because he himself is a cheerful giver, and he invites us to be like him! He has marked out for us the way of generosity, giving his life on a cross, being broken in the sacrifice of love to achieve the mighty ministry of salvation, giving himself when we were not worthy of it.

The Christian must try to reproduce in his or her own life today something of the nature of God's love. This means, in practice, that we must give ourselves unstintingly. Our giving must be independent of the response from the beloved. To give is to live. Our gifts show forth our love for the living God.

This faith is structured and predicated upon promises—the promises of God, which are from everlasting to everlasting, merciful and majestic, and the promise that I make to God as a steward of his gifts.

$ MONEY TALK

Permission to reprint this article has been given by Stewardship Education, Presbyterian Church (U.S.A.)

Why Do We Make Stewardship So Difficult?

THE REVEREND DR. ROBERT W. BOHL

Of all the things we do as Christians, one of the things we do the poorest is what we call stewardship. Why do we make stewardship so difficult? We neglect it, abuse it, run from it, deny its importance, and, in most cases, believe we are doing a better job with it than we actually are. As proof, we know that many give only 2.5 percent of their income to the church. Whatever happened to tithing? Whatever happened to real commitment to Jesus Christ?

The first and greatest tendency when something is wrong is to find someone to blame for it. We pastors blame our seminaries for not showing us how to teach good stewardship habits—and then we blame church members because they don't do what we tell them. Church members blame clergy because they are so inept, so afraid, and so uncreative when speaking about money.

A stewardship disease called "cirrhosis of the giver" is going around. Many church members in leadership positions suffer from this peculiar disease. Pastors have been advised by pastor-nominating committees that, to be a success, they should never speak about money in the church.

"Mum's the word," pastors have told me. "If Jesus had wanted me to speak about money in the church, then he himself would have said something about it."

I always respond, "He did. Half of the parables speak about the issue of being good stewards." Yet most clergy don't mention the word *money,* and most members are very happy about that.

One reason congregations have such poor stewardship is because they think stewardship is fund-raising. They think it is how you support the church's budget. They think it is the clergy code word for money. They think it is something you do one Sunday in November. But where you find a vibrant, exciting congregation, you will find that they have made stewardship, first of all, a spiritual matter. Stewardship begins the moment a person confesses Christ as Lord. Stewardship is everything we do—how we live out our commitments once we call Christ Lord.

Set Goals

Why do we make stewardship so difficult? I don't know all the answers, and I know that correcting centuries of poor stewardship habits won't happen overnight. But imagine what can happen if you begin to take just one little step—and celebrate that little step.

Start by establishing a focus. You cannot help people develop good stewardship habits without firm, specific, clearly articulated goals. Ask members to increase their giving by 1 percent of their income each year, until they reach the goal of tithe. Increase the mission side of your church budget by a bigger percentage than the operating budget, until you give away more than you spend on yourselves.

Stress Mission

Second, remember that people never give according to their means, but according to their understanding of the needs. If we let people do what they are, by nature, inclined to do, they will do nothing. Churches that experience growth in stewardship do not start with the budget. They start with a clear, precise description of the mission needs. A good stewardship program tells people all year long what is happening.

Healthy stewardship is not concerned with what people have, but with what they do with what they have. The apostle Paul asked Timothy to share this statement with the Christians in Ephesus: "For we brought nothing into the world, so that we can take nothing out of it; but if we have food and clothing, we will be content with these" (I Tim. 6:7-8). I don't want to contradict or challenge Paul, but the truth is that we do take something out of this world when we die. We take the record of what we have done with what God has given to us to use while we are alive.

So don't apologize for asking people to give to the mission of the church of Jesus Christ, and don't be afraid to stress the needs.

Keep It Biblical

Third, keep stewardship biblical. This does not mean blasting biblical texts at each other. Keeping it biblical means teaching theology to people—stewardship theology.

Dietrich Bonhoeffer wrote:

[G]race is costly because it calls us to follow, and it is grace because it calls us to follow Jesus Christ. It is costly because it costs [us our] life, and it is grace because it gives the . . . only true life. It is costly because it condemns sin, and grace because it justifies the sinner. Above all, it is costly because it cost God the life of His son . . . and what has cost God much cannot be cheap for us.

Authentic Christian stewardship cannot be developed apart from a sound biblical and theological basis.

Jesus said, "If any want to become my followers, let them deny themselves and take up their cross and follow me" (Matt. 16:24). We all know, don't we, that there is not much self-denial going on in our churches, not much cross-bearing, and therefore not many who are really following Jesus. But you can't develop good stewardship habits if you don't first have people firmly committed to Christ and the church.

The needs of the world are so massive. We can't satisfy all the existing needs or cure all the problems, but that is no excuse for doing nothing, though many people (and churches) make that their excuse for being such poor stewards. But suppose it is true, and I believe it is, that one day we will have to explain to God both what we did and what we failed to do, in our askings and our givings to the mission work of the church of Jesus Christ.

A Loving, Caring Ministry

CHARLES F. "SKIP" ARMISTEAD

Before graduating from seminary, I vowed to never preach or teach about money. I reasoned that helping persons with their spiritual life would produce the money needed for ministry. I also didn't like the stigma of "All that preacher wants is money."

I never spoke about financial giving during my first two years in ministry. I focused on "spiritual matters." As time passed, I noticed that no matter how much I helped persons with their prayer life, worship, Christian education, missional outreach, jail ministry, marriage, family life, vocational choices, and all the other areas of their lives, the issue of money continued to arise. Eventually, I realized that a person's relationship with money *is* a spiritual issue. Helping persons grow in their relationship between God and money, and their lives become a fulfilling ministry. I then acknowledged that God did not ask me for my vow.

Whether our church members are wealthy or broke, helping people learn to trust God to guide the use of their financial resources, or lack of them, is spiritual growth. Helping persons to trust God to provide, when they have little or nothing, is spiritual growth. Helping persons who "have" to share with those who "have not" is spiritual growth.

Helping persons grow in their relationship with God and the money they possess (or wish they possessed) is one of the most loving, caring ministries a church can provide. For if anyone struggles, worries, or is bitter about their financial situation, then "money" most likely has control of them, instead of God helping them control it. Even church members who get upset at our talk about money as a spiritual issue is a sign that money is a god attempting to be in control.

SMALL GROUP STUDY

Small Groups and Money

MARYLE ASHLEY

The Christian life is not lived in isolation. As Jesus showed, the call to the Kingdom is a call to community. His disciples provided companionship on his mission, and themselves became powerful witnesses who kept the Christian faith alive. Similar aspects of support and growth occur again and again when small groups of disciples gather in Jesus' name.

Companionship, badly needed in exploring money issues as a difficult dimension of your life, can make the difference between staying on the journey and turning back.

Working with money is hard work. Basic values about money (like its psychological security, associated power, and seemingly necessary accumulation) are called into question by a Christian perspective (like the source of ultimate security, ultimate power, and satisfaction in intentional sharing).

Such a reversal of acquired values can stir up a storm within. That is a good time to have companions in the boat with you. Not only can they admit their own fears over this journey (thus making yours less unique and more manageable), but they also can help you recognize the Lord's presence when he comes to calm the storm. Forming or joining a small group to work with money can be an important step toward spiritual maturity.

GETTING STARTED

All any group ever needs to start is someone to invite it to begin. If you are the "someone," issue your invitation—announce it at church, make it a Sunday school class, post a flyer on bulletin boards, make a few phone calls. The chances are that if you are interested, so are others.

HINTS ABOUT GROUPS

If you have ever been in a group, you might recall some of the things that seemed to "work" and others that did not. Material on groups abounds, and you might want to brush up a little before you issue your invitation. Here are a few key points to keep in mind:

1. *Size*—Keep the size manageable—not more than twelve—even if you must arbitrarily limit the size or form two groups. A group larger than twelve will be too large for each person to have an opportunity to share and be heard. (When working with money, regular sharing is important.) A minimum size of four or five is recommended, so that there is some diversity in the sharing.

2. *Commitment to Meet*—The life of a group grows as its members come together to meet. If every member is present at every meeting, the group grows evenly and steadily. If, however, members drift in and out (no matter how valid their reasons for missing), the group does not grow together. For a relatively short-term group, regular attendance will be imperative. You might make attendance at each class a requirement for participation, and talk about why at the first meeting.

3. *Be Faithful*—Once the parameters of the group are set—how many weeks it will be, what time it starts, what time it ends—follow them faithfully.

4. *Break Bread Together*—After the Resurrection, whenever Jesus appeared to the disciples, he ate with them—a common everyday act that allayed the disciples' fears. The same breaking of bread through a simple fare—doughnuts and coffee, fruit and cheese—also relaxes a group and brings it closer right away. If you try it, see how quickly others in the group volunteer to bring the refreshments next time—a good indication that commitment to the group is forming.

5. *Centering In*—At the beginning of each session, take a few moments to be quiet together. You might read a Scripture verse, or just sit quietly. These moments are invaluable for collecting oneself and turning the focus to the present.

6. *Sharing as Led*—Although you have heard it a thousand times, one more reminder on keeping group sharing free and voluntary is too important to miss. In sharing times, you may need to get things started, and often the level of your sharing will determine what follows—honesty calls forth honesty. But you will need to trust what follows; let others share as they are willing and able. Resist the urge to "go around the circle" or force anyone into sharing. As trust grows through the group's regular contact, those persons less eager to share will open up.

7. *Avoid "Head Trips"*—Keep the questions and responses at a personal-experience level: Not the "What should our economic policy toward Latin America be?" but more the "How did you feel when you learned that you pay more for an apple grown in this state than for a banana imported from Latin America?"

8. *Scattering*—Before ending the session, take time for prayer.

SUGGESTED OUTLINE

The outline of group sessions which follows suggests a format with exercises, questions, and Scripture that a group might use for eight weeks. By the end of eight weeks, you will be ready to keep going on your own, or even scatter out like the disciples, starting new groups. Once the Holy Spirit descends and new creative energy touches your group, the faith will be spread.

The content for each week aims at a balance among: (1) Scripture or Bible study; (2) psychological aspects, especially an awareness of feelings being raised while looking at money; and (3) sociological dimensions that connect this learning to the reality of the global society. If you do not finish all three dimensions in one session, try to continue with the material the next session, so that the group does not become unbalanced—possibly focusing only on Scripture and feelings. All three dimensions are essential for growth.

WEEK 1
The Christian Perspective: Seeing God as Giver

Scripture: Psalm 24, Psalm 50

Theme: All things come from God.
We are blessed by the grace God gives.
We give back out of gratitude.
We give back in joy.
We give through prayer obedience, seeking God's will, loving others, sharing with others, and giving our money.

Feelings: Take five minutes of silence to reflect on your own life. Where is God Giver for you?
Your family
Your home
Your church
Your paycheck
Where are you Giver for yourself? What

do you feel that you yourself have earned? Form subgroups of three or four to discuss where you feel God as Giver and where you feel yourself as Giver.

Grounding: Read Leviticus 26:3-5, 9-13; Luke 12:22-34; John 3:16.
In small groups, discuss your reaction to each passage. Name God's gifts in each one.
Discuss ways we freely receive those gifts. Or do we receive them graciously?

Assignment: To share with the group, write down:
Your earliest childhood memories of money—one positive experience and one negative experience.
Reread the Scripture passages discussed in this session.

WEEK 2
Taking Stock: Where Am I?

Scripture: Psalm 8, Psalm 49

Theme: There is no right and wrong feeling about God as Giver.
Feelings are not moral; feelings are real.
Knowing your feelings is important.
Your actions as a Christian are important.
Feelings and actions many never line up. ("If it feels good, do it" is not a moral guideline.)
There is tension living as a Christian in a non-Christian world.
Don't judge yourself or try to be something you are not.

Feelings: Share the assignment from the last session in small groups.

Grounding: Examine the reality of money in life today. Discuss these questions:
Who are the wealthy?
Who are the poor?
Where do you fit?
(This discussion is not to deal with "shoulds" and "oughts." Be as honest as possible.)

Assignment: Write down some of your recent experiences with money—one that left you feeling good and one that was not so good. Be prepared to share.
Reread the Scripture passages from this session.

WEEK 3
Where Is My Security?

Scripture: Matthew 6:33

Theme: Where do you put your hope for security?
It is important to be honest and to be aware of what makes you feel safe.
Security lies in one thing you cannot do without.
In American society, money is probably the number one security.
Money buys comfort and pleasure.
Money signifies power, influence, and prestige.
Most people want to be rich.
Living in this culture, we are swept up in a life of accumulating money.
For Christians, God is security. Anything we place between God and us is an idol. We sometimes try to compartmentalize our lives. (I make money for the practical needs of life; God can be in charge of my spiritual life.) But everything is God's. Our problem lies in not being able to let God be our security. We can't believe it. We hear in our heads that God loves us and will never leave us, but we're afraid to live as if that is true. Our growth as Christians depends on our trusting God more. It is a lifetime process.

Feelings: In small groups, share the assignment from the last session. Determine whether your "good" and "bad" feelings about money dealt with security.

Grounding: To believe that God loves us and to shift that knowledge and belief from the head to the heart, do the following exercise for five minutes:
● Sit still, in a relaxed position

● Close your eyes.
● When your breathing slows, repeat in your mind: God loves me.
● Hear the words; feel the words; believe the words; rest in the words.

Assignment: Each day this week, spend at least five minutes meditating on "God loves me." Reread the Scripture passage from this session.

WEEK 4
Giving Out of Grace

Scripture: Deuteronomy 14:22-29; Malachi 3:6-10; Matthew 23:23

Theme: Giving to God is your response to grace: realizing that all is given by God; trusting in God for security; experiencing the peace and depth of God's love. We respond in gratitude. Giving a tithe is one way to respond to God's grace.

Feelings: In small groups, talk about tithing. Do you now, or have you ever tithed? If so, how did your start? What happened? How do you feel about tithing? Is it a burden, a joy, an "ought"?

Grounding: Review the Scripture passages. What would you have done differently this week, if those passages guided your life? As a group, determine what your congregation would be like if 50 percent of the current givers tithed?

Assignment: Look at your present level of giving. Figure what percent of your gross income you give through the church. Commit to increase your giving by 1 percent.

WEEK 5
Giving Out of Joy

Scripture: 2 Corinthians 8

Theme: It is said that it is better to give than to receive. Joy is the reason.
The unexpected return on giving and the

sense of joy encourages more giving. It is impossible, by the world's standards, to receive by giving away.

The world says to cling, hold on, accumulate. God says to let go, open up, be free. There is release in giving. There is joy in giving that transcends understanding.

Feelings: In small groups, reflect on these questions:
What was the most fun you ever had in giving a gift?
What do you like to give?
To whom do you enjoy giving? Why?

Grounding: Christmas baskets prepared and given to needy families have been a standard outreach experience for many churches. Remember what those times were like. Identify the kinds of giving involved: money, time, food. Which kind of giving gave you the most joy?

Assignment: Think of three ways your group could give with joy. Make notes of any joyous return you receive from giving.

WEEK 6
Giving Out of Justice

Scripture: Amos 2:7-8; 5:7-11; 5:24

Theme: Justice is another motive that stimulates giving. As we grow as Christians, we become aware that our brothers and sisters are worldwide and connected to us through Christ. We also become aware of the inequities of living conditions in other countries, and within our own nation and town. From our unity and our desire to share what we have with the family of God, we give out of a sense of justice.

Feelings: Name the living conditions of your town, the nation, or the world that bring you happiness? Sadness? Anger? Hopelessness?

Grounding: Share some of the ways the group can give out of joy.
Discuss how to "pray" the newspaper/ TV/radio.

Commit to one another to take these steps as you read or listen to the news:
Who is this person or group?
How am I connected to them?
What is my prayer on their behalf?
Hold that person or group in God's presence that day.

Assignment: Pray the newspaper every day. Note your responses, and what happens.

WEEK 7
Expanding Gratitude

Scripture: 2 Corinthians 9

Theme: Our spiritual journey never ends. Our love for God grows. As our love for God increases, our love of unnecessary things decreases. As we become more and more grateful, we can become aware of where God's grace is being laid.

Feelings: Take a few minutes to reflect and recall a grace moment from the past week. Share in small groups.

Grounding: Write down ten things you are grateful for. Share with the group.

Assignment: Each night, reflect on the day that is ending. Write down the occurrences you are grateful for.

WEEK 8
Continuing the Money Journey

Theme: This is the last group session. This is not the end of the money journey, but another beginning. Take time to evaluate and the ways you may choose to continue. Letting go and responding to God's grace is a lifetime process.

Feelings: How do you feel about the group experience?
What went well?
What could be improved?
Where do you feel you grew?

Grounding: Write down one specific thing you will do because you had this group experience. Place it in an envelope, address it to yourself, and ask another member of the group to mail it to you in six weeks.

Assignment: Trust God. Live in joy. Give out of gratitude.

PART TWO

PROCLAIMING THE WORD

Introduction

DON JOINER

The problem with the word *stewardship* is not the word itself, but the corruption of that word as it is used in the church. If we placed an announcement on a sign in front of the church that next week was "Stewardship Sunday," most people would panic, hold on to their wallets—or stay at home! The only time we use the word in the church is when we are trying to get people to give.

Stewardship is a faith-fulled word that refers to "what we do after we say yes to Jesus Christ." It is a celebration of the truth of God's love in our life. It is a word that describes how we respond in our total life, after we have discovered our receivership. It is an affirmation that we are first receivers; in response, we become gracious givers.

How your church defines stewardship directs the organization of ministry in all areas. If defined as "money," all that is done will be directed toward how to get it. If we define it as a relationship between receiving God's love and responding in faith and action, we will help others to experience that rela-

tionship and celebrate the "life of the steward."

Frank Colclough's article shows how one church changed stewardship from money raising to an expression of the life of that congregation. George Englehardt and Norma Wimberly provide a model for Stewardship Sunday which may not be a part of a fund-raising program.

Patricia Wilson-Kastner helps pastors broaden their stewardship preaching style from money-centered to faith-centered sermons. She takes stewardship to the higher level of a way of living, not merely financial giving.

Those seeking help for sermon preparation, devotional material, and worship resources will find this section full of support. The funding ministry of the church can be fun. Brian Bauknight raises the laughter level with his list of humorous stewardship illustrations. Gil Miller, as only he can, provides two short skits to be used in stewardship programs, events, worship, or training.

 NEWSLETTER

Always Talking About Money

ANONYMOUS

Not long ago, someone said, "Our preacher is always talking about money, and he makes me tired." That started me thinking. Just how much talking should a preacher do on the subject of money?

Before I tried to decide the matter, I made a hurried trip through my New Testament and arrived at some very interesting and surprising discoveries.

I may have missed a few, but I found that Jesus had

preached at least thirty-one sermons on the subject of money and possessions. Out of the thirty-nine parables, at least thirteen of them deal directly with the question of money.

Now, if our pastor preached on money at the same ratio, he would devote one third, or about seventeen sermons, of his total year's preaching program to that matter. And I confess, that would sound to me like a lot of money talk.

But Jesus was never the pastor of a church, and maybe he did not know how much trouble too much money talk makes inside a congregation. But Paul knew. He founded a whole string of churches and was the pastor of several, and he knew how people such as we are feel about such things.

I didn't have time to read all of Paul's letters carefully, but I did discover that in one of his sermons, he quoted Jesus as having said that "it is more blessed to give than to receive." I couldn't find that in any of the four Gospels, and I decided that it must have been one of Jesus' sayings that was remembered by the people but was not included by any of the Gospel writers. That made me think that Jesus must have done even more talking about money than is recorded in the New Testament.

In addition, I found Paul warning his churches again and again against the sin of covetousness. Apparently that was a problem in some of the congregations. And in one case, to the Thessalonian church, he talked pretty straight, telling them that if a man would not work, he was not to eat. Evidently they had some folk up in that town that were trying to live off other people.

One of the most interesting things I discovered as I skipped through my New Testament was that the apostle Paul took up the first great Christian collection. It must have been just a little like one of our modern campaigns, for he had a committee in every church who were responsible for collecting and forwarding the money, and the people were expected to give something every week!

He insisted that it should be done in a systematic and orderly fashion, not haphazard or by chance. It sounded just a little like an every-member canvass, to me.

The principal difference was that Paul's great collection was taken in behalf of some kind of missionary project. It seems that a lot of the Christians in Jerusalem were in desperate need, and the money was collected to help feed them, not spent on the local budget. It must have been a good big collection because it took a considerable group of men to transport it to Jerusalem.

That collection meant a lot more to me when I read somewhere that the first Christian churches were made up of slaves, working people, women, widows, and only a very occasional man of affairs. There was a depression on in the East about that time, and business was at a standstill in many cities. But Paul never let up on the subject of that collection. And the people gave generously.

As I have thought it over, I am glad our preacher does ask for money a good many times. That means that we are a church that is doing things. We are always attempting just a little bit more for Christ's sake. I think I would be ashamed of ourselves if he did not have to ask for money. It would make me think that we were in the peanut business.

So Pastor, go on preaching about money. Preach about it just as Jesus did, as Paul did, and as the saints and martyrs did. We're with you, for the responsibility—the stewardship for it—belongs to all of us, and not just you alone.

MONEY TALK

Permission to reprint this article has been given by Stewardship Education, Presbyterian Church (U.S.A.)

Revitalizing the Congregation Through Biblical Stewardship

THE REVEREND DR. FRANK D. COLCLOUGH

One of the joys I have experienced during my twenty-four years of ministry were the sixteen years I served as pastor of the Goodwill Presbyterian Church in Mayesville, South Carolina. During the 1950s and early 1960s, Goodwill was one of the largest African American churches in the United Presbyterian Church (USA). Located in a rural farming area, the congregation, through the mid-1960s, was composed primarily of sharecroppers, farmers, and day laborers. Even though the membership was relatively large, the congregation was not self-supporting. It depended upon aid and subsidy from governing bodies to meet essential obligations. Very little was given to mission and benevolence. The church saw itself as an object of mission, not as a participant in mission.

I became pastor of the Goodwill Church when the primary source of livelihood for church members was shifting from farm work to employment in professional vocations and industries that had moved into the area. The church's annual budget was growing;

45

however, individual giving was not increasing in proportion to the higher earned income of the membership. Church leadership continued to make special appeals to raise enough money to prevent the church from ending the year in the red.

A continuing annual decrease in aid and subsidy, as well as the fact that the presbytery had placed the church in a category for self-support within the next two to three years, made it clear that something had to be done other than fund-raisers, rallies, and special appeals as methods of financial stewardship.

I decided to initiate a stewardship education project within the congregation as a part of my studies at McCormick Theological Seminary. The intent was to move the congregation from an emphasis on fund-raising (to support the mission and ministry of the church) to a broader understanding of the mission of the church—what it means to have faith in God, to accept Jesus Christ as Lord and Savior, and to be a church member.

A crucial focus of the project was providing the opportunity for every church officer and key leader to study the Christian tradition and Reformed heritage, and to come to grips with their own personal convictions about God and the mission of the church. Understanding who we are and whose we are must always precede the challenge to give a proportionate amount of our income to the work of the church. Stewardship technique is secondary to understanding mission and creating excitement within the congregation about that mission.

> Stewardship is an expression of congregational life. When people are not taught why they should give, many give for the wrong reasons, reluctantly, or not at all. What one gives in terms of time, talent, and money to support the church is directly related to the depth of one's faith in God and one's understanding of the mission of the church. Local church leaders cannot make the assumption that everyone has a mature understanding of mission and stewardship. Rather, there needs to be an intentional and continuous effort of education in these areas.

In many of our congregations, norms and values about stewardship need to be altered. A surprising number of church members equate stewardship solely with the giving of money to support the church's budget. Because of this, new ideas and broader concepts about stewardship are needed. Teaching the theological basis for stewardship begins with God, God's earth, and what God has done for us through God's Son, Jesus Christ.

Stewardship is centered in the conviction that everything we have—time, talents, money, health, air, water, property, relationships, the Gospel—is given to us by God. We simply hold these gifts in trust. Since all things come from God, it is impossible to separate stewardship from the totality of life. Life, itself, is stewardship.

The theological perspective taken in initiating this project at the Goodwill Church was that people should give to the church in response to what God has already done for them. It is the job of the church leadership to help people understand this concept. Paul wrote in First Timothy 1:15, "The saying is sure and worthy of full acceptance, that Christ Jesus came into the world to save sinners." This is the very heart of Christianity, the supreme claim of its faith. It is the vital pulse of Christian belief that God has visited us in Christ—because God cares for us. In Christ, God desires that the lost be found, the wrong be set right, that whose who sit in darkness see the great light of their salvation. Nobody else could do for us what God in Christ did for us.

Those who take the vows of church membership and profess Jesus Christ as their Lord and Savior need to develop a stewardship philosophy that compels them to give in response to what God has done for them. A task of the church is to enable church members to experience the grace of God in their lives, so that they, in turn, might freely respond through their gifts, that others might also know and experience that grace. The project at Goodwill Church was not a two-month campaign held during the stewardship renewal season to secure pledges for the next year's budget. It was a year-round effort of workshops, Bible studies, group discussions, worship services, and sermons on mission and the theological basis for stewardship. the project achieved its objectives and helped to raise the mission and stewardship consciousness of the congregation, resulting in self-support and more money for mission and benevolence.

I learned some valuable lessons through that project:

> In any program of stewardship, the pastoral leadership must be the starting point.
> An elderly member once said to me, "Mr. Preacher, we'll go as far as you lead us. If you don't lead us nowhere, we aren't going nowhere."

1. In any program of stewardship, the pastoral leadership must be the starting point. If the minister(s) is not committed to a program of stewardship, if he or she is not willing to set the example through faith and action, it will have little chance of success. The minister(s) must have the conviction that it is his or her duty to teach, preach, and practice what being a good steward is all about. An elderly member once said to me, "Mr. Preacher, we'll go as far as you lead us. If you don't lead us nowhere, we aren't going nowhere." Of course, I believe in shared leadership; the point is, the minister(s) is the key to creating the proper environment and attitude for faithful stewardship.

2. The emphasis should be on the giver, not the gift—on the person, not the money. The main thrust of a stewardship sermon should be on bringing men and women into total surrender to Christ, not on finances. Paul uses the example of the Macedonians in appealing to the church at Corinth for a generous offering: "For, as I can testify, they voluntarily gave according to their means, and even beyond their means, begging us earnestly for the privilege of sharing in this ministry to the saints . . . they gave themselves first to the Lord" (2 Cor. 8:3-5). When people have given themselves first to the Lord, then they give of their resources freely and willingly.

3. A successful stewardship program has a plan that reflects the needs of the congregation. A congregation must, first of all, determine what the needs are and where it wants to go. Then it can begin to draw upon appropriate resources to help meet those needs. Our denomination produces excellent resource materials to assist local churches in the implementation of their stewardship program. However, the starting point is at the local level.

4. A successful stewardship program must be year-round. Workshops, training sessions, and sermons on mission and stewardship need to be given throughout the year. Mission interpretation through real-life stories is crucial. In stewardship, as in every other Christian discipline, one can never let up.

5. There is the tendency to separate stewardship from Christian education, evangelism, and other areas of church life. All these areas are interrelated and need to be seen as such when developing a stewardship program for the local church.

6. The congregation needs to feel some ownership in the process. One way to do this is to keep the membership informed. The session is responsible for developing the annual budget. It makes good sense for the session to share the budget with the congregation, interpreting it within the context of mission. This ensures clarity to givers about their connection to Presbyterianism and what mission they enable to take place through their gifts. Also, there needs to be full disclosure to the congregation about the income and disbursement of all receipts.

7. An enthusiastic attitude by the pastoral and church leadership is crucial. The ministry of the church is God's work, and God will supply what is needed to accomplish the work. Taking God at God's word and knowing that God will supply our every need is reason enough for excitement. And when the leadership gets excited about the things of the Lord, that excitement has a way of spreading throughout the congregation.

PLANNING TOOL

Stewardship Sunday

GEORGE ENGLEHARDT AND NORMA WIMBERLY

Stewardship Sunday can occur anytime within the liturgical or program year!

Consider initiating and sponsoring a Stewardship Sunday celebration each quarter, or once per season of the liturgical year. Talk to the chair of the worship committees or your pastor to verify the dates and emphasis of each season, and then determine ways you can work together. If you choose to have additional program activities related to each special Stewardship Sunday, coordinate with the appropriate educational group or leadership team.

ADVENT

Some churches initiate a property inspection and evaluation during this time. In a worship service, consider a special thanksgiving for property, buildings, supplies, and grounds. Begin to see that we are stewards of all things of this world. For youth, encourage a clean-up, paint-up, fix-up project. For children, organize a time to plant flower bulbs on the church grounds.

Advent Litany:

Leader: God, we hear your call to justice and righteousness.

People: **As your people, we hear your call to liberation and reconciliation.**

Leader: God, we hear your call to peace and shalom.

People: **As your people, we hear your call to harmony and wholeness.**

Leader: This is the season of expectation.

People: **During this Advent season, may we reach deeper levels of devotion and discipleship, of sacrifice and servanthood.**

Leader: This is a time of growth and renewal.

People: **During this worship, may we catch a new vision of the reign that Christ came to establish on earth.**

EPIPHANY

The gifts of the Magi to baby Jesus signal a time for us to affirm all the gifts we receive from God, as well as our individual response to God's gifts. On Epiphany Sunday, host a gifts-discovery workshop, with sessions for all ages in the congregation!

Offertory Prayer for Epiphany:

Lord, we know that you are the Creator. You made everything. We appreciate your generosity, and we would like to be generous with our gifts in all areas of our lives. We pray that you will help us discern those gifts and use them wisely. We thank you for your Son, Our Lord. Amen.

LENT

During Lent, a suggested emphasis is renewed commitment to be faithful stewards of our bodies. During the worship service, lift up special prayers of gratitude for good health and for healing of members who suffer. During the offertory presentation, ask your pastor to include Romans 12:1 as a guiding passage for gathering and presenting the offering.

If your congregation has a special mission project each year, invite the children and youth of the church to hold a bike-a-thon or walk-a-thon. An event of that nature can highlight the mission project, as well as good exercise habits.

EASTER

During the Sundays of Easter, you may want to emphasize Stewardship of the Gospel and host a special Bible study of the four Gospels, particularly utilizing the Gospel of Luke and Acts. During the worship services of this season, ask the lector or liturgist to read the Gospel in the midst of the people—from one of the aisles, rather than from the lectern or pulpit.

A Call to Confession for Eastertide:

We do not always know what to do with the empty tomb, Lord. We do not always know where we are going. However, with your help, we can achieve clarity of vision of where we've been. Let us silently, with honesty, open-mindedness, and willingness, take an inventory of our days. In this moment of personal, individual, and community confession, let us face our shortcomings with the courage of the resurrection.

PENTECOST SEASON

Although Easter is the holiest of days in the church year, the church historically was born on Pentecost. A reminder of the Gospel tradition would be appropriate preparation for the "Birthday Party." Consider this litany as a song of new birth and renewed commitment.

A Litany of Stewardship:

Leader: Maker of heaven and earth, by whose design we have come to life, in whose image we have been cast, and by whose kind providence opportunity and responsibility have come our way,

People: **Help us to know that we are accountable to you, the owner of all things seen and unseen.**

Leader: Thank you for the time of life, for you are the giver of both life and time.

People: **Help us to use all our hours in ways that will please you.**

Leader: Thank you for the ability to learn and do many things.

People: **Help us to develop and use our skills in ways that will advance your reign.**

Leader: Thank you for money and what can be accomplished with it.

People: **Grant that our earning, spending, investing, and giving will be acceptable in your sight.**

Leader: Thank you for the resources of the earth.

People: **Help us to responsibly use the soil, air, and water, so that future generations will know your abundance.**

Leader: Thank you for health of body and mind.

People: **Help us avoid all habits and abuses that unnecessarily reduce our physical and spiritual well-being.**

All: **Thank you for the Good News in Jesus Christ that has forever changed the human outlook, given us new birth and eternal hope.**

SEASON AFTER PENTECOST

This lengthy season offers us the opportunity to pay closer attention to the gifts and miracles of everyday living. A "Gratitude List" is one way to open our eyes to the extraordinary in the ordinary. Encourage each Sunday school class to set aside time for each person to make a list of at least twenty things for which they are grateful. With small children, this can be done on newsprint, with the leader recording each thing the children name. At the beginning of each administrative meeting during this season, ask the members to name things about the congregation to add to a community "gratitude list."

Thanksgiving Prayer:

Great are the blessings you give us each day, O God. As we depart from this time of worship with newly thankful hearts, help us to pay closer attention to each miracle in which we partici-

pate. Keep us ever mindful of the wonders of life. Help us to trust in your mercies and goodness, which are new every morning. Amen.

THANKSGIVING

During the service of Thanksgiving, which may correspond to a celebration Sunday at the end of a financial-commitment program, consider a time of personal witness to God's giving. Some congregations include a witness time each Sunday, or one Sunday a month, just before the dedication of the offering. If this is not a regular part of worship, consider carefully the persons invited to share their testimony. During this time, someone may discover that they *want* to give a witness based on their Gratitude List!

A Prayer of Confession for Thanksgiving:

Christ, you call us to live lives of gratitude, yet we are prone to grumbling. You call us to be faithful, but our days are marked by infidelity. You call us to live in solidarity with others, but we treat our brothers and sisters as strangers. You call us to be generous, but we respond with closed fists. You call us to stand steadfast in your love, but on occasion we commit ourselves to the company of evildoers. Forgive us, O Christ, and direct our hearts to the compassionate love of God.

In the fall, or whenever you conduct a financial emphasis, coordinate your efforts with the Finance Committee and financial commitment team. Get involved with the development and communication of a narrative budget. Volunteer to share your witness of the way God is working in your life through the mission and ministry of the congregation.

Stewardship Sunday can become an event when your church's spending plan tells the exciting story of your congregation's mission, rather than its misery! A narrative budget, instead of a line-item budget, can accomplish that for you. When loyal members and friends find themselves reflected in the story of your church's ministry, they are more motivated to give than when asked to analyze and compare an accounting manager's presentation.

Develop a narrative budget or spending plan that tells the unique story of your church. What is special and irreplaceable about your congregation and its mission in the lives of members and the community? You may want to select four or five specific areas of ministry, and then divide all proposed spending for the fiscal year into these categories. You will find that Worship, Christian Education and Faith Nurture, Missions, and Pastoral Care are categories that apply to almost any congregation.

Using these categories, working committees and staff can shape the "budget vision" and translate every line item into percentages that fund the ministry of each program area. The goal is to enable people to see that they are giving to support mission and ministry, not to simply pay bills!

(For example: Calculate how much of the pastor's time or staff time is used in preparing for worship each week. That percentage is then extracted from salary, benefits, parsonage costs, utility expenses, insurance, and so on included in the category of Worship.) All proposed expenses are spread by percentages into your story categories. At the end of this process, you have a narrative budget that tells a story and describes a vision that may have been hidden behind your line-item budget.

Don't forget about giving beyond your church. Supporting the connectional mission is a great strength of our denomination. Add appropriate payments to the story of your congregation's mission, describing what each accomplishes in a sentence or two. As part of your mission, factor in overhead expenses which support the service organizations that use your facilities. That is also mission! The commitment that is revealed in your story is probably deeper than you imagine.

On Commitment Sunday, when you emphasize financial commitment, share your narrative spending plan. Include a simple graphic to show the percentage of the total budget that each category represents. It can be helpful to show bottom-line dollar amounts here. For example, a brief description of the activities

> "I have a very strong feeling that the opposite of love is not hate, it's apathy."
>
> —BUSCAGLIA

and programs in Christian Education, together with the community-building groups and events you provide for, shows that 31 percent of your budget supports the vital ministry of Christian Education and Faith Nurture.

Recruit someone willing to give a personal witness to each category. A choir member or liturgist might speak about worship. A Sunday school class officer can offer a word about experience in Christian Education. A member of a group that meets in your building can be invited to thank the congregation for its mission with them. Someone else may share how they were supported by the pastor during illness or death. Even apportionments come alive when given faces and voices! Why not have a retired, respected pastor express gratitude for the pension your giving provides?

Stewardship Sunday becomes an event when everyone discovers that they are all a part of the church's story. You will have helped them make the connection between financial stewardship and your church's ministry. Visioning, answering God's call, need not be limited by line-item balances, or even by projected deficits. Fully balanced spending plans call for little faith. Manageable projected deficits within the context of the story and the call of a congregation become invitations to grow in giving. Faith and experience declare that God does not call us without providing what we need!

The Finance Committee and Stewardship team have major roles in encouraging givers to grow in generosity and joy on the shared journey toward tithing, putting God first in all we do.

Whenever you declare a Stewardship Sunday, you are reminding fellow Christians of our commitment to offer all that we are to the Lord—not just our financial resources. Regular reminders can become a part of a year-round stewardship education program.

Open your minds, your hearts, and your imaginations—the possibilities are without limit!

DEVOTIONAL

The Holy Spirit Inspires Faith and Imparts Spiritual Gifts

A Devotional Reading of First Corinthians 12

D O N A L D   W .   J O I N E R

Leader: Now I want to give you some further information in some spiritual matters. You have not forgotten that you were gentiles, following dumb idols just as your impulses led you.

Reader One: We all have different gifts, but it is the same Spirit who gives them.

Reader Two: There are different ways of serving God, but it is the same Lord who is served.

Leader: God works through different persons in different ways, but it is the same God who achieves those purposes through them all. Each person is given a gift by the Spirit, so that gift may be used for the common good.

Reader Three: One person's gift by the Spirit is to speak with wisdom, another's to speak with knowledge.

Reader Four: The same Spirit gives to another faith, to another the ability to heal, to another the power to do great deeds.

Leader: The same Spirit gives to another the gift of preaching the word of God, to another the ability to discriminate in spiritual matters, to another speech in different tongues and to yet another the power to interpret the tongues. Behind all these gifts is the operation of the same Spirit, who distributes to each individual, as the Spirit wills.

UNISON: **As the human body, which has many parts, is a unity, and those parts, despite their multiplicity,** **constitute one single body, so it is with Christ. For we were all baptized by the Spirit into one body, whether we were Jews, Greeks, slaves or free, and we have all had experience of the same Spirit.**

Reader One: Now the body is not one member but many.

Leader: If the foot should say,

Reader Two: "Because I am not a hand I don't belong to the body,"

Leader: does that alter the fact that the foot is a part of the body? Or if the ear should say,

Reader Three: "Because I am not an eye I don't belong to the body,"

Leader: does that mean that the ear is not part of the body? After all, if the body were all one eye, for example, where would be the sense of hearing?

Reader Four: Or if it were all one ear, where would be the sense of smell?

Leader: But God has arranged all the parts in the one body, according to God's design. For if everything were concentrated in one part, how could there be a body at all?

UNISON: **The fact is there are many parts, but only one body.**

Leader: So that the eye cannot say to the hand,

51

Reader One: "I don't need you!"

Leader: nor, again, can the head say to the feet,

Reader Two: "I don't need you!"

Leader: On the contrary, those parts of the body which have no obvious function are the more essential to health;

Reader Three: And to those parts of the body which seem to us to be less deserving of notice, we have to allow the highest honor of function.

Reader Four: The parts which do not look beautiful have a deeper beauty in the work they do,

Reader One: while the parts which look beautiful may not be at all essential to life!

Reader Two: But,

Reader Three: God has harmonized the whole body by giving importance of function to the parts which lack apparent importance,

UNISON: **that the body should work together as a whole with all the members in sympathetic relationship with one another.**

Reader Four: So it happens

Leader: that if one member suffers

Reader One: all the other members suffer with it,

Reader Two:
Reader Three: and if one member is honored all the members share a common joy.

Leader: Now you are together the body of Christ, and individually you are members of that body.

Reader Four: And in Christ's Church God has appointed

Reader One: first some to be messengers,

Reader Two: second, some to be preachers of power;

Reader Three: third, teachers.

Leader: After them he has appointed workers of spiritual power;

Reader Four: persons with the gift of healing,

Reader One: helpers,

Reader Two: organizers,

Reader Three: and those with the gift of speaking in tongues.

Leader: As we look at the body of Christ do we find all are messengers, all are preachers, or all teachers? Do we find all wielders of spiritual power, all able to heal, all able to speak in tongues, or all able to interpret the tongues?

UNISON: NO,

Reader Four: We find God's distribution of gifts is on the same principles of harmony that God has shown in the human body.

Leader: You should set your hearts on the best spiritual gifts.

 SERMON HELP

Theology of Stewardship for Preaching

PATRICIA WILSON-KASTNER

When I was a child growing up in a Roman Catholic family, *stewardship* was not a word we used. It was too "Protestant." But we all knew that how you used your money was very important. If you had a quarter, you could buy a couple of Mounds, savor the chocolate, coconuts, and almonds, and endanger your immortal soul because you were so selfish, or you could put the quarter in a tin can for the missions and ransom the soul of a pagan baby, both saving a soul and receiving credit from God for doing good.

Our theology may have been a little askew by more mature standards, but we learned early that what we did with our money was important not just for us, but it mattered to God, to Mary, to angels, saints, and poor struggling missionaries, and children like us all across the globe. I am still grateful for that youthful vision, because it opened me to the notion that money was not dirty or unimportant. Rather, it was a wonderful instrument to help others, even if I could not see them or reach out to them myself.

I also learned early on that money was like toys and cookies—even if I wanted them all for myself, sharing was the better way to behave. If thousands and thousands of us shared our nickels and dimes and quarters, children like us who lived in many different places would be baptized, learn about the faith, receive an education, and grow up to be teachers and nuns and priests (my horizons were more narrow in those days).

I remember those days with appreciation because that youthful experience was formative for me. I have grown and changed much, but still depend on those roots. Each of us, I suspect, can point to experiences that were equally vital for our growth as Christians, and which gave a form and shape to our feelings and thoughts about stewardship. Sometimes those experiences were positive and offered us strong roots in which to ground our more adult ideas and practices. For others of us, early ideas about stewardship were painful or inadequate, and they need to be changed, or even replaced before we can open ourselves to a healthy and constructive theology of stewardship.

Even though I didn't have a particularly helpful vocabulary in my youth for expressing what stewardship was, I had experiences that taught me about the reality of stewardship in my life—that stewardship is about my whole life, with its time, talent, and money. But never ought I to minimize the importance, I learned very early, of my stewardship of money. My money can help or hurt others as well as myself, and being responsible about my use of money is essential to my Christian life.

"The joy of giving is as often overlooked as the giving of joy."

—DAVID BARTON (1924–   )

"Why is the church always talking about money?" people sometimes complain to clergy, especially to the preacher who has just finished a stewardship sermon. Some reasons for talking about money are obvious—because no institution can survive without money; because the church distributes money and services to needy people and to organizations that serve the community and its people; because clergy and lay church workers and their families need food, clothing, and shelter; because church buildings are used by community organizations and individuals who often have no access to comparable facilities; because we have valuable artistic and cultural monuments to restore and maintain for our children, and those buildings take money. But the real reason, the deep reason the church talks about money is that money is very important to the human heart. I learned that in my childhood experiences with money and missions, and I never want to forget that early lesson.

We like money and value it. Not because we enjoy the little pieces of paper and the coins for themselves, but because of the power, the status, and the comfort that money indeed can buy. In our twentieth-century culture, money is an important sign of our personal power and status. The "price tag" is both a real and a symbolic designation of our society's measurement of value. In twentieth-century America, economic worth is perhaps the most important single criterion of social significance.

Our time and talents also all have economic value, as well as the specific usefulness of each gift to God's service. Stewardship encompasses both our use of money, and our valuable time and varied talents. How we use all our resources is an important indication of our commitments. Our checkbook and our calendar indicate the way we spend our money and our time, and these will usually tell us whether we are really converted to loving God and neighbor, or whether these sentiments are still just words.

As a preacher over the last twenty years, I have become extremely conscious of my own need to be aware of my experiential and theological grounding for preaching about stewardship.

I have found this clarity encouraging and energizing for my preaching, and in my teaching about stewardship to congregations. Such clarity is essential, because stewardship is, I believe, a critical indicator of the spiritual health of a congregation. People who don't give according to their ability are not, in my experience, committed to the Christian life, no matter how much they may protest their devotion. Their situation is somewhat like that of the children in my class who prayed loudly for the mission schools overseas, but spent all their nickels and dimes on Hershey bars. Despite the words of their mouths, their hearts were not committed.

Any person or any congregation that takes seriously its baptismal commitment wants its dedication to ministry and mission to give life to its stewardship activity. The preacher is designated, through ordination or delegation of the preaching responsibility, to articulate to the congregation its theology of stewardship, its

> The preacher is designated, through ordination or delegation of the preaching responsibility, to articulate to the congregation its theology of stewardship, its beliefs that feed its theology, and the experiences that reinforce the truth of its beliefs.
>
> The laity put stewardship to practice in the marketplace of everyday life. But the primary work of the preacher in worship is to make explicit the connection between the theology of commitment to God, and our practice of stewardship in the world.

beliefs that feed its theology, and the experiences that reinforce the truth of its beliefs.

Of course it is essential for laity to speak about their experience and beliefs about stewardship. Their words offer a "real-life" credibility indispensable to the practice of stewardship. The laity put stewardship to practice in the marketplace of everyday life. But the primary work of the preacher in worship is to make explicit the connection between the theology of commitment to God and our practice of stewardship in the world.

That brings us back to the centrality of stewardship in the Christian life. Stewardship emerges in our life from our conversion of hearts to God, and our growth as members of God's people. The centrality of money, and our use of our time and talents, are vital parts of our human life. They express our control over life, our capacity to give and receive value, and they are signs of our importance. We do like money and control over our resources. That's why it is not easy to give. Children must learn to share. Only as they learn to love and care for another can they willingly share with one another.

That's why I believe firmly that good stewardship can't be forced on anyone; it grows from our love for God and others, and our desire to show this love through the church. For this same reason, stewardship is a lifelong process. Stewardship matures as we grow in love and in our desire to share. Our Christian maturity shows when we want to give—to maintain the church, which is of such service to us and to others. The preacher expends maximum effort to encourage and to teach the congregation how to grow in stewardship.

Chiefly, our Christian maturity expresses itself when we give because we love and want to show our love to God and one another. Such maturity is not a matter of years, but of relationship to God. As children of God and sisters and brothers of one another, we want the use of our resources—our time, money, talents—in the service of God and of one another in this world. The preacher's sermons intentionally and directly encourage such development.

Sermons thus best present stewardship to the congregation as our loving responsibility for the use of all our resources; that includes giving to church and other groups to support the worship and work of the church, which have no other means of support than our contributions. Such regular giving is also important as a sign of our own belonging to God's people, our desire to give from our own substance to dedicate our money, time, and energy directly to God's work.

Stewardship, the preacher proclaims, is an expression of our desire as baptized Christians to contribute to the mission and ministry of the church. In the process of our growth in faith, we awaken to the awareness that prayer and generous service are equally important to the fullness of the Christian life. From a practical point of view, it is vital to our Christian maturity both to pray regularly, with attention to our own love and obedience to God, and to give of ourselves through time, talent, and treasure. Frequently, that will involve us in establishing goals for ourselves to help us learn to give better and more freely. Just as learning to ride a bicycle is both joyous freedom and disciplined practice, so good stewardship (as well as good prayer) involves careful effort and a loving heart.

Stewardship, to look at it another way, is not an option for the Christian life; it is a necessity. In sermons, most people receive their most direct teaching about Christian stewardship. Through their preaching, clergy thus must affirm as clearly and straightforwardly as possible the biblical roots of the church's belief and teaching about stewardship. These three statements express the biblical experience of God, which is, in my experience, most crucial to the Christian theology of stewardship:

1. God the Creator is present and active in all of our world.
2. God became incarnate in Jesus Christ.
3. Through the Holy Spirit, God calls us to share Christ's mission in restoring the world as God in love created it to be.

Those deceptively simple statements form, in my experience, an essential grounding for a theology of Christian stewardship. Without such rooting, one is simply engaged in Christian fund-raising. That exercise is laudable and necessary, but it is not Christian stewardship. Christian stewardship grows from an understanding of God, God's relationship to us, and our response to God. Because of that connection, I want to suggest to the preacher the significance of these theological assertions for stewardship.

1. *God the Creator is present and active in all of our world.* God is the Creator of the world and of everything in it. I have just returned from paying a visit to a neighbor whose young-adult child died unexpectedly from an undetected heart problem. The visit

shared one characteristic with many other visits: There was very little of comfort to say to the bereaved. The child was gifted, friendly, good, beautiful, and now is dead. In the parents' eyes, the world "happens," and we are thrust into it. There is no ultimate rhyme or reason for anything. Culture and love are the only comfort we can offer one another, and they are the sole boundaries which protect us from the utter capriciousness of the universe.

To adapt Einstein's phrase, there are many people in this world who believe that God plays dice with the cosmos. For most of them, there is, however, not even any God. The game of dice happens, and we experience the result. This way of perceiving the world is quite distinct from the Christian assumption that there is a God who made the world and cares about the universe and its multiform life. Even the Christian who is angry and feels abandoned or betrayed by God believes that there is a God who has failed the believer's expectations.

That bedrock belief is uttered in the first words of the Bible: "In the beginning, when God created the heavens and the earth, the earth was a formless void, and darkness covered the face of the deep." The story of creation, as the priestly writer recounts it, is the effortless progress of the creative God's commanding of a living order of many creatures, made out of formless chaos. Against the background of a Middle Eastern mythological system which regarded creation as the act of divinities overcoming monsters, or explained it as the unforeseen product of divine fertility, the Hebrew Scriptures portray the world as the product of God's intentional activity.

> Are all of us to follow the Gospel teachings on money and possessions? I don't know. It probably calls us beyond where we would want to go, to a freedom from and a freedom for—but how that works out for each of us is not clear to me. What is certain is that until we can claim that inner freedom, we will be unable to claim Christian discipleship. It is also true that the by-products of this kind of living are powerful enough to set fire to the earth.
>
> —DORIS DONNELLY

In this theological perspective, God created all things because God chose to do so. God was not, according to Genesis, compelled to create. God wanted to make something good. The author of Genesis writes, at the end of the account of the creation of each item, that "God saw that it was good." Everything that exists in the universe was created by God, and everything that was created is good. These two statements are the root and direction of all Jewish and Christian beliefs about creation. They also are the source of the theology of stewardship.

God is the creator, and creation is good as it comes from God; God is thus to be praised as the source of everything that is. God made the earth, sky, water, land, birds of the air, and fish of the sea. God also made human beings, with their loves and desires, sexualities and energies. The human desire to care for the world, to work, to be valued, to have a place—all are part of God's creation.

Humanity's basic character is described by God in the words of creation: "Let us make humankind in our image, according to our likeness; and let them have dominion over the fish of the sea." What is the image of God? The questions may be best expressed as: How does God behave toward human beings? What sort of dominion does God exercise toward us? The response offers us the key toward being in the image of God.

God made us to be to the world what God is to us—the one who cares for life and makes justice and peace. It is thus absolutely true to assert that God made us to be stewards; stewardship is our way of being in God's image toward creation. We are made to be responsive to God's self-revealing activity, to love one another and the world as God loved us. In the account of Adam and Eve in Genesis 2, we see, from a different tradition, the same sort of relationship of humans to creation in the naming and caring for the animals. Biblical "dominion" is not domination and exploitation, but love, care, and concern for the good of creation.

2. God became incarnate in Jesus Christ.

William Temple, Archbishop of Canterbury during World War II, observed that Christianity is the most materialistic of religions. By that he meant that though Christians believe that God made the material world and that it is good, we also believe that God voluntarily became a part of creation, as well as remaining the Creator. Matter is essential to our vision of God and God's relationship with us.

> In the beginning was the Word, and the Word was with God, and the Word was God. . . . All things came into being through him, and without him not one thing came into being. . . . . And the Word became flesh and lived among us, and we have seen his glory.
>
> (John 1:1, 3, 14)

Jesus Christ, the Word of God, through whom God made the world, became part of the world. He lived in a family, ate and drank with sinners, told stories about money and its use, and commented upon the political and social, as well as the religious structures of his day. Jesus was "tested as we are, yet without sin" (Heb. 4:15).

For us, the incarnation of Jesus means nothing less than that God has irrevocably become a part of the created world in its totality. There is no "sacred" and "secular" division, because not only did God create all things, God shared, through Jesus, in everything of this world. In God's economy, everything is both holy and worldly.

Because of the Incarnation, we are able to say that all of us, our selves, abilities, goods, actions, belong to God through God's Incarnation in Jesus. In this sense, through Christ, all of our life is a part of God's life. That is the specific Christian twist to stewardship. God not only created us to be stewards, and revealed to us that we are made to behave towards the world as God behaves towards us, in the person of Jesus, God shares in all of our life and becomes a steward.

Jesus' own life is an expression of stewardship as God would have us live. Furthermore, through the death and resurrection of Jesus, we and our whole world are offered to God and accepted by God. Jesus' life in the world, and our lives as disciples of Jesus, express God's acceptance, love, and use of the world as holy, as "pure as the first light Eden saw play."

3. Through the Holy Spirit, God calls us to share Christ's mission in restoring the world as God in love created it to be.

As Christians, we profess that God calls and invites us to be part of the church that is the Body of Christ, the people of God. In Ephesians 1:10, 22-23, Paul (or his disciple) expresses his insistent faith that the church exists for the redemption of the world, "a plan for the fullness of time, to gather up all things in him, things in heaven and things on earth. . . . He has put all things under his feet and has made him the head over all things for the church, which is his body, the fullness of him who fills all in all."

The *raison d'être* for the church is not primarily its own support or the satisfaction of worshiping God well, but the continuing redemptive work of Christ in the world. What the earthly Jesus began and perfected in his relationship with God, the earthly church continues in time, in our relationship with God and our spreading of God's good news in Jesus Christ. As Paul reiterates in Romans 8, this redemptive activity extends to the entire world. The creation, Paul asserts, awaits its redemption with longing, as we "who have the first fruits of the Spirit . . . wait for our adoption, the redemption of our bodies."

The redemption to which we look forward, the Apostle teaches, includes all creation. In the biblical world view, "Spirit" and "body" are not opposites. The body can, and is created to be, Spirit-filled, in the sense of being open to God's influence and guided by God's Spirit. The role of the baptized Christian in the church is to restore the world to God through the Spirit whom Jesus has given us.

This restoration of the world is the goal of our vocation as "servants of Christ and stewards of God's mysteries" (1 Cor. 4:1). Every aspect of our lives, our time, our money, our abilities, our play, our prayers, our sex life, our desire for power, our love of nature—all are drawn into our vocation as stewards of God's mysteries. We are entrusted with the ongoing work of redeeming the time, of sharing in the rededication of the world to God through our use of all that is part of the world.

To speak of stewardship is to address our sharing in the Holy Spirit's work of sanctifying the entire world. Stewardship is thus not simply a matter of giving some money or dedicating some time. Stewardship is the word we use for the Christian's vocation to

> Stewardship is the word we use for the Christian's vocation to "restore all things in Christ." It is an expression of the Christian's relationship to the whole world, and to everything in it. Probably the preacher's most significant role today is to make explicit this connection between stewardship and the redemption of the world, and to insist upon it again and again and again.

"restore all things in Christ." It is an expression of the Christian's relationship to the whole world, and to everything in it. Probably the preacher's most significant role today is to make explicit this connection between stewardship and the redemption of the world, and to insist upon it again and again and again.

Summary. Our planning and our contact with our congregations flourish best if we return again to the theological source of our preaching and teaching about stewardship. Stewardship is a gift of love that flows from a heart dedicated to God. We are God's creation, redeemed and accepted in Christ, and sharing Christ's mission and ministry to the world through the transforming power of the Holy Spirit. God welcomes even the meanest gift offered with only a little love, but good stewardship invites us to more. Our hope in Christian stewardship is to increase in ourselves our dedication, our love, and our desire to give ourselves and our resources to God. Again and again, in different ways and under different guises, the preacher will ask: Why settle for less?

A Sermon in Shoes

One afternoon in Chicago, officials gathered at a train station to await the arrival of the new Nobel Peace Prize winner. When he stepped off the train, the officials came up with hands outstretched, telling him how honored they were to meet him. The man thanked them, and then, looking over their heads, asked if he might be excused for a moment. He walked through the crowd until he reached an elderly black woman who was struggling to carry two large suitcases to a bus. He picked up the bags and escorted the woman to the bus, then finally returned to the welcoming committee. Later, a member of that committee was telling a friend about the event. He summed it up by saying, "I think that was the first time I ever saw a sermon walking."

The man who had delivered that graphic sermon was the missionary doctor who had spent his life helping the poor in Africa, Dr. Albert Schweitzer.

Seeing the need, then doing what Jesus would do. That is stewardship of our time. It will say more to those around us than our position or our words. And it gives anyone a chance to be a walking sermon!

 SERMON HELP

Stewardship Humor

BRIAN BAUKNIGHT

A minister prayed, "Protect us from members of this church who, when it comes to giving, stop at nothing."

—From a church newsletter:
The mustard-colored pledge cards you were mailed were treated with a coated substance that will begin to emit smoke fumes within ten days. Cards not returned by June 30th will begin to self-destruct, releasing an unpleasant order. Your Stewardship Committee hopes you will protect yourself from these hazards by returning the cards immediately to the church office.

—A typographical error in the church bulletin:
Anyone wishing to live should drop off their pledge card at the church office!

Three men went to church, and when it came time to pass the offering plate, the three discovered that they had no money. Not wanting to be embarrassed, one fainted, and the other two carried him out.

A college student had this message on his dorm phone answering machine:
"Hi! This is Fred. If it's the phone company, I sent the money. If it's Mom or Dad, please send money. If it's a friend, you still owe me money. If it's the financial office, you didn't loan me enough money. If it's a female, leave a message—and don't worry, I've got plenty of money."

A man called the church office and said to the secretary, "I want to talk to the head hog at the trough."
The secretary said, "Sir, we don't speak about our minister here that way."
The man replied, "I want to give the church $10,000."
The secretary said, "Wait just a minute. The big pig himself just walked through the door."

A cartoon depicts two persons marooned on a desert island. One of them is standing at the water's edge, gazing into the distance with an extremely distraught and worried face. The other is sitting back against the palm trees, perfectly relaxed. "Don't worry," he says, "I know we'll be found soon. My church pledge is due this week."

Attributed to the late Bishop Gerald Kennedy:
"Church supply houses now market an offering plate that responds to your gifts. When the offering plate is passed, if you put in a $20 bill, it plays the 'Hallelujah Chorus.' If you put in a $10 bill, it rings a bell. If you pass the plate without putting anything in the plate, it takes your picture."

Garrison Keillor tells of a letter written from a local church to one of its members who was not present on pledge dedication Sunday, and therefore did not fill out a pledge card:
"Dear Anne and Joe: We missed you last Sunday, Pledge Sunday. Since you were not present to fill out your pledge card, and to make it easy for you, we have completed a pledge card for you. Thank you for being so generous. Your Finance Committee."

A young child wrote this note to his pastor:
"Dear Minister:
I'm sorry I can't leave more money in the plate on Sunday, but my father didn't give me a raise in my allowance. Could you give a sermon about a raise in my allowance. It would help the church get more money!"

A wealthy man had lived a rather rough and intemperate life. When he became ill and was told he was going to die, he called the preacher and asked him to come for a visit. When the minister arrived, the man said, "I know I have not lived an exemplary life. But do you suppose if I gave $50 to the church, I might be able to get into heaven?"
The preacher said, "I don't know, but it's worth a try."

Our culture now has "lite" everything on the market: butter, cheese, syrup, even beer. A suggestion arose regarding what a "lite" church might be like: perhaps a 45-minute worship service, a 7% tithe, and only 8 of the 10 Commandments. And you get to choose which eight!

 DRAMA

Horatio Amplebucks and Son

GILSON MILLER

CAST OF CHARACTERS:

Horatio..
Son..

COSTUMES: Horatio wears a three-piece business suit; the son wears jeans and sweater.

Horatio Amplebucks has made a fortune selling paperclips. He has built an empire and is a die-hard capitalist. He worked hard to achieve his success, and he finds it difficult, if not impossible, to understand feelings of compassion. He persevered, overcame obstacles, and pulled himself up by the proverbial bootstraps. He runs his industry in a dictatorial style and has managed to run his family the same way. Now he wants to pass all this on to his son. But his son is reluctant; he finds it difficult to convince his father that there is more to life than making money.

Father and son stand facing each other.

Dad: Son, I'm so proud of you, graduating from Big Bucks University. How many fathers can boast of a son who led his school's polo team to a national championship? And while you were doing that, you managed to graduate "magna carta." Or was that "magna comma"? I had to quit school in the sixth grade to support our family. And now you are standing on the threshold of a great career with the family enterprise, "Paper Clip Conglomerate." Why, our family has been clipping the public for more than forty years!

Son: (shyly) Dad, there's something we need to talk about.

Dad: (ignoring his son) Yes, Son, some day all this will be yours. (Makes sweeping motion over his empire.) Did I ever tell you how all this started?

Son: Yes, Dad, several times. There's something I need to discuss with you.

Dad: (ignoring the son) Yes, it all began when your granddaddy made that first paperclip with his own hands. I can still see him in that cold, dimly lit room, hunched over that mass of wire. (Dad gets emotional.) His hands were bruised and bleeding. His eyes were bloodshot. I get misty when I think of all he did for us, how he often stayed up all night. He twisted pretzels during the day. I don't know where he found the stamina. His kids were dressed in rags and hungry. The babies were crying. Mom had consumption. What a story! Did I forget anything?

Son: You forgot about the hole in the bottom of his shoe. Dad, there's really something I need to talk about.

Dad: Well, one night he made that final twist and formed the perfect paperclip. He pulled on his boots and made his way to the patent office. Of course, it was 18 miles across several mountains, a swollen river; and there were wild animals, too. And here we are today. Son, one day you will carry the torch for the company, Paper Clip Conglomerate (salutes as he says it). One day you will sit behind that big oak desk, or is it teak? I know it's been hard on you, just polishing paperclips all these years. But now that you are graduating, you will be in a position to take over!

Son: That's what I want to talk to you about, Dad!

Dad: Yes, our empire stretches all the way to those smoke stacks. The EPA hates those things, but to me that smoke means we're making money! See those trucks out there at the main gate? (Comments to himself that they are behind schedule.) That's how far this business has grown. Who knows—one day we might even venture into safety pins!

Son: Dad, I have something to tell you, and it *can't* wait any longer. I don't *want* to carry the torch in the family business. I want to be a missionary to the natives of Bongo Bongo and live in abject poverty.

Dad: Yes, now that you've got that out of your system, let's talk about your starting salary with the company. How does $40,000 sound?

Son: Dad, I'm serious. I know it must sound crazy to you, but serving people is what I really want to do!

Dad: Sure, Son. Now, of course, when you start here at the company, we'll throw in a new car. How does a Porsche sound to you?

Son: Dad, how can I convince you that I'm serious about this?

Dad: Son, I'm gonna pretend this conversation never took place. No one has ever said no to Horatio Ampelbucks, and I don't intend for my own son to be the first. Now, why don't we just forget those barefoot heathens, and we'll talk tomorrow about your position with the company.

Son: Dad, you don't seem to understand. I have been thinking about this for a long time. Remember when you sent me to the Caribbean last year? Well, I left the resort and wandered around one of the islands. I couldn't believe what I saw on the other side of the island. There are a lot of hungry people down there who need medical help and education. Something inside told me: This is where you belong. This is where you can help someone. I found a place where I could make a difference. I know I'm not going to see any drastic changes; but I feel if I could improve things for even a few people, it would be worth it.
I've signed up for language training. I'll be leaving next week. Please understand.

Dad: Son, this is getting ridiculous. I could buy any one of those islands if I wanted to. But there's nothing on them except squalor, filth, and suffering. The land isn't fit to grow much of anything. The people are illiterate. You don't want to go down there. You might wind up with a knife in your back, or some rare tropical disease. Your mother would be worried to death. Stay here and enjoy all the advantages. This is where you will be happy, not down there in that hell hole!

Son: Dad, that's where you and I are different. All my life I have had everything I wanted. Yet I never really felt that I was helping to improve things in this world. I have always lived in your shadow, and you assumed the things that were important to you would be important to me. Now I realize there are things that money can't buy. Let's face it—most of this (hands sweeping over the empire) will crumble one day, and then what do we have? I want to contribute to something that will last.

Dad: Son, you sound just like your Aunt Helen, God rest her soul. She worked for the church all her life. She sacrificed. She was always helping someone, listening to their problems, helping them financially, and when she died, she wasn't able to give a cent to her children. That won't be the case with you. All this (sweeping gesture to the empire) will be yours one day. That is, if you give up this silly idea of throwing your life away in the jungle.

Son: I liked Aunt Helen, and maybe she influenced my decision. She was generous in every sense of the word. I think she left her kids and me a rich legacy.

Dad: Yes, and look what it got her—a big funeral with some nice words at the grave. Why, I own everything (sweeping gesture) you can see for miles.

Son: Dad, what good will any of this be to you or me in 100 years?

 # SERMON HELP

Drawing the "Enough" Line

A Sermon Starter

Ephesians 2:13-18; Luke 16:19-31

BETSY SCHWARZENTRAUB

The story of Lazarus and the rich man is not about whether we're rich or poor. It's about whether or not we're connected, and whether we care about the connection that already exists between the strong and the weak.

Jesus tells about a rich man (whom tradition names Dives) who lives in a nice home with a front gate, wears fine purple linen, and eats well every day. Lazarus lives in the dust at that gate, wears rags, and is perpetually hungry.

What should Dives do? Jesus doesn't tell us. There isn't one "right thing" to do—except to notice, and somehow to respond out of their connection to each other.

It's easy to feel guilty, thinking that money can solve the problems of all the Lazaruses in the world. Even those who live like Dives can feel like Lazarus sometimes—vulnerable and afraid. They may get sick or old, or lose their job in a deflating economy. Here's the point: Lazarus isn't the only one who is vulnerable. Dives is vulnerable too. They are part of each other. Lazarus knows that, even if Dives does not.

Jesus continues the story. Soon Lazarus dies, and then Dives dies. Lazarus goes to heaven to be with Abraham. Dives is on the other side of the line, in Hades, looking at Abraham and Lazarus across a great chasm. The essential connection between Dives and Lazarus has been severed.

Who drew that line between them? Not God. Dives had drawn that line. It's the "Enough" line that separated him from the poor in his life and kept him safely distanced from people who suffer. It broke his unity, his communion with them. This is the line we draw between "us" and "them," whoever they may be: the poor, the embarrassments, those we wouldn't be caught dead with. It's a line that says, "There isn't enough to take care of them all, so I draw the line here in my caring. I won't be connected with this anymore." This line becomes a gap between us, an uncrossable chasm.

Where's the Good News in this? The "Enough" line doesn't exist unless we put it there! God wants us all to be with Lazarus and Abraham! Every Lazarus, whoever has suffered evil in this life, will be in heaven. In Christ, God has erased that dividing line between the rich and poor, the haves and have-nots, the worthy and worthless. In Christ Jesus, we who once were far off from each other have been brought near by the blood of Christ. His life was placed over the line as a bridge, bringing us both to God in one body through the cross.

> ## "He who gives to me teaches me to give."
> *—DANISH PROVERB*

 SERMON HELP

It's in the Bag!

True (?) Story

II Corinthians 8:8-15
Hymn: "We Give Thee But Thine Own"

TERRY WAYNE ALLEN

An older man walked into a new-car dealership. One of the sales representatives greeted him and asked if he could help. Yes, he could. He was going to buy a new car and wanted to see what was available. The salesman noticed that the man had a rolled-up paper bag clutched tightly in his hand. They strolled the grounds and, over a period of time, the man carefully examined more than a dozen new cars. He was particular about his needs and tried each one carefully. Finally, after making a selection, they went inside to write up the sale.

The salesman quoted a price and they agreed. He asked the older man, "How would you like to pay for this?"

The man looked at him and said, "If God wants me to have this car, this bag will be full of money!" He loosened his grip and opened the bag. It was empty!

Great story! I assumed it was full of cash, didn't you? But to the dismay of the salesman, he had wasted his time and effort.

This story reminded me of Paul's second letter to the church in Corinth. In 8:12, he says, "For if the eagerness is there, the gift is acceptable according to what one has—not according to what one does not have." But I'm not sure that an empty bag was what Paul had in mind!

- Share some thoughts on how we bring gifts that are long on "show" and short on substance.

  I hear Paul saying that you should give from what you have to give. Don't worry about giving what you don't have or cannot give.

  If you are short on paying your "shared ministries," celebrate what you *can* pay and resolve to do more.

- Be sure to let everyone know how the funds are used. We can do so much more together than we can individually.

- Share some localized examples of World Service/Judicatory benevolence. Talk about a pastor's education fund or another specific program.

> "We are called to share generously from what we already have, so that all may have enough. Don't worry about giving what you don't have. Give generously and willingly of what you do have, and all will be blest!"
>
> —JOE DOMINQUEZ AND VICKI ROBIN, *YOUR MONEY OR YOUR LIFE*

Pontius' Puddle

 MEDITATION

A World Communion Day Meditation

LEE DOMANN

A lot of people would be surprised and shocked if they knew the real-life stories of some Christians, including Christian pastors. Some pastors, like some of you, have had to try to find God in all the wrong places before they could come to a spiritual awakening and an understanding of God's forgiving grace. I'm one of those.

Back in the late sixties and early seventies, I found myself in some settings that weren't always that healthy, spiritually or physically. Back then I was a pretty big fan of jazz, and found that fact to be a really good excuse to wander in and out of some of the dimly lighted clubs along Main Street in Kansas City, Missouri. One of them was a notch or two above the rest, where you had a somewhat better chance of at least walking out alive. It was simply called Milton's. Milton was the first name of the owner, who doubled as bartender.

For a dollar or so, you could sit in the corner alone, or with friends, in a black leather booth and drift away on the sweet recorded sounds of Count Basie, Dizzy Gillespie, Charlie Parker, and John Coltraine. Jazz was all that came off the old reel-to-reel tape machine.

I once heard a song (not at Milton's) called "Church Pews and Bar Stools." The chorus goes like this: "Church pews and bar stools both hold God's children / weary from playin' life's game / And they all need some place to lay down their burdens. / Church pews and bar stools are a whole lot the same."

I suspect there's a lot of truth to that, though at least one fellow begged to differ when he heard the song.

"Yeah, maybe so," he said, "but I have to say I've never seen anybody fall off the back of a church pew!" Good point. So there *are* some differences! Major ones, of course.

Yet the fact remains that we all *do* seek comfort where we think we can find it, whether it turns out ultimately to be the right place or not. And I remember a lot of sad, lonely people at Milton's place. Sad faces. Sad conversations. In the midst of the laughter and joking around, there was the ever-present feeling of "something's missing."

One of the sadder sights at Milton's was the big cork board over by the pay telephone. It was nearly always filled with bad checks, hanging from rusty thumb tacks older than the building itself. And above the checks was a sign that politely invited these particular customers to please pay their bills as soon as convenient. Sadder still was the fact that a lot of people who had signed those checks—people Milton genuinely loved and cared about—never did pay up. And you'd never see them again. Maybe they were con artists. Or maybe they just felt guilty. I tend to believe the latter. I suspect most were just too ashamed to come back.

And I suppose there are spiritual con artists in Christ's church. In fact, I'm convinced of that, though I can't prove it. Some are behind the pulpits; some sit in the pews. Some sit at home and complain about both the preachers and the pew sitters. Yes, there are a

---

Do you care enough to give the very best?

Take your son, your only son, whom you love, and go . . . (Genesis 22:2).

God knew Abraham's values. He knew what Abraham considered most important for daily happiness, security, and identity. And he knows the same of us.

God's great love for each of us constantly calls us to a steadfast dependence on our relationship with him—not on our jobs, our possessions, or even our earthly relationships. He wants us to see ourselves first as people committed to his plan for blessing our lives.

To help make that a continuing possibility for Abraham, God tested Abraham's willingness to obediently return the most cherished possession God had given him. Not because God needed the sacrifice. Abraham needed it—in order to keep first things first.

Where is God calling you to look at your values and see his priorities today?

few spiritual con artists in the church, I do believe. But I don't think their total number can hold a candle to the total number of those folks whose overriding feeling is one of guilt. Some know why they feel that way, and others don't. Some stand behind pulpits, not feeling worthy to be there. Some sit in pews, not feeling worthy to be there. But many, many more sit at home or stand on street corners, not feeling worthy to be in church—or to be anywhere, for that matter.

What a shame. What a shame to feel as if you've spiritually bounced a check somewhere. And either you remember it all too well, or you can't remember it at all. What a tragedy, in light of God's forgiveness—a forgiving love so powerful that a man like Paul, once a scoundrel and murderer, could be swept away by that love and have his life forever changed, in spite of himself. Paul, a forgiven sinner who was given the gift of compassion, to the point that he could plead with his fellow Christians in those early years of the church, "Be ye kind to one another, tenderhearted, forgiving one another, even as God for Christ's sake hath forgiven you."

In a few minutes, we'll gather once again around the Lord's table, together with millions of other Christians throughout the world on this World Communion Sunday. When we do, I pray we'll all feel that we belong here, no matter what we've done or said in this past week that we regret. Or no matter what we've done that we *should* regret, but don't, either out of callousness or out of ignorance that we did anything wrong. I pray that no matter what spiritual "bad checks" we've tried to pass off in the totality of our lives up to this point, we'll nevertheless remember this morning that God has already forgiven us through Jesus Christ.

I don't know whether Milton called himself a Christian. I do know that some folks would judge him because of what he did for a living. I hope I never do, and I hope you won't either, because Jesus didn't judge the Miltons of his day. His message to them was the same as it was to the rabbis—"It's between you and God," he said. But I believe Milton received the spirit of the living God into his heart more than a lot of people do. I believe that because Milton knew the meaning of forgiveness. And I know this because about two or three times a year, in the classified ads in the *Kansas City Star* would appear the following words: "All debts forgotten. All is forgiven. Please come home. Love, Milton." He'd clip it out of the paper and tape it to the tiny window on the front door of his lounge, so you'd see it if you were one of the guilty or the ashamed standing outside on the sidewalk, wondering whether to come in.

I'm glad God's forgiving love appears, is mirrored, and is reflected in our world in such unexpected ways and places—sometimes even through the most unlikely people. I figure that if Milton the bartender knows something about forgiveness, then I, too, have some hope when I partake of the body and blood of Christ today. It makes me grateful that God doesn't nail my spiritual bad checks up to some celestial corkboard. It makes me grateful that the only nails involved in this whole thing are the nails that went through the hands of Jesus on a cross. It makes me grateful that he was sent to let us know that it is possible to be in the form of a human and still have the capacity for divine compassion, love, and forgiveness—to have the capacity to destroy and retaliate, and yet choose instead the tougher, but infinitely more rewarding, path of wholeness and reconciliation.

The forgiveness is there. All you and I have to do is accept it. "All debts paid. All is forgiven. Please come home. Love, God." Amen.

 # SERMON HELP

Stewardship Sermon Starters

BETSY SCHWARZENTRAUB

The multicolored thread of stewardship weaves throughout the fabric of the scriptures, touching on all of life as a gift to be celebrated, invested, and shared. Here are some of the lectionary texts (Cycles B and C) for the year ahead:

April—Fifth Sunday of Eastertide   Acts 8:26-40

Showing Up

Acts 8 describes how Philip witnessed to the Ethiopian official, answered his questions about the scripture, and baptized him, all at the Ethiopian's request. Philip's actions not only transformed a person's life; they affected the course of a nation.

It wasn't Philip's idea to be there in the first place. The road to Gaza was a wilderness road—hardly the place one would choose to be. But God's angel ("messenger" in Hebrew) said to go there, and Philip was willing to obey, no questions asked.

Faithful stewardship begins with our willingness to be in the right place at the right time, so God can do something beautiful through us. As stewards, not the Owner and Author of life, we can't see the whole picture or know the reasons God calls us to obey. But once we are clear on God's message to us, our first act of stewardship is simply to show up. If we do, God will use us in surprising and influential ways.

May—Ascension Day   Ephesians 1:15-23

A Living Network

Those who like to explain miracles scientifically become nervous when we talk about Jesus' ascension into heaven. In usual human experience, people don't just rise off the earth like that. It's a humbling reminder of how much about Jesus is beyond our understanding and control.

But why is Jesus' ascension important to us? We find one reason in Ephesians, which says that Christ reveals "the greatness of God's power for us." The cosmic God of Jesus, Sovereign of glory, has not hoarded either wisdom or revelation (direct experience of God). Through the Mystery of God in Jesus, we are receivers of this power, wisdom, and grace.

God gives all of this to us, not as atomized individuals, but as the living network of the church. We are a community of stewards of the Gospel, an interwoven net of "God's power [put] to work in Christ." God has done this, not just for Jesus, but "for the church, which is his body, the fullness of the One who fills all in all."

June—Third Sunday After Pentecost
I Samuel 16:14-23

Weaving in God's Design

No one on earth could have designed such an entré to the royal court! Israel's king Saul was tormented by a demon and began to look for a musician who could soothe his troubled spirit.

Enter David, who could play the harplike lyre, was

prudent in political places, had good presence, and could double as a bodyguard. Little did Saul know that David would take his place one day as king.

Leslie Weatherhead describes God as the Master Weaver of life's design, who asks human assistants to thread through different colors and textures from the back side of the loom. Only the Master can see the work of art that is being woven. Like David and Saul, we are stewards, meant to be trusting assistants, weaving in God's design.

July—Eighth Sunday After Pentecost   Mark 6:7-13

A Freeing Authority

In most of our human organizations, "authority" connotes an accountability chart that works from the top down, receiving legitimacy and power from the one who is over us.

But Jesus demonstrated a different kind of authority— freeing empowerment instead of mindless imitation. When he sent out the disciples two by two, he gave them no formula for healing or business cards to gain acceptance. In fact, he instructed them to travel light, use their discernment, and make sure they spread the message of the Good News, no matter how it was received.

Christ sends us out in the same way, as stewards with the kind of authority which empowers us as well as others, through faithful, thoughtful obedience. Like those first disciples, we return from our journey surprised by the healing, repentance, and joy that follow in our wake.

August—Twelfth Sunday After Pentecost
II Samuel 18:1, 5, 9-15

Difficult Choices

Joab was King David's chief military steward, managing the country's armies on his behalf. David told Joab and his top commanders to deal gently with his son Absalom, who had marshaled a rebel force against him.

Here was an incredibly difficult decision. When David spoke this way about Absalom, was he talking as a grieving father about his rebellious son? Or was he commanding as a king, about the rebel leader who was trying to seize his throne? Joab had to decide whether to be loyal to the king or to the kingdom. He chose the kingdom, and slew Absalom himself.

Honest-to-God stewardship involves ethics—why we do what we do. Often it meets us in the midst of ambiguous situations. God doesn't give us an easy formula for making choices in our daily lives. In every dimension of our living, we must face the values of the One to whom we are accountable, and put ourselves on the line in the way we think God would have us go.

Whether he was right or not, Joab chose. As God's stewards today, we also face tough decisions, and must do the best we can to discern and act upon God's will.

September—Sixteenth Sunday After Pentecost
James 1:17-27

Living as First Fruits

Sometimes we approach the scriptures, asking, "What should I do? How should I live in response to God?" But these questions put the emphasis in the wrong place. We should begin every time where the Bible begins—not with our response, but with God's initiative of grace.

James puts the message directly: "Every generous act of giving, with every perfect gift, is from above, coming down from [God]." First John echoes his statement: "We love because [God] first loved us." Whenever we give our time, our compassion, our skills or perspectives, our finances, assets or concerns, we are giving out of what we have already been given by God, the most generous Giver of all, Creator of both life and love.

Hearing God's Word results in action, and when we live in a way that fulfills God's purpose, says James, we "become a kind of first fruits of God's creation." In agriculture, the first fruits of each season herald a new harvest, a new beginning of abundance and fruitfulness for a particular crop. In Christian living, when we care for people and reflect God's holiness, we become the first fruits of a new kind of human being—one who is made in the image of Christ.

October—Twenty-first Sunday After Pentecost
Genesis 3:8-19

The Blame Game

Genesis 2:15 tells us that God put Adam in the garden of Eden "to till it and keep it," as a good steward of the earth. Even the name *Adam* emphasizes this fact, since it comes from *adamah,* which means the soil or the earth. Human beings were meant to be good caretakers of the earth, in as mutual a way as "Adam" came from "adamah." (See Genesis 2:7.)

So how are we doing today as stewards of the earth?

About as well as did Adam and Eve (whose name is related to living beings and to the name of God). They violated their stewardship trust by challenging God's sovereignty. Adam played "The Blame Game" on Eve, and Eve played it on the snake. The result was that they were kicked out of the garden, estranged from the very earth out of which they had been formed.

We are not the only ones paying a high price for our estrangement. So are the species that are dwindling toward extinction: the fish in polluted waters, animals on toxic land, plants and trees in fouled air. The Blame Game results in hiding, fear, and destruction.

But the Good News is this: We can claim our purpose on earth and our identity once again, God's Adam and Eve. We can become the good stewards our Creator intended us to be. There is still hope—for the garden and for us.

November—Twenty-fifth Sunday After Pentecost
I Kings 17:8-16

Down to the Last Drop

The tough thing about trust is that it demands so much. Elijah may have known that God stood behind his demand for food, but the widow certainly didn't know it. She had to take what he said on faith and give food to him first. Only then could she prepare what she knew to be her family's last meal before starvation.

We may not have been down to our last crumb of meal and ounce of cooking oil, but there have been times when we were convinced we had nothing left to give. Our caring, our time, our money, our abilities—we have felt totally depleted. And yet in giving to the last drop, we find a strange replenishment that is enough to sustain us.

God's resources never end. The blessings may not come in the form or manner we expect, but they are always there—especially when we think we're giving it all away. Jesus gave away his very life, all the way to the end—and in the process received life for all of us, both abundant and eternal.

In this age of scarcity, we are stewards of God's abundance. What Good News we have to share!

December—Fourth Sunday of Advent   Luke 1:39-55

Passionate Stewardship

God has a way of fulfilling promises that seems to turn them upside down.

Take Mary and Elizabeth. Who would have

expected unwed Mary to carry the Messiah, or her cousin Elizabeth to bear John the Baptist, who would herald his reign? Nevertheless, these two women, who were not counted as people of consequence in their local region, were bearers of God's promise fulfilled—the holy God come into human flesh, embodying God's message of repentance and forgiveness.

As stewards of the Gospel, we are not dispassionate, unaffected proclaimers of a foreign message. Like Mary and Elizabeth, we were created to live out the Word of God's love—in our bodies, our hearts, our hopes, and our relationships. The promise of God's Word fulfilled on earth in human lives and action matures within us, from one stage to the next.

Mary grew in her understanding of the connections between her miracle birth and the purposes of God on earth. She knew that God's gift of Jesus ultimately would bring distributive justice, the rich and the poor leveled out, powerful people humbled, lowly people fed. As the carrier of God's Word Incarnate, she models passionate stewardship for us all.

January—Third Sunday After Epiphany
Nehemiah 8:1-6, 8-10

Joy

"How then shall we live?" the people wondered, as they wept in awe and guilt after hearing the Law of God for the first time.

Children of former exiles, they had returned on foot to the ruined homeland of their parents and ancestors, determined to begin anew. But in that far-off country, they had never heard the story of Israel's God and God's chosen people. Now they wept for all they had not known, and for that part of their lifetime that had not been lived out of such a vital, personal relationship with God.

"How shall we live?" is the bottom-line stewardship question. How can we show—by our priorities, our passion, our tears, and our joy—the loving relationship that God offers us all?

Nehemiah answered all who gathered before him that day. "Go your way, eat and drink and share portions with those who have nothing, for this day is holy to our LORD! And do not be grieved, for the joy of the LORD is your strength!"

The stewardship question—the way we live out God's covenant relationship with us—brings us through tears to a deeper, lasting joy.

February—Second Sunday in Lent
Genesis 15:1-12, 17-18

A Covenant of Grace

It must have been an eerie sight that night, even for trusting Abram. God had promised what seemed impossible by human logic: descendants as numerous as the stars for this childless old man; a land on which to live; and after four generations of suffering, a victorious return.

"But how shall I know this?" Abram had asked. The answer was an odd instruction from God, so that all levels of sacrifice animals, from the most expensive to the poorest offering of all, lay cut open and stacked against each other in the deepening dark.

As Abram watched, a smoking firepot appeared, and then a flaming torch. They passed through the air between the halves of the sacrifices, extending the priestly ritual of burnt sacrifices for healing and forgiveness.

God had literally "cut a covenant" (which is what the Hebrew phrase means) with Abram in a way that he would never forget. It was an agreement between God and Abram, based not upon anything earned, but entirely on grace.

Grace. Free gift. This is the foundation for good stewardship. All that we are as God's people, we have received and are to use for God's service.

March—Maundy Thursday   Luke 22:7-20

A Living Legacy

There's no question that our generation will leave a legacy of some kind for our children and their children. The question is, What kind of legacy will it be? What will we leave behind in values, in resources, in priorities, for them to manage, invest, and share in their lifetime?

On the evening before Jesus' death, he summarized all that he had taught and done throughout his lifetime and intentional ministry. As he handed out bread and passed around the cup, he said, "This is my body which is given for you. . . . This cup is the new covenant in my blood."

Jesus gave a unique legacy to the world that is different from anything we might leave behind. His legacy is alive now in the lives of every successive generation of disciples, and in the Holy Spirit to energize and guide them. It is a constantly new and renewing covenant, offered to us by God on the other side of achievement or failure, beginning anew with God's mercy and love. We are stewards of this living legacy, which lives on through us to future generations.

 HANDOUT

Stewardship by the Book

Bulletin Bits Based on the Sunday Gospel Readings, Cycle B

SHARON HUECKEL

(1st Advent—Mark 13:24-37)

We are the servants of God, each with his or her own task. We will be judged good stewards if, at his coming, he finds us ready and conscientiously pursuing the tasks to which we have been called.

(2nd Advent—Mark 1:1-8)

Today's Gospel speaks of preparation and anticipation. John prepared his people's hearts with the baptism of repentance and spoke with confidence about the coming of the Messiah. We have been baptized with the Holy Spirit—are we prepared for and anticipating the Lord's *Second* Coming?

(3rd Advent—John 1:6-8, 19-28)

John the Baptist seemed to know and rejoice in what God was calling him to be and to do. Do I understand the role the Lord is calling *me* to? Am I prepared to use my gifts and talents in the service of God?

(4th Advent—Luke 1:26-38)

It was through Mary's "Yes"— "Here I am, the servant of the Lord; let it be with me according to your word"— that the promises of God found fulfillment. But the Lord never forces our assent. When *we* hear God's call, may we, like Mary, be willing to say "Yes!" with love and trust.

(Christmas Day—Luke 2:1-14 (15-20) or
*   Luke 2:(1-7) 8-20 or John 1:1-14)*
Today we have been given a Savior! The Word Incarnate dwelling among us! How can we show our gratitude for so great a gift? To love with all we have and are is only a beginning!

(1st Sunday After Christmas—Luke 2:22-40)

When Mary and Joseph brought Jesus to the temple, they offered the sacrificial gift "required by the law of the Lord." An offering of a particular size or kind is not "required" here when the gifts are received. But is my gift proportional to the blessings I have received?

(2nd After Christmas—John 1:(1-9) (10-18)

Today's Gospel teaches us that from the fullness of Christ "we have all received, grace upon grace." Understanding this, good stewards strive to be accountable before God for all these gifts, giving as graciously as they have received.

(1st After Epiphany—Mark 1:4-11)

The Baptism of Jesus reminds us that through baptism, we too are God's beloved sons and daughters. May our discipleship be such that one day God will say of us, "With you I am well pleased."

(2nd After Epiphany—John 1:43-51)

Nathaniel was a skeptic, asking sarcastically, "Can anything good come out of Nazareth?" Jesus knew that and called him anyway. The Lord knows us, too, through and through, and calls us, despite our shortcomings, to follow him in love and use our gifts in his service.

(3rd After Epiphany—Mark 1:14-20)

There is an urgency in today's Gospel as Jesus calls his first disciples, Andrew and Simon, James and John. Each one follows Jesus *immediately,* unhesitatingly abandoning nets, boats, father, and fellow workers. To what is Jesus calling *me?* What must I abandon in order to follow him?

(4th After Epiphany—Mark 1:21-28)

Lord Jesus, I acknowledge your authority in *my* life. Cast out all that is unclean in me, that I may follow you with clearer vision and a pure heart.

> "The people of hope are those who believe that God created them for a purpose and that he will provide for their needs as they seek to fulfill his purpose in their lives."
>
> —*JOHN PAUL II*

(Transfiguration—Mark 9:2-9)

In the Gospel today, Peter yearns to do something to make concrete the Transfiguration event. But the answer to him—and to us—is to be still, to listen to Jesus, and to wait for his direction before we act.

(Ash Wednesday—Matthew 6:1-6, 16-21)

Today's gospel reminds us that our giving must always be done without expecting a reward. For if the world sees and applauds our generosity, we have already been rewarded! Instead, may the giving of our time, talents, and treasure be for the glory of God alone!

(1st Lent—Mark 1:9-15)

Stewardship is the hallmark of our discipleship. It is the next step, after we repent and believe in the good news, and the way we help to bring about the coming of the kingdom of God.

(2nd Lent—Mark 8:31-38)

Jesus says today that his followers must be prepared to give up *everything*, even life itself, to follow him. In the face of that uncompromising standard, how can we not give back in gratitude some portion of the many gifts with which God has blessed us?

(3rd Lent—John 2:13-22)

Jesus' anger in today's Gospel is directed not at those who came to the Temple to offer sacrifice, but at those who sought to profit at their expense. The Lord always receives with joy our sacrificial gifts of money and time!

(4th Lent—John 3:14-21)

"Those who do what is true come to the light," says the Gospel, "so that it may be clearly seen that their deeds have been done in God." May our living and our giving testify that we have seen—and are determined to follow—the Light of Christ.

(5th Lent—John 12:20-33)

"Whoever serves me must follow me," says Jesus in today's Gospel, "and where I am, there will my servant be also." In what ways is Jesus inviting *me* to follow him? What service is he asking of me?

(Palm Sunday—Mark 11:1-11 or John 12:12-16)

The colt upon which Jesus made his triumphant entry into Jerusalem was given without hesitation when the owner was told that the Lord needed it. Do I give as readily and as cheerfully to the Lord's work?

(Easter—Mark 16:1-8 or John 20:1-18)

Those who faithfully followed the Lord until—and after—his death were the first to hear the good news of his resurrection. May we who follow the Risen Christ be as steadfast and persevering in faith and good works!

(2nd Easter—John 20:19-31)

Jesus' word to all believers—to those frightened first disciples cowering in the upper room, to "doubting" Thomas, and to us—is "Peace." But it is an active, not a passive, peace—"As the Father has sent me," Jesus says, "so I send you."

(3rd Easter—Luke 24:36b-48)

The disciples in today's Gospel came to know Jesus in the breaking of the bread. Whenever we share what we have with those who are in need, we too discover Jesus in our midst.

(4th Easter—John 10:11-18)

To be good stewards, we must be good shepherds, willing to lay down our lives for those committed to our care, not mere hired hands who run off, leaving the sheep to be snatched and scattered by the wolf.

(5th Easter—John 15:1-8)

In today's Gospel, Jesus says that God is glorified when a disciple, grafted in Christ, produces abundantly and bears much fruit. The disciple must then be a good steward of that abundance.

(6th Easter—John 15:9-17)

Jesus' commandment is that his disciples love one another, even to the point of laying down their lives, if necessary. What gifts of myself—my skills and talents, my time and resources—will best demonstrate my love for God's people?

(7th Easter—John 17:6-19)

Jesus is the perfect steward—watching carefully over all who had been entrusted to him by the Father, then sending them out into the world in service. May I similarly protect and wisely use the gifts entrusted to me!

(Pentecost—John 15:26-27; 16:4b-15)

Today's Gospel reminds us that the Father, who already had given his Son for our salvation, also sent his Spirit to lead us to the truth. As witnesses and recipients of God's abundant self-giving, we can be numbered among his disciples only if we respond with gratitude and generosity.

(Trinity Sunday—John 3:1-17)

God's love for us was so great that he gave even his own Son that we might have eternal life. Our love, too, will be measured by what we are willing to give!

(2nd After Pentecost—Mark 2:23–3:6)

The Gospel's Pharisees were scrupulous about doing exactly what—and *only* what—the law required. Jesus challenged their thinking by giving what was *needed,* not simply what was owed. Do I give what I feel I must, or what I know I can?

(3rd After Pentecost—Mark 3:20-35)

We believe ourselves to be the brothers and sisters of Christ by virtue of our baptism. But do we also pass the more rigorous test in today's Gospel—"Whoever does the will of God is my brother and sister and mother"?

(4th After Pentecost—Mark 4:26-34)

Like the sower in today's Gospel, I scatter as seed my gifts of time, talent, and resources; and I trust that, by God's grace and in God's time, these small gifts of myself may grow and flourish, and help to bring about the kingdom of God.

(5th After Pentecost—Mark 4:35-41)

In today's Gospel, the disciples set off in the boat at Jesus' invitation. When the storm arose, they had only to ask him, and the storm abated. When we use our gifts and talents in his service, we too can be assured that he will be with us to see that good work to completion.

(6th After Pentecost—Mark 5:21-43)

On his way to heal the rich man's daughter, Jesus is touched by—and heals—a woman with a chronic illness. In my daily work, do I put my gifts at the service of those who ask for my help? Am I available and willing to be used by others I meet along the way?

(7th After Pentecost—Mark 6:1-13)

In the Gospel today, Jesus sends the disciples out with no possessions at all, utterly dependent upon the providence of God and the kindness of those they meet. Am I carrying any "baggage" that hampers my effectiveness as a disciple? Do I trust God enough to leave it behind?

(8th After Pentecost—Mark 6:14-29)

Herod gave Salome the grisly gift her mother suggested because he had promised to give her whatever she asked, and he would have been embarrassed to renege on his promise. What motivates my giving? What promises have I made, and to whom?

(9th After Pentecost—Mark 6:30-34; 53-56)

In today's Gospel, Jesus had planned to slip away from the crowds for a few moments of peace and a little rest. When he saw the people gathered, however, he put his needs aside to meet the needs of others. Sometimes, as good stewards, we are called to do the same.

(10th After Pentecost—John 6:1-21)

It is too great a burden for any one person to feed the multitudes. Even six months' wages, Philip says in today's Gospel, would not be enough! The miracle is that sharing God's gifts *always* results in abundance— five thousand fed, and twelve baskets left over!

(11th After Pentecost—John 6:24-35)

The crowd in today's Gospel demanded a sign of Jesus, wanting to know what "work" he did to inspire their faith. The very "bread of life," he gives himself to feed their deepest hunger. How does what I give "feed" others?

(12th After Pentecost—John 6:25, 41-51)

Jesus gave his very self as bread for the world. How do we, as disciples, respond to our Savior's example of total self-giving? How much of ourselves are we willing to give to others?

(13th After Pentecost—John 6:51-58)

"The living Father sent me," says Jesus in the Gospel today, "and I live because of the Father." Good stewards know that life is a gift from God and that they, too, are sent to use that gift in the service of others.

(14th After Pentecost—John 6:56-69)

Hearing Jesus speak of himself as the bread of life, some chose not to follow him, complaining, "This teaching is difficult; who can accept it?" May we remain faithful amid the unbelief of our own time and declare, like Peter, "We have come to believe and know that you are the Holy One of God."

(15th After Pentecost—Mark 7:1-8, 14-15, 21-23)

Jesus quotes the prophet Isaiah and says of the Pharisees of his day, "This people honors me with their lips, but their hearts are far from me." Dear Lord, let that not be true of us! Help us always to love and serve you with pure and generous hearts!

(16th After Pentecost—Mark 7:24-37)

Jesus healed all who came to him. The need and the faith of the sufferer were all that mattered. Our stewardship, too, must extend beyond the boundaries of denomination or nationality. Whenever there is need, there we can use our gifts in God's service.

(17th After Pentecost—Mark 8:27-38)

Discipleship is costly! "If any want to become my followers, let them deny themselves and take up their cross and follow me," says Jesus in today's Gospel. What sacrifices am I willing to make to be numbered among his disciples?

(18th After Pentecost—Mark 9:30-37)

Today's Gospel contains the key to good stewardship—"Whoever wants to be first must be the last of all and servant of all." So, must I give of my time and talents to others? Absolutely! To all who ask!

(19th After Pentecost—Mark 9:38-50)

The Gospel today is full of grave warnings about the seriousness of sin. But it also contains the reassurance that the smallest act of kindness—just a cup of water given in Christ's name—will be remembered and rewarded.

(20th After Pentecost—Mark 10:2-16)

Children receive gifts with joy and delight. We, too, can "receive the kingdom of God as a little child," if we receive joyfully the gifts God has given us. We are good stewards when we use those gifts gratefully, praising God as the source of all we have and are.

(21st After Pentecost—Mark 10:17-31)

In today's Gospel, Jesus asks the rich young man to give away all that he has in order to have treasure in heaven. But the rich man is unable to free himself from his possessions, and so he goes sadly away. Does what *I* own keep *me* from following Jesus?

(22nd After Pentecost—Mark 10:35-45)

Good stewards must not argue about who is the most important. Today's Gospel says clearly that those who aspire to greatness must humbly serve the needs of all. Even Jesus came not to be served, but to serve.

(23rd After Pentecost—Mark 10:46-52)

Jesus heard the cry and met the need of the blind beggar in today's Gospel, in spite of the clamoring crowd. Do I hear those who cry out for my help? Am I willing to help, even in the face of noisy opposition?

(24th After Pentecost—Mark 12:28-34)

What percentage does God ask of me as a good steward? *All* of my heart, *all* of my soul, *all* of my mind, and *all* of my strength!

(25th After Pentecost—Mark 12:38-44)

The widow in today's Gospel gave all she had to the work of the Lord, putting her two copper coins into the temple treasury. Faithful stewards give all that is asked and trust the Lord to be faithful to his promises.

(26th After Pentecost—Mark 13:1-8)

Jesus' description of the last days sounds as contemporary as this morning's headlines. His counsel to today's disciples is also the same now as then—be faithful, do not be led astray. For just a few verses later, he assures us, "The one who endures to the end will be saved."

(Christ the King—John 18:33-37)

Pilate asks Jesus if he is a king. We must ask that question, too. Is Christ sovereign in my life? What homage do I pay him? Can others tell by my actions and attitudes that he is Lord of my life?

(*Thanksgiving Day—Matthew 6:25-33*)

Today's Gospel is often preached as an invitation to trust in God. Today we see in it also the reason for thanksgiving—everything we have and are is graciously given by our loving God. As good stewards of these gifts, we must rejoice, be grateful, and be generous, too!

 # DEVOTIONAL

Fabulous Fortunes

Second Corinthians 8:1-7

DONALD W. JOINER

Few television shows make me stop what I'm doing to watch what's happening. *Night Court* is one exception. The star is Harry, sometimes magician, sometimes comic, and sometimes judge. Another key actor is Bull, a large, bald bailiff.

In one particular episode, Bull is helping an electrician string some wire. Bull is on the roof of the courthouse when lightning strikes. His shaven head and his height draw the lightning—he is hit by the lightning and knocked out. The scene opens with Bull lying on the couch in the judge's chambers. His face is blackened, his clothes torn and smoking.

A doctor is looking at him in wonderment: "He should have died when the lightning hit him. In fact, he was technically dead for a brief time, but it looks as if he is going to be all right."

When Bull recovers, he relates that he heard a voice and saw a bright light—which he interprets as God. He is sure he heard: "I'm not ready for you yet—go and give everything you have to the needy." Bull removes his life savings from the bank and begins handing it out to anyone who is in need. A long line forms in the courthouse cafeteria where Bull is enjoying his new role.

When all but one crumpled bill of his entire life savings has been given away, Harry confronts Bull with the news! It wasn't God he heard! In the confusion of the lightning strike, Bull had misinterpreted what the electrician said to him. Saddened that he had given away his life savings, Bull is now seen in a darkened courtroom. His large head is in his hands. A rather nondescript old man in rumpled clothes comes walking into the courtroom. He asks Bull to show him where to find the man who is giving away the money. He is obviously in great need. Bull pulls his long body up, reaches into his pocket, and pulls out a crumpled bill. He offers the last $100 of his life savings. "I was saving it for food—but here, you take it."

As the grateful man leaves the courthouse, the scene pans to Harry standing there. He had entered the courtroom in time to witness the whole scene. He calls out to Bull, "It's a hard habit to give up, isn't it?"

> "I do not believe one can settle how much we ought to give. I am afraid the only safe rule is to give more than we can spare."
>
> —C. S. LEWIS

After Harry leaves, Bull begins talking to God. It is clearly a new relationship for Bull. He explains to God that he really thought he was doing God's will. Besides—it felt good! Now what should he do? He had given away his life savings. Could God give him a sign? There is a long silence in the dark courtroom as Bull stares through the skylight.

Then another man enters the room. He represents the city, which is anxious to avoid a lawsuit from Bull's electrical accident. The attorney offers Bull $20,000 to sign the papers releasing the city from liability. Bull hesitates while he considers the offer.

The attorney says, "Okay then—$27,500—but that's our final offer." Bull grabs the papers and signs them as the attorney fills out the check. When the attorney leaves, Bull walks quietly across the dark courtroom. Then he stops, looks up and simply says—*"THANKS!"*

MONEY TALK

Possessing Our Possessions

EARL F. LINDSAY

Acts 5:4—"While it remained unsold, did it not remain your own? And after it was sold, were not the proceeds at your disposal?"

As an itinerant United Methodist pastor, I have lived in a variety of places. I was born and raised in a community of less than one hundred out on the Dakota prairie. I also have lived in Chicago, Boston, San Francisco, and Milwaukee. Strange as it seems, in every one of those diverse communities, there were two kinds of people—I don't mean the rich versus the poor, or the central city versus the suburbs. I mean the opposite ways that many seek to find worth for their lives. To see the truth more clearly, I name these two opposite sides of town the "Secular City" (thank you, Harvey Cox) and the "City of God" (thank you, Saint Augustine).

The citizens of the Secular City are the largest in numbers—the survival of the fittest is the rule of their life, and they are brutal to any who get in their way as they rush toward what they consider success. Material success at any cost is the goal of their life! The City of God is a smaller part of the community. It is a group of citizens who believe that better people are more important than bigger profits. Their satisfaction and joy come from sharing what they possess, rather than from larger accumulations.

The truth is that most of us, at one time or another, try to be part of both communities. Some of us start out in one community and end up in the other. We start out with good intentions and rather pure motives, but as our life absorbs the brutal blows and our experience prepares us for bigger payoffs, we succumb to the highest bidders and discover we belong to a different crowd.

Acts 5:1-10 is the story of a couple who started out for the "City of God" and died in the "Secular City." In them, we recognize how good people can become possessed by their possessions.

Ananias and Sapphira started their married lives with high ideals. They believed so strongly in the good side of people that they voluntarily joined a new kind of community. They would serve God and humanity by selling all they had and giving the proceeds to the community. The idea was that each person would give according to what they had, and everyone in the community would receive according to what they needed. They truly wanted to help build the City of God. It was so idealistic—so pure in motive! But the Bible tells us that they did not really throw everything into the pot! They secretly made a pact to hide some of their resources and thus build a little Social Security system for themselves! You see, they wanted to *live in* the City of God but *live by* the rules of the Secular City. They had betrayed their ideals, and that destroyed both their credibility and their caring community. Ananias and Sapphira became possessed by their possessions.

Can we become so possessed by our possessions that our sense of fulfillment evaporates? Can wealth and security be bought for too high a price? I don't mean that poverty makes anyone righteous; it could even make one bitter. But can we get to a place in our life where we know the price of most everything but the value of nothing?

Do we teach our children to share with the same enthusiasm that we teach them to accumulate? We have encouraged them to get to the top and have tried to provide them with the tools to get there; but have we helped them experience the joy of giving as well as receiving? Have we praised their acts of service, or is it just their accumulating that we compliment?

The City of God isn't as well advertised or as large as the Secular City, but it has groups of people who find their satisfaction in caring for more than themselves. They give money, and they give themselves. That's where Ananias and Sapphira missed it. They wanted everyone else to do the giving.

But the citizens of the City of God had discovered an inner peace that comes from sharing. It is never experienced when only accumulating is emphasized! The Gospel is saying, "Let's not work just for money; let's make money work for us. Let's keep it our slave, and not allow it to become our master!" Let's possess our possessions, rather than be possessed by them!

Wallace Petty was a pastor from an earlier generation. He tells about serving in his first parish and how

73

much both he and his wife enjoyed the people. When the time came to move to a new parish, the congregation presented them with a beautiful chest of silverware as an expression of their appreciation for the years together. It was expensive, and certainly a sacrifice for this proud but poor congregation. It was also something more expensive than the Pettys had ever owned. As a result, they found themselves very protective of their gift. They locked it up in a safe place; they insured it; they polished it with regularity; and when they were away for a few days, they would take it to a neighbor's for safekeeping!

Dr. Petty says, "One day I realized that we had become nursemaids to a chest of silver. We didn't own that silver. That silver owned us. So I placed the silverware in a safe place and taped a note to the box: 'Dear Thief, if you need this more than I do, take it.' "

The Pettys would not be possessed by their possessions. Both Ananias and Sapphira were good people, but their good side was destroyed by the lure of the Secular City. Greed gripped them until it strangled the real life out of them—the fun, the joy, the meaning. They had more "things," yet they had nothing!

We come to God's house each Sunday morning—not because everything said or sung will be profound, but to bring our life back into focus; to loosen the grip that greed gets on our life; to keep our idealism from being suffocated; and to allow our wholesome side to rise to the surface. We can renew our citizenship in the City of God.

 SERMON HELP

When Things Keep Us from God

BRADLEY G. CALL

Luke 12:13-31

C. William Nichols tells a story about a college football coach who was talking to a new recruiter on his staff: "You know, there's a certain kind of player who seems to have all the right statistics, but if you put him in the game and he gets knocked down, he stays there. That's not the kind of player we want. And there's another kind of player who can get in the game and get knocked down, and he'll get back up; but if he's knocked down again, he'll stay there, too. That's not the kind of guy we want either. And then there's a third kind of player who can get knocked down and get back up, and if he's knocked down a second time, he'll get back up a second time. Even if he gets knocked down a third or a fourth or a fifth time, he keeps getting back up."

"Yeah, coach," said the recruiter. "That's the guy we want, right?"

"No," replied the coach, "we want the guy who keeps knocking all those people down!"

There's somebody who keeps knocking people down—young couples whose marriages would otherwise be happy; bright, energetic people who could discover the cure for cancer or AIDS or other crises we face. There's a tyrant loose in our society creating havoc. That tyrant's name is "money."

Money can be a cruel master, causing people to do all sorts of things they wouldn't ordinarily do—lie, cheat, deceive, forsake their values, their church, even their family. Money can be a cruel tyrant. And the only way to transform that tyrant is to turn it into a servant.

A man came up to Jesus one day and said, "Teacher, get my brother to divide his inheritance with me." It's a story that not only shows us how things can keep a person from happiness, but how things can divide a man from his own brother. Here is a man who is willing to sacrifice what he already has—his relationship with his brother—in order to get what he thinks will bring him satisfaction.

To a lot of people, the measure of success in life is something tangible: money, accomplishments, things that yesterday were only dreams. Some people are looking for their fulfillment in things. Yet Jesus said that a person's life doesn't consist in the abundance of things. True happiness doesn't come from pleasures or possessions, but from purpose.

To illustrate that, Jesus told a story about an entrepreneurial landowner whose farming operation was immensely successful—one of approximately three dozen stories (we call them parables) which Jesus told throughout his ministry. Of those three dozen, one-third have to do with money or possessions. Apparently Jesus saw the potential for money or possessions to shape our lives, and he wanted to help us develop a healthy perspective on them.

From all indications, the man in Jesus' story wasn't a bad guy. Jesus didn't call him a sinner. He doesn't say he was corrupt or had pulled any shady deals. He wasn't a thief. He hadn't mistreated any of his employees. He seems to have been one of those people who had worked hard, and whose hard work had paid off. He had mastered the techniques of his trade. He knew how to care for the soil. He knew which seed to plant for greater yields. He knew the right time to market his product to get the best price. He seemed to be the kind of person you would want to have running your operation or watching over your investments.

Things were going so well for this guy that he didn't have enough room in his barns. To not tear down his undersized barns and build bigger ones would have been considered by many of us, to be foolish. So why was Jesus critical of him?

Part of the answer may be found in the words the man used: "my crops . . . my barns . . . my grain . . . my goods," even "my soul." Someone has said the man had an "I problem"—"I will do this," "I will do that," "I need," "I have." The pronouns tell the story: "I," "me," "my," "mine"—these are what drove him. Get all you can, accumulate, store up.

But God says that in the end, "How foolish! These things—whose will they be when your soul's time is up?"

Jesus says we are to beware of every kind of covetousness, for life does not consist in the abundance of possessions. Covetousness is not the desire to enjoy possessions, so much as the desire to have just for the sake of having. After all, in Proverbs 3:9-10, having "barns . . . filled with plenty" and "vats . . . bursting with wine" is depicted as the blessing prepared for those who honor the Lord with their "substance" and "first fruits." So we shouldn't construe that Jesus is condemning "having," per se; what Jesus criticizes is the tendency to identify "life" with "things."

One thing that is clear from the comment Jesus made at the close of this parable is that he considered it foolish for someone not to take into consideration an accountability to God. I believe you will agree that some people are what may be called "functional atheists"—that is, they believe in the existence of God, but it makes no real difference in the way they live their lives. They have no sense of their own personal accountability.

They are the creation of their environment, they believe, and God is so gracious, loving, and forgiving that God certainly wouldn't hold them accountable if they degrade their lives and demean their existence. But doesn't it make sense that the great God who granted us the gift of life, who gave us talents and abilities and opportunities, should hold us accountable for the use to which we put them? Wouldn't it be foolish to assume otherwise? It is a foolish assumption to think that what we have is ours alone, when it is not.

Another thing that is clear from the parable is that it is a foolish assumption to think that physical life is not terminal. We never know when our last day of life on this earth may be, but we do know that we will live for eternity. Every day we live contains 1,440 minutes, or 86,400 seconds, for us to spend or invest. Each day of this earthly life, the bank named Time opens a new account. It allows no carry-over balances, no overdrafts. It we fail to use the day's deposits, the loss is ours. There are lot of things we can do with the time we are given, but it is a foolish assumption to think we can plan and plan, and never plan for eternity.

You have to be very careful about the assumptions you make—they can prove to be very costly sometimes. It is foolish to assume that we can live our lives being accountable only to ourselves, or that we can find meaning in life in the word *more*. The rich man in Jesus' story gathered a lot of treasure for himself, but in the end, he had failed to gather anything of ultimate and eternal value.

We have so much. There is so much we could do. Someone put it like this: If the world were reduced to a global village of 100 people, 80 of them would be unable to read; only one would have a college education; 50 would be suffering from some form of malnutrition; 80 would be living in substandard housing. In this same village of 100 people, 6 of them would be Americans who have one-half of the entire income in the village, leaving the remaining 94 percent to live on the other half.

The man's problem isn't just that he talks to himself, but that he talks only to himself. He plans only for himself. He doesn't seem to be aware of the unseen partner in his enterprise, or of the people around him who could benefit from some of the fruit of his labor and truly make his life richer.

The farmer was foolish—not because he didn't plan ahead, but because he didn't plan far enough ahead. He thought more of himself than of others, more of his body than of his soul, and more of time than of eternity. He was able to see beyond the current market, but he couldn't see beyond this world—and so his story ends with the ultimate tragedy of souls who shut out the beauty of life that God intended.

This story reminds me of that old sketch done by Jack Benny, who made a career out of appearing to be very tight with his money. One sketch was worked into his show many times. He would be standing in a dark place and accosted by a would-be robber. The robber would poke a gun in his ribs and say, "Your money or your life."

There would be silence. The robber would say with greater forcefulness, "Your money or your life!" Again there would be silence.

Finally, in exasperation, the robber would say, "Mister, didn't you hear me? I said, 'Your money or your life!' "

And Jack Benny would reply, "I'm thinking! I'm thinking!"

Jesus' story challenges us, in the midst of an uncertain world, to examine our priorities. It is a story in which our Lord holds out before us our ultimately accountability to live our lives meaningfully, building relationships with God and people, so that when the day is over and we are headed for home, we can feel good about the way we lived, the difference we made, and the welcome we will receive.

 # SERMON HELP

Two Kinds of Giving

BRADLEY G. CALL

Mark 12:41-44

Suppose you have a friend who is a widow, and she calls you on the phone, saying, "I just wanted to tell you that I'm liquidating all my assets, selling everything I own, and giving it all to the church next Sunday." What would you think? A lot of people would probably advise her to hold on, not do anything rash, to wait until some financial advising could be done, until she could come to her senses.

Today, as a way of confronting us with ourselves and the world around us, consider the story we call "the widow's mite." Jesus sat down to watch worshipers contribute money to the temple treasury. Now how many people do you know who do this? Why did Jesus do it? Because he knew it said something about their faith. The original text says that many wealthy people "threw in" much. The sound of heavy coins told everyone how much they were giving, and by "throwing" them in, they could make sure that others would hear how "religious" they were. (By the way, it doesn't work with paper money, unless you get a really big wad!) Nowadays people have to find more creative ways of throwing their financial weight around—and some do!

Some would have us stop the lesson right there, advocating that the story shows that no one should know how much you give, since the amount obviously

is secondary. But it's not secondary. And the story isn't intended to show us that no one should know. In fact, the story would be pointless if we didn't know how much the widow put in, and that it represented a commitment of her whole self. What the story really tells us is that the measurement of our commitment is not in how much we give, but in how much we hold back.

> ## The measurement of our commitment is not in how much we give, but in how much we hold back.

Author G. Campbell Morgan says that two mites were about 1/96th of a denarius, and that a denarius was worth about 17 cents by today's standards. So if you want to see how much she put in, calculate 1/96th of 17 cents. That wasn't much. All the more striking, then, when Jesus said that she had put in more than all the rest of them. (Note that he didn't say she had put in more than *any* of the rest of them, but more than *all* the rest of them—combined!) Why would he have said that?

"For all of them have contributed out of their abundance; but she out of her poverty has put in everything she had, all she had to live on" (Mark 12:44).

She put in everything she had. Not *most* of what she had; *all* of what she had. Not just "leftovers," symbolic tokens, not a "tithe," not her "fair share." What she put in was her future, her trust, her faith, her life. Whatever she had, whatever summed up her whole being, her existence, her life—that is what this woman offered that day.

Some of us may think that what she gave was foolish—even reckless. How was she going to live? The funny thing is, I don't think even God expects such a commitment from us. Security is so basic a need that today we would consider the widow exemplary if she had given 1/10th of her coins—maybe less! But she gave it all!

What would move someone to give that much? You know, my mother-in-law (also a widow) is like that. She gives to her church. She gives to a variety of charities. She has given so much of her money to a wayward son that the rest of the family is worried about how she is going to get by. She has been tapped so many times by so many people that no one can understand why she keeps on giving. Some even think it is foolish. But I don't think that is ever an issue for her. She simply gives because she loves and because she thinks she can. That's all there is to it for her.

There was another lady in one of my previous churches (also a widow) who was just like that. Naomi came to me one day and asked how she could decide which charities she should cut because she couldn't continue to give at the level she had been giving. She was distressed because she thought they all were worthy. I know that Naomi did without a lot of comforts herself because she wanted to be a giver. It was important to her. It was an expression of love, an expression of who she was and who she wanted to be.

Naomi didn't set out to be noticed, but she was noteworthy. My mother-in-law doesn't expect any praise, but she is praiseworthy. The widow Jesus pointed out was intending only to be an ordinary, though faithful, worshiper, but she became an example of devotion for all of us. Some of you know people like that. Some of you probably are people like that. Some would call such givers foolish. I wonder what Jesus would say.

Why did the widow give the way she did? Because she believed in the work of God. The work of the temple was important to her, and she wanted to support it. She freely dropped her two coins in the box, for she knew that in so doing, she was part of something bigger than herself. There is a certain dignity about being able to give to something we believe in. It says that we are not simply takers, but givers.

Winston Churchill once said, "We make a living by what we get, but we make a life by what we give." The widow in the temple that day knew that. And some of you do, too.

Jesus' act of singling out the widow and her seemingly small gift reminds us that a gift cannot be measured by its size or impact alone. It must be measured against the balance one retains after the gift is given. It really has little to do with the actual money itself; it has to do with the depth of our love, our faith, our discipleship.

Mother Teresa has said: "It's not how much we do, but how much love we put into doing it. It's not how much we give, but how much love we put into giving."

MONEY TALK

Discover Joy

BRIAN K. BAUKNIGHT

"May the God of hope fill you with all joy and peace in believing, so that you may abound in hope by the power of the Holy Spirit" (Romans 15:13).

Two women were discussing their sons, both of whom were sophomores in college. One asked the other, "What does your son intend to do when he graduates from college?"

"I'm not sure," came the reply. "But from his letters, I think he intends to be a professional fund-raiser."

Some people contend that most preachers are professional fund-raisers. Yet a single truth should undo such a notion: Christian stewardship is not fund-raising. Christian giving is responsive discipleship. Vital congregations are not supported by dollars, but by disciples.

I may be a strange breed of preacher, but I enjoy

preaching about money. One reason? When I am preaching about money, I am not really preaching about money! I am preaching about discipleship. Jesus talked more about money than any other subject, except the kingdom of God. Sixteen of the thirty-eight recorded parables of Jesus concern the use of money or possessions. Jesus was training disciples, calling them toward the Kingdom.

My call is the same. I rejoice in that call every day of my life. Paul wrote to the Roman church: "May the God of hope fill you with all joy and peace in believing, so that you may abound in hope by the power of the Holy Spirit."

His message is a message of joy. I want to examine the possibilities within that message, in the context of giving. Our call through this text is a call to "discover joy."

Giving Is Joy

Giving itself is a joy. Part of the Christian journey includes the development of giving habits, a giving lifestyle. That process is joy!

Someone told me the story of three small-town preachers who were discussing methods of getting rid of bats in their bell towers. The Presbyterian minister said, "I tried shooting them, but all I succeeded in doing was putting holes in the roof."

The Lutheran minister said, "I tried something very different. I trapped them and took them 25 miles outside of town. But in less than 24 hours, they were all back!"

The Methodist minister spoke up: "I got rid of every bat," he said. "None are left."

"How in the world did you accomplish that?" the others queried.

"It was easy," came the reply. "First I baptized them. Then I confirmed them. Then I asked them to support the church with their prayers, their presence, their gifts, and their service, and I gave them a box of offering envelopes. And I haven't seen them since!"

Some congregations live in a similar mood. Talking about giving will drive people away. They are convinced that conversations about giving should be avoided whenever possible.

Someone has said that the most sensitive nerve in the human body runs to the left hip pocket. I know churches that live by that conviction. Yet the exact opposite is true: giving is a joyous, freeing, lifting experience.

Karl Menninger reportedly once said, "Money giving is a good criterion of a person's mental health. Generous people are rarely mentally ill people."

Giving is the way of the Kingdom. Giving is joy.

Tithing Is Joy

Then we become even more specific. Tithing is a joy. You say, "Uh-oh, preacher. Now you're meddling. Giving may be a joy, but not tithing."

Someone sent me a cartoon recently. It shows a young couple greeting the minister after a worship service. The woman holds a small baby in her arms.

"I'm sorry for the crying of my child in the service, Reverend," she says. "I tried to quiet him, but he's just starting to teethe."

"I understand about the baby," the minister replied. "What I don't understand is why your husband was crying."

"Oh," she said, "he's just starting to tithe."

Some people weep in the mere anticipation of tithing. Tithing is too painful. Tithing costs too much. Tithing is simply not a realistic issue.

The exact opposite is true. Tithing is indeed a joy.

Recently, I met a man who is a member of a church near San Francisco. He and his wife retired three years ago. Only since retirement have they decided to tithe. He gave me a marvelous testimony: "We are probably more content and more satisfied than we have ever been in our entire lives. And we definitely have better control of our finances than ever before. Starting to tithe has been a joy."

A clergy colleague has responsibility for his elderly aunt—his mother's only remaining sister. She is in her eighth decade of life. Recently, he helped her move into a retirement home. Her monthly income is $1,550. The retirement home fees are $1,150 per month. The nephew was helping her put together her finances and calculating her fixed expenses in light of the change.

He said to her, "Virginia, this is going to be very tight. You can just barely make it."

"Did you figure in my $155 tithe to the church each month?" she asked.

"Oh my, Virginia. No way. You will have to cut back. There simply isn't enough."

His aunt looked straight at him and said, "Nephew, I don't care how you do it. But you do it. You put my tithe at the top of my list!"

A couple made this statement to a friend of mine:

We have never regretted our decision to tithe. We have enjoyed our lives even more since we made the 10 percent commitment. We do not have much, but we do not need much. And God has been more than sufficient for us.

What a wonderful witness. And it reflects the joy of tithing.

You will never be in a better position to tithe than you are today. Furthermore, the decision to tithe is usually not made with calculators or with pencil and paper. The decision to tithe is made on your knees and from the heart. Tithing has very little to do with mathematical formulas.

I was surprised to learn recently that President Abraham Lincoln tithed. Little is known about Lincoln's true spirituality or his theology. But he tithed. He said that his tithing was a witness to the fact that God owned everything he had.

Whenever I speak of tithing, someone always asks, "OK, I'll consider tithing; but must it all go to the church?"

My response is simple. The decision must be made by each individual. My own decision is to give the full tithe to the church. I was taught from the earliest time I can remember that the church is God's best hope for this world. I tithe it all to the church. But an amazing truth has followed that decision: Enough money always remains to give something to other worthy causes as well. I can never remember a time when that promise of God was not true.

Tithing is a joy in the greatest adventure of Christian discipleship. I pray that many of you will discover that joy.

Beyond the Tithe: Even Greater Joy

And there is more! To move beyond the tithe is even greater joy.

I remember a story about a Baptist minister who preached a marvelous and moving sermon on tithing. When he finished, one of the inspired deacons rose to his feet. "A tenth is not enough," he cried. "Each of us should give a twentieth!"

Sometimes, God calls you beyond a tithe as your next step in discipleship. God calls you to this wider dimension of discipleship.

God has called my wife and me in this direction in recent years. Tithing had literally become too easy. There was no growing edge to our giving. In a recent year, in recognition of all that was before our church, we committed 15 percent of our income to the general operating budget of the church. We needed to allow God to stretch us.

I was feeling pretty good about that decision. Then, not a week after we had made our decision, I met a young couple who were giving 18 percent! And they were looking for ways to stretch it to 20 percent in the coming year! More important than the numbers: They were radiantly alive, full of joyous energy and faith. The challenges of God toward faithful discipleship and trust never end.

Sometimes God calls you beyond a tithe because you have what the Bible calls the "gift of giving." Scripture illuminates many spiritual gifts. Paul and other New Testament writers mention at least 25 gifts. One of those gifts is the "gift of giving." One word defines that gift: *generosity*. Paul writes that those who have the gift of giving should be "generous and ready to share" (I Tim. 6:18; see also Rom. 12:8). Such giving brings joy.

You may be a believer who has the gift of giving. As other believers who have that gift relocate or retire, new disciples are called. God regularly calls new persons to the "gift of giving."

I can only promise that in such giving, you will discover joy! Just recently, one of my members with this spiritual gift said to me, "Remember! Don't hesitate to ask me. I want to give. I need to give. I really enjoy giving!"

Joy in Being the Church

Great joy permeates the church these days. I have never felt such jubilation on behalf of the church as I feel right now. New ministries continually appear on the horizon—ministries of inreach and outreach. Somewhere I read this quotation: "The future belongs not to those who have all the facts, but to those who have a vision." The church of Jesus Christ is never short on vision. I call you to joyous giving in faithful discipleship to match that vision.

The story is told of an old-timer who was watching one of the first steam locomotives start on a trip. He looked at the huge iron horse with its massive wheels and pistons, shook his head, and said, "They'll never get 'er started!"

Just then, the steam began to surge through the components of the engine. The huge wheels began to turn. The pistons moved back and forth. Gradually, the train moved down the tracks, picking up more and more speed as it moved along. The old-timer shook his head again and quipped, "They'll never get 'er stopped."

If my joy in giving is at all contagious, and if you who also know the joy of giving are similarly contagious, there will be a momentum that is unstoppable! And God will be praised.

 DRAMA

The Pizza Party

GILSON MILLER

Ephesians 4:25-32

Cast of Characters:
Upper Level—3 characters
Lower Level—7 characters

Costumes:
Upper Level people are dressed very nicely.
Lower Level people are dressed in old, dirty, tattered clothing.
They wear no shoes.

Props: 3 stools, card table, 4 coffee cans to elevate the table legs, 3 empty soft-drink cans, 5 pizza boxes.

Setting: Three people are seated around a large, elevated table enjoying pizza, colas, and other junk-food items. Underneath the table crouch seven people—three adults, two teenagers, two children.

(UL indicates Upper Level of table; LL indicates Lower Level—the people under the table.)

UL #1: That Louise can sure bake a mean pizza! If I keep eating like this, they will expel me from Weight Watchers.

UL #2: Could you believe Reverend Sleeptalker last Sunday? Trying to convince us that we should share with all those hungry people in other parts of the world.

UL #3: The nerve of that man, trying to make us feel guilty. It's just a gimmick, using all those gross illustrations about starving children. We need to take care of our own, right?

UL #1: Yeah, I wonder if he is really in touch with how much things cost today. These designer jeans were $68! I mean, he doesn't expect us to walk around without any pants on, does he?

UL #2: This is one pizza party ole Sleeptalker isn't going to wreck!

LL #1: It is so crowded down here. I wish we had a little more room. I can hardly move.

LL #2: I wish we had some food! It gets harder each night to watch my little ones go to bed hungry.

LL #3: Hey, listen! I think I hear someone. It sounds like some kind of party right above us. They are laughing. How long since we've had anything to laugh at?

LL #4: I wonder if they can hear us?

LL #5: They haven't heard our cries for years. Why should tonight be any different?

LL #6: Hey look—food! It must have fallen from their table. *(Wild scramble for the stray piece of pizza from the table.)*

UL #1: You know, I'm worried about my car. Its almost two years old, and when I look at the prices of new ones, I'm not sure I'll be able to afford another full-sized car like I've always driven.

LL #1: I wish we could afford to buy some shoes. It would help so much for the long walk to the market.

UL #2: I'm having a dinner party this weekend, and I just can't decide what to serve. Do you think I should go with the prime rib or lasagna?

LL #7: Mom, I am so hungry. When will the pain in my stomach go away?

UL #3: We just priced braces. It's going to cost more than $2,000! There's only a small

80

irregularity in Julie's teeth, but I couldn't have her going though life with imperfect teeth. It might affect her self-esteem. The dentist said the braces really weren't necessary, but I want my daughter to be attractive in every way. I don't want her to feel deprived.

LL #2: If we don't get our child to the clinic, he will soon die. But the nearest doctor is more than 50 miles away, and we have no money.

UL #1: We have tried turning down our thermostat to save some on utilities, but we don't want anyone to feel uncomfortable, right?

LL #3: Who gets the blanket tonight? Sometimes I can't wait for morning and the sun to come out and warm things up. It gets so cold at night.

LL—ALL: Help, please help us!

UL #1: Did you hear something?

UL #2: Yeah, the sounds of my overworked stomach trying to make room for more pepperoni and anchovies.

UL #1: No, I thought I heard someone crying for help. And it sounded like it was coming from right under this table.

UL #3: That's what too much pizza will do for you. Let me check under there and see. *(Lifts tablecloth and peers under table.)* Nope, just one of those little fishes you dropped.

LL—ALL: Please help us! Just a little food would help so much. Don't ignore us. We need you. *(These statements can be said simultaneously.)*

UL #1: *(Handing one of the LL folks a piece of pizza.)* Here, I know this isn't much. How come there are so many of you down there?

LL #3: You need to understand that it's like this all over the world. While three of you feast, seven of us starve.

UL #2: What are you doing, poking around down there? Did you lose your contact? Maybe you're feeling light-headed from your aerobics class.

UL #3: She's always been a little dizzy.

UL #1: No, really! You have to believe me. *(Looks under table again.)* There are people down there calling for us to help them. They are hungry and cold and have no medical help. Worst of all, they have no hope.

UL #2: Sure, and next you'll tell us that Reverend Sleeptalker is the pope! I think that sermon really got to you last Sunday. Don't believe everything you hear. All the food that's sent to those people sits in warehouses and rots. Or it gets sold on the black market. Eat, drink, and forget your imaginary seven under the table.

UL #1: I don't think I can. I can't ignore them. They are people, too. They have pride and dignity, and they love their children.

UL #3: Well, don't wreck our party with your guilt trips. *(To #2)* Let's take the pizza and find someone who wants to have fun. Goodbye and good riddance to you, too. *(He is speaking to the seven on LL. They exit down left aisle, laughing, leaving #1 reaching under the table to the people on LL.)*

PART THREE

MONEY MANAGEMENT IN THE CHURCH

Introduction

DON JOINER

Whenever I tell people that I specialize in helping churches understand how to fund their ministry, most respond, "I couldn't do that." When I'm introduced, there seems to be a semi-apology for what I do. However, helping churches discover the excitement of raising funds for ministry is the most fulfilling work I have ever done! Donald Messer, in his article, says it's time to get away from the "fear" and lift fund-raising to "a noble art."

After all, helping fund ministry in the church is to help people see that their giving is purposeful, faithful, and exciting.

"The old way isn't working!" But we still cling to the familiar ways of doing things in the church. This is a new day—and Tim Ek's article lists some of the myths to be exploded.

One of the trends in financially healthy congregations is to have a vision of ministry and the willingness to work toward that vision. Glenna and Roy Kruger provide positive steps a church can take to increase the funding level for the vision. To do planning, we must understand the dynamics of the church. Each church is different. Robert Wood Lynn's article

asks: Who are your members? How is your congregation different? Then Greg Pope provides some practical tools for understanding the particular demographics of your church.

Some churches need something to celebrate. "We can't do that" usually derives from a lack of funds or a perception that people don't want to give. One of the prominent needs in many churches today is lack of funds for maintenance. Buildings suffer from neglect when there is no money left in the budget for repairs. For some churches, this leads to disgrace—even an "institutional depression" about what is possible in ministry. Wayne Barrett's Miracle Sunday program is a way to raise more money than you ever have before. He shows how to raise from 55 percent to 300 percent of your annual budget in one Sunday!

This part of THE GUIDE is full of practical tools to improve your funding program: sample letters to send to members year-round; a creative way to view your quarterly statements, twenty fund-raising ideas to see you through the short term; and a way to look at different levels of giving. Finally, Don Stoner brings us back to why we give as he leads us through a "Litany of Gratitude."

 MONEY TALK

The Noble Art of Funding Ministry

DONALD E. MESSER

Does anyone ever grow up planning to be a professional fund-raiser? Does any mother or father ever say to their child that they hope they will devote their life to asking other people for money? Does one list on one's passport: occupation, money-raiser? What happens to a conversation on an airplane or at a cocktail

party, when you happen to mention that you devote all your time to asking for gifts?

Church fund-raisers have an image problem. Temple money changers, despised tax collectors, and medieval indulgence sellers have not been honored historically. Contemporary scandals by the Jimmy

Bakkers and Jim Swaggarts, scams by the Oral Roberts and the Pastor Blairs, skiddishness by pastors and laity about asking for money—all have helped devalue the worth and work of those called to raise resources for the life of Christ's church. The scandals, scams, and skiddishness force us to change our understanding of what it means to commit our lives to the Christian ministry of fund-raising.

Moving Beyond Stereotyped Images

Critical to accepting God's gift of the noble art of fund-raising is to move beyond the stereotyped images that we encounter, create, accept, internalize, or perpetuate. Mention to someone that you are engaged in fund-raising, and you will detect from that person's body language, if not their words, a degree of discomfort stemming from preconceived images of who you are and what you do. These misunderstandings are distorted perception. Briefly, let us examine some of these stereotypes that are disturbingly persistent, both within and outside Christian communities.

"The beggar with the tin cup" image suggests that we are engaged in activities worthy of only a minor contribution. Historically, begging has had a worthy religious connotation in some cultures and times; but in our own culture, its negative dimensions outweigh any positive perspectives. When most people think of beggars with tin cups, they don't associate that image with medieval monks, but with derelicts or "moonies" on street corners or in airports.

A second image, *"the bureaucrat with a computer,"* rates only a little higher in the public's estimation. Churning out documents and mass mailings, the church bureaucrat spins out a web of appeals and photocopied materials. The individualized computer letter and the impersonal phonathon become the major means of ministering. The bureaucrat often only itinerates between the computer and the coffee pot!

Third, the image of *"the hustler with tricks"* suggests a person willing to engage in any activity or scheme in order to get money. Integrity is sacrificed

on the bed of compromise. Flamboyant promises and fervent pressure characterize the deceptive trickster who may reach goals, but leaves a trail of carnage.

A fourth image is of *"the careerist with a license."* Obviously, this is the most positive of the images cited, since career professionals, at their best, represent high standards and competent skills. Yet in the life of the church, it also often presumes a lifestyle or identity of haggling, "left the ministry" for the land of conferences, the language of annuities, and the legalese of tax consequences. Ordination certificates may appear to mean little more than licenses received from specialized training in planned giving.

Over the past twenty years as a college and seminary president, I have known personally the beggar with a tin cup, the bureaucrat with a computer, the hustler with a bag of tricks, and the careerist with a license. I have witnessed their successes and failures, their strengths and weaknesses. The stereotypes engendered by these images prove to be barricades, keeping the brightest and most promising from becoming fund-raisers and prohibiting the church from fulfilling its urgent mission in the world. Each has some strengths.

On a more positive side, the beggar dramatizes that money is needed now for immediate needs; the bureaucrat does the careful planning necessary; the hustler gets out of the office and meets the people directly; and the careerist brings competence to the work. Ultimately, such images, however, can be self-defeating and discouraging. What is needed is a move beyond these stereotypes to revisioning fund-raising as a noble art and a ministry in the economy of God.

> "The important thing is to be willing to give as much as we can—that is what God accepts, and no one is asked to give what he has not got."
>
> *II CORINTHIANS 8:12*

Fund-Raising As a Calling

Those of us who work within the context of the church must understand fund-raising as a calling from God. As laity and clergy seeking the reign or kingdom of God on earth, we must experience what it means to be summoned, even commanded, by God to achieve God's liberating and loving initiatives in the world. Christian fund raising is more of a calling than a career, more of a vocation than a job, more an opportunity than an obligation.

Like many in the church, I formerly accepted the notion that asking people for money was undesirable, if not degrading. However, I was converted and in a most unusual way.

I was a seminary student in Boston when Martin Luther King, Jr., called white clergy, laity, and seminarians to join African Americans and others on the demonstration lines in Selma, Alabama. We decided to send two bus loads to march and represent our school. I was elected treasurer, and chosen to raise funds to pay for the buses. Believing deeply in the cause, and sensing the urgency of finding sufficient funds, I plunged into the task of asking persons to give money to cover the costs of the buses. I discovered a new and deeper spirituality as I understood and exercised the calling of fund-raising. I learned that asking for money is at the heart of Christ's mission and ministry in our time.

Christians, lay and clergy, who embrace fund-raising as a calling are not stereotypical beggars, bureaucrats, hustlers, or careerists, but active agents of reconciliation in a hurting world. We like raising large amounts of money—not for its own sake, but for the large amount of good it does, both for the donor and the cause of Christ we represent. We know there are more needs to be met than we can reach, but we labor on without experiencing "compassion fatigue," because we ultimately believe that the future belongs to God. By our asking, we plant seeds that we hope will yield fruit in God's great harvest. We believe the Talmud when it says that "in saving one life, we save the whole world."

Fund-Raising for Christ

By accepting the task as a Christian calling, we may help others and ourselves to fulfill the noble art and ministry of fund-raising.

First, raising money for Christ's work is a pastoral calling. Instead of primarily picturing ourselves as professional fund-raisers, we should portray ourselves as practical theologians, committed to helping donors understand the spiritual joy of giving and enabling the monies to fund worthy projects. We are not indulgence sellers, offering or guaranteeing salvation, but pastors who seek to connect the practical and the theoretical. We help others to create a legacy of love.

Fund-raisers need to be professional, giving people the best information available and providing the proper legal and tax counsel. Fundamentally, what we offer is a spiritual ministry, helping people to expand their vision of how they can love God and their neighbor. As practical mystics, we help persons translate their best stewardship hopes into practical ways of caring for others. Our pastoral task, whether we are clergy or lay, is to help others understand how miraculous dollars can be.

Undergirding our work with prayer, Christian fund-raisers pray, "Thy kingdom come, thy will be done, on earth as it is in heaven." We live by grace, not by works. Prayer provides the courage to ask for truly sacrificial responses. Prayer lifts our vision and highlights our hopes. Prayer entrusts God to be at work. Often the answers to our prayers may be different from what we had imagined, but in time, we are confident that God's will shall be manifest. We believe that truly, the future belongs to God.

Second, we are called to look for and contact persons who can and will give generously to advance Christ's Kingdom. We need to cultivate the practice and reputation of always being alert to possible donors.

If we keep our networks open and our own sensitivities alert, we can often find people in the most unexpected places.

I recently had a call from a friend, telling me about a retiring chief executive of a Fortune 500 company whom I might ask for a donation. However, obvious signs of wealth are not the only, or often the best, leads to givers. I used to visit a woman in her very modest duplex bungalow in Grand Junction, Colorado. A social worker, she lived a simple life, dedicated to saving her money so that she could endow scholarships for seminarians. When she died, she had accumulated almost a million dollars for that purpose. Another couple who were active church members had never been on anybody's list of rich people, but when they died, they left a million dollars to The Iliff School of Theology to establish an endowed chair in preaching.

Third, be contagiously enthusiastic about the cause you represent. I cannot imagine raising money for something I don't believe in myself. Not only would my integrity be threatened, but my interest would betray a lack of excitement about what could be achieved through sizable gifts.

If one believes in a cause, the clock means little. The fund-raising careerist may want to work 9 to 5, putting off tasks for another day. When fund-raising is a calling, however, there is a passion that pushes us beyond the minimum required. We like visiting in people's homes. We don't mind driving distances to make contacts. We don't easily become discouraged. Fund-raising is seldom easy, and the results are rarely quick. Like women and men who fish, we try to make sure we have as many lines in the water as possible, in hope of "catching" something great and grand for the work of Christ.

Fourth, it is never right to rob Peter to pay Paul. John R. Mott, a great lay evangelist and fund-raiser, raised millions of dollars for the work of Christ in the world. He said it was his life rule "not to be a party to letting a person cut off, omit, or reduce his gifts to one part of the work of Christ's Kingdom in order that he may respond favorably to my appeal on behalf of some other part of the Christian cause . . . . Christ is not divided, and His work should not be."

The temptation is sometimes to "steal" a donor or downgrade the need or importance of the other, but robbing Peter ultimately rapes Paul. Undermining other programs and organizations demeans our calling as Christ's ministers.

In working with estate plans, it is a wise policy to encourage people to remember the needs of their families and local churches. Though we may work for different agencies or concerns, our calling always is to uplift the church and world in general, not to do anything that would hinder or hamper Christ's mission of liberating love.

Fifth, we should never despise or depreciate small gifts. In the sight of God, we are never sure what is a small or large gift. Obviously, we should encourage people, in John Wesley's language, to "gain all you can, save all you can, give all you can." The problem with human nature, of course, is that for many of us, by the time we have gained and saved all we can, we no longer have any appetite for giving all we can.

Truly, no giver is too insignificant and no gift too small not be merit the time, attention, and love of those who have been called to be fund-raisers for Christ's Kingdom.

Sixth, it is always a good time to ask for money to advance Christ's Kingdom. Do not apologize for seek-ing monies to help the church and its agencies to extend ministries of education, love, compassion, and service. The immediacy and urgency of our calling prompts us to ask now.

Conventional wisdom always suggests that this is a bad time for initiating a campaign or asking for a gift. We are either entering a recession or still recovering from a recession. People either have just lost money on the stock market or have it all invested and can't get it out right now. Commitments have already been made and economic conditions don't seem quite right. I believe I have heard every reason for not giving that has ever been uttered.

> People won't give if they truly don't have the money. None will give more than they should. People know how to protect their self-interest and don't generally over-give to charities. In twenty years, no person who contributed to the causes I represented ever went bankrupt or was hungry for a single day because of a gift they had given.

Times were desperate in the days of Jeremiah. The city was under siege with the enemies at the gates, the wells drying up, and the children crying. Jeremiah had warned the king about whoring after false gods and following false prophets. He told him disaster was coming, and his worst possible projections happened. Thanks to his prophetic and public forecast, Jeremiah was jailed.

At this moment of great despair, God told Jeremiah to buy a piece of land controlled by the enemy. Without blinking, Jeremiah bought the land, signed the documents, and had the deed sealed in a safe deposit jar to keep for a long time. With great defiance, Jeremiah declared to the king: "Thus says the LORD of hosts, the God of Israel: Houses and fields and vineyards shall again be bought in this land" (Jer. 32:15).

This act of supreme faith epitomized Jeremiah's faith in God. When others despaired, Jeremiah invested in the future, believing that his people under God had a new destiny. Eventually, the land would be liberated, the siege would be over, and the recession would end. Even when times are tough, Christians believe that the future will be better. There are always Christians willing to invest in God's future Kingdom, if we but ask now.

Vision-Bearers of God's Kingdom

As vision-bearers of God's Kingdom or Reign of Love on earth, we can embrace the noble art and ministry of fund-raising. The potential good that you do cannot be measured today. Few fund-raisers ever see the fruits of their labors or hear the appreciative applause of those who benefit. Ours is a labor of love that transcends time and place, rooted in the realm of the eternal.

As vision-bearing fund-raisers, think not of yourselves as being beyond the local church or having left the ministry, or being peripheral to the pastoral work of Jesus Christ. Rather, image yourself in the center of God's great mission and ministry, seeking to be faithful to the Great Commandment:

"Love the Lord your God with all your heart, and with all your soul, and with all your mind. . . . And . . . love your neighbor as yourself" (Matt. 22:37-39).

 MONEY TALK

Misconceptions About Giving

TIMOTHY C. EK

During my days as a pastor, and now even more as an administrator, I have become aware that we often are guided by perceptions we have accepted as true, when unfortunately, many are not. To continue making assumptions based on these "myth conceptions" can severely limit planning for stewardship programming.

Here are twelve examples of myth conception that I have encountered in the church:

1. We can't tithe because our members don't have the resources.

For those in a congregation where no member is able to purchase a new automobile, own a home video recorder, afford an out-of-state vacation, have air-conditioning, or send children to private colleges, this statement could be understandable. However, such a congregation is rare in America. The truth is that generosity has much more to do with our attitude than our possessions. Some of the most generous people I have ever met (especially in third-world countries) live on almost nothing. The spiritual health of a congregation is dependent upon its willingness to model the sacrificial giving love of Christ and his submission to God's will for his life and resources. The church that "cannot afford" to be generous is usually the church that does not understand the Lord's heart or his message.

2. Our church must address its own money problems first.

Most local church money problems are related to lack of leadership, fresh ideas, and a sense of mission. Hudson Taylor once said that "God's work done God's way will never lack resources." The apostle Paul said it best, of course: "God is able to make all grace abound toward you" (2 Corinthians 9:8). Money problems are the surface issues that ought to challenge church leadership to take a deeper look at the mission they are seeking to accomplish.

3. Asking for financial commitment will drive people away.

Lyle Schaller counters this by saying, "You can raise as much money as you ask for." We can be sure that if we do not ask for it, somebody else will. People love to give when they feel their gift can make a difference.

Jesus challenged potential disciples to always count the cost, reminding them that following him would demand a total-life response. He was never afraid to call people to commitment.

4. Our income is tied to the income of our members.

This statement is no longer as true as it once was. There have been dramatic changes in our culture since

1960. A large percentage of Americans now have significant accumulated assets—thus (especially when there are capital-fund drives or new mission opportunities) members will often use resources from their accumulated assets to give their support. Churches that fail to recognize that members can and want to give, both out of current income and accumulated assets, will fail to utilize all the resources God has provided for the church to accomplish his mission.

5. *Budget expenditures should never exceed projected church income.*

It is not unusual for a local church budget committee to review last year's income, determine the inflation rate changes, and set the budget for the new year accordingly. This is not a mission-driven or faith-sized approach to local church budgeting. The local church budget ought to be the mission statement of the congregation, to demonstrate its priorities for helping to fulfill Christ's Great Commission. While the budget committee is responsible for providing prudent guidelines, a budget always should be set with a "faith factor" that encourages the church to stretch beyond its expectations and allow God the opportunity to prove his faithfulness.

6. *Giving will increase with higher attendance.*

Higher attendance does not guarantee higher income. The exact opposite can be true. It usually takes new members three years to grow in their understanding of stewardship to a point that is equal to that of other members of high-expectation congregations.

When new members are drawn into the church, they often bring with them demands for local-church programming that carries very high costs—costs they may not yet understand or be committed enough to support. Thus, churches that are experiencing rapid growth need to be aware that they must provide education to assist new members in becoming disciplined stewards, or they will quickly discover they do not have resources to maintain the programs that have attracted new people. Until then, churches should remember that ministry costs in excess of $15 per member per Sunday!

7. *The pastor should not know what people give.*

This is a concept that seminaries helped instill in a whole generation of pastors. It is much akin to believ-

ing that a doctor should not be aware of a patient's symptoms until just before the operation.

The assumption seems to be that pastors will cater to the rich if they become conscious of their gifts. Be that as it may, if the pastor is one to whom people from the church and community turn when they have problems that require counseling, certainly the pastor can be trusted to know the giving patterns of the members. Spiritual health and maturity are directly linked to what Christians do with what they have.

This maturity also relates to choosing church leadership. A pastor needs to know that all leaders are active, disciplined givers. Leaders can never lead others beyond their own level of practice. In short, this myth conception can hinder the pastor from exercising essential leadership in the church.

> A pastor needs to know that all leaders are active, disciplined givers. Leaders can never lead others beyond their own level of practice.

8. *The pastor shouldn't be involved in stewardship and fund-raising.*

This perpetuates the old agnostic heresy that there is something inherently evil and nonspiritual about dealing with money and material issues. Jesus' own example is an important counter to this idea. If the pastor is unable to share involvement in shaping the stewardship program of the church, he or she will be unable to help shape a vision for mission or build a budget to support it.

John Maxwell notes that 89 percent of what people do is what they have seen modeled. Pastors must model by their own lifestyles and teachings that stewardship is vitally linked to the spiritual health both of individuals and the local church family.

9. *People who are committed will give generously as the Lord leads.*

While this statement sounds good, it is unsubstantiated in consistent practice. Right beliefs, and even right commitments, do not always translate into right actions. Ironically, people who regularly make and keep commitments to pay off mortgages and credit-card debts consider themselves somehow beyond the need to make a commitment of their resources to God. Even the most committed may not always "feel led" to exercise the discipline needed to follow through on commitments.

Church leaders, therefore, must be challenged to keep the issues of stewardship before their people as they call them to specific and sacrificial commitment.

10. You can't ask the same people to give again and again.

Because church leaders do not want to be perceived as always asking for money, and because money seems to be one of the most private areas in our culture, we often fall prey to this belief. It justifies our willingness to share financial ministry needs with people. Interestingly, fund-raisers point out that the best prospects for future gifts are people who are already giving. These people give because we have a relationship with them; they trust us, and feel a part of the ministry.

While we need to be sensitive to how subsequent appeals are made, we must recognize that past donors are inclined to follow up previous gifts with further commitments, in order to guarantee that the ministry they have supported can continue to flourish.

11. The best giving plan is a unified budget and reduced special appeals.

This has been a favorite theme in most denominations since the early 1940s. Close evaluation of gift-request patterns within these denominations, however, reveals that it has not really been their practice since the 1960s. In light of today's giving climate, I believe the church needs to utilize both the unified-budget and the designated-giving approaches as ways to enlist support of ministries.

The unified budget provides an efficient and focused way of receiving broad ministry support that assures a stable income source—especially for areas of ministry that are vital to the ongoing mission, but may not have a lot of appeal to the donor. The challenge for church leaders will be to find a middle ground, to minimize the negative sides of both the unified and the designated-giving approaches and accentuate the positive aspects of these approaches.

12. The church has done a poor job of teaching stewardship.

While it is true that many churches struggle to find resources to support their ministry, there are many evidences in our culture that the church has been far more effective in teaching stewardship than we have realized. Corporations influenced by leaders who are members of the church now designate 3 to 5 percent of their corporate income to support charitable causes.

In today's culture, 84 percent of all charitable giving comes from individuals. This is another reflection on the influence of the church. The Independent Sector indicates that church givers are much more generous to nonchurch charitable causes than are nonchurch persons.

I was once told that if the church teaches people illusionary theology, they are setting people up to be disillusioned. To live with false expectations is to set ourselves up for failure. This is also true in the area of stewardship.

If we allow misconceptions to direct our thinking in stewardship planning and practice, we are going to miss opportunities and resources that God had provided to his people in order to accomplish his purpose.

I was once told that if the church teaches people illusionary theology, they are setting people up to be disillusioned. To live with false expectations is to set ourselves up for failure. This is also true in the area of stewardship.

If we allow misconceptions to direct our thinking in stewardship planning and practice, we are going to miss opportunities and resources that God has provided to his people in order to accomplish his purpose.

PLANNING TOOL

Proclaiming Through Planning

GLENNA KRUGER AND ROY KRUGER

Have you glimpsed God's vision for your church? Are there special ministries and needs that God has called your church to fulfill? What are the unique resources God has given that enable you to respond? How can you get from questions to implementation of God's plan? We will explore the many benefits of a thoughtful planning process and help you get started.

WHY PLAN?

Planning is a great process to encourage people to talk about your church—to dream and pray together about new possibilities. Planning can put enthusiasm back into the life of your congregation as people share their hopes and visions for ministries. Planning stimulates creativity and fresh ideas from a cross-section of the congregation. It can lessen misunderstandings, clearly define expectations, and produce a commitment from individuals regarding the future direction of their church.

Planning helps you make the most of your resources. You can't expect to fund every ministry known to exist in every church. Establishing priorities and budgeting for key programs is good stewardship.

Planning also helps you acknowledge progress. If you have a plan to increase mission giving, roof the building, or start a ministry for singles, you will be able to measure your progress, celebrate the success, and evaluate the outcome.

THE PLANNING COMMITTEE

Involvement of all members of your congregation is crucial to the successful planning process. We all have more sense of ownership in organizations that we have helped start, in processes we have designed, or in goals we have helped to establish. In a small church, your planning committee may serve only to organize the process, while the whole congregation participates at some level. In large churches, you may need to delegate the task to a planning committee that not only organizes the process, but produces the actual plan. Be sure the planning committee represents a good cross-section of your congregation and involves a variety of ages, experiences, and points of view.

This group can develop its own level of commitment to the planning process through creating a mission statement for its own work. Committee members can decide questions such as:

- What is the committee expected to accomplish?
- How will it gather information from the congregation?
- How will it communicate back to the congregation?
- Will it investigate programs in other churches that might be adaptable?

You may want to divide the work among subcommittees that focus on specific topics. Goals can be developed by each committee and pulled together into a single document.

STEPS FOR CREATING A CONGREGATIONAL PLAN

Now we're going to take you step by step through the planning process. You can use this as an outline for your planning committee.

Step One: Developing the Vision Statement

Vision statements should reflect the core values of the Gospel, have a sense of passion to unite people, and be easily remembered. It's different from doctrinal statements or creeds that you may use. Those statements define specific beliefs and interpret the Gospel for a whole universal body of Christians.

Your church vision statement is specific to your local congregation. It's a temptation to make the vision statement too broad. Perhaps you fear placing limits on God if you try to be specific about your focus. However, a good vision statement helps to clarify your long-term direction, focuses your energies on specific goals, and gives enough boundary that you don't waste resources.

Your church is composed of a unique combination of elements that interact with one another in a special way. Your church is different from the one across town because of its size, location, polity, talents of parishioners, background of professional staff, and types of visitors. That's why your own church seems like home when you come back from visiting another on vacation.

Your vision discussion should start with an examination of what makes your church unique. Consider such items as:

- your location
  — near the poor, or families, or universities
  — a small town with many small churches or a large metropolitan area
  — a growing (or dying) community

- the demographics of your congregation
  — how many children and youth
  — number of families
  — percentage of retired persons
  — number of year-round residents

- your resources
  — the size, condition, and flexibility of the building
  — skills of professional staff
  — available volunteers
  — amount of income

This self-examination should lead you to an understanding of how you might uniquely serve God where you are. You could also develop some radical new thinking about making major changes. Is it time to plant a new church by sponsoring a core group from your church to begin a new congregation? Is it time to open up the building to new uses never before thought possible? Are there people "knocking on the door," asking to share in your resources?

At our church, you can choose among a Baptist service in three languages (English, Spanish, Cambodian), followed by a Presbyterian service in Korean. During the week, the hungry are fed in our dining room, street kids have a place to hang out and have some fun, and senior citizens have weekly activities organized by volunteers. These are missions that can happen when you have a great building in a downtown area.

A vision statement allows church committees to develop specific action plans that are consistent with the direction underscored in the vision statement. Even small task teams should develop a simple statement of purpose that gives all members the same frame of reference for their activities.

Constantly communicate your vision statement and keep it very visible. Have it printed up on poster board and display it prominently throughout your building. Print it on every newsletter and every bulletin, so that each member can articulate it and constantly reflect on what is being accomplished.

Here's an example of a vision statement from a small suburban congregation:

"The mission of Community Baptist Church is to be an open and inclusive community that brings people to faith in God through Jesus Christ. We seek to be an inviting people, reaching out to our community and the surrounding region through:

— worship that brings people to an experience of God's loving presence and action in their lives;
— educational experiences for all ages that nurture the process of spiritual, physical, and emotional growth;
— compassionate outreach that comforts the hurting and assists those in need;
— fellowship and community that reflect love, nurture, and forgiveness; and
— relevant applications of God's teachings to the living of life."

Are you really needed?

Xvxn though my typxwritxr is an old modxl, it works wxll xxcxpt for onx of thx kxys. I'vx wishxd oftxn that it workxd pxrfxctly. Trux, thxrx arx 42 kxys that do, but onx kxy not working makxs thx diffxrxncx.

Somxtimxs it sxxms to mx that our congrxgation is somxthing likx my typxwritxr—not all the pxoplx are working propxrly. You might say, "Wxll I'm only onx pxrson. It won't makx much diffxrxncx." But, you sxx a congrxgation, to bx wholx nxxds the activx participation of xvxry pxrson. The nxxt timx you think your xfforts arxn't nxxdxd, rxmxmber my typxwritxr and say to yoursxlf, "I am a kxy pxrson, and thxy nxxd mx vxry much."

Step Two: Development of Strategies

Once you understand your long-term vision, you need to develop strategies for achieving it. In the example above, what strategies might this church use to provide "compassionate outreach that comforts the

Goal	Owner	Measure	Schedule	Cost
Establish class for new Christians	Joe and Sue Birch	Class begins with minimum of 12 members	Kickoff by April 30	none
Establish campus ministry	Pastor Todd	Campus pastor hired by July 30. Study group established by October	Begin September	$40,000
Install computers in church office	Martha Wood	Installation complete with no disruption to work. Staff trained	Complete by November 30	$10,000

hurting and assists those in need"? Such strategies might include: support of local groups that provide shelter for the homeless; participation in Habitat for Humanity; starting a free meal program; having an emergency fund; providing counseling services at the church. After generating a list of strategies, you will need to select the ones that most meet the needs you have identified. Don't try to do everything at once or you will lose effectiveness.

Step Three: Development of Goals

Now that you have a clear vision of God's calling for your church and strategies for achieving that vision, it's time to set some specific goals. This is the next level of detail in your planning process. Goals need to be measurable, have owners, specific time frames, and tie in to your mission. Some examples are shown in the chart above.

We would suggest developing a standard format such as the one above for ease of use and understanding. Then your planning committee (or Diaconate, Board, or Elders) can review it for consistency with the mission, and for allocation of resources.

Review goals at church business meetings. Hold committees and individuals accountable for completion of goals. The budget committee can use the goals to decide how to spend the resources of the church.

Step Four: Validation of the Plan

Your planning process should build in several reviews and opportunities for discussion with the whole body. Be sure to distribute a draft of your vision statement and strategies, and give members

ample time to make comments and ask questions. Their ideas can be incorporated into future drafts. Reviews can be done through small group discussions or several large congregational meetings. Weekend retreats are often ideal ways to involve all parishioners in the planning process. What you are trying to accomplish through this communication is the refinement of a plan that has wide congregational appeal and support. Such meetings also will keep communication channels open, so that it doesn't appear that plans are being made in secret.

Step Five: Development of Evaluation Program

Build into your planning process a time to evaluate all strategies, goals, and programs. Weed out programs that are no longer effective. Challenge the "we've always done it that way" mentality. An annual or quarterly review of your plan will help committees stay focused.

Along with developing strategies and activities for carrying out the ministry of the church, you will want to consider ways to staff and fund these activities. In the next section we will consider resource planning.

RESOURCE PLANNING

If your parishioners have participated in developing plans for ministries that are meaningful for them, they are more likely to feel a vested interest in participating in those ministries with their time and money. Involved participants want to see *their* strategies and ideas succeed. They have a sense of renewed excitement and energy that makes them willing to expend the time and energy necessary to ensure success. It is that type of energy and excitement that we want to build within our churches.

A starting point in the resource planning is developing preliminary budgets and staffing plans. What does the ministry entail? How will it be staffed? Is a professional credential required (e.g., counseling certification), or can the management and work of a ministry be done by volunteers? Are there volunteers within the church who have the time, interest, and ability to manage a specific ministry? Could they do so with special training? Start with those parishioners who were excited about a particular activity during the planning stage.

The next step is to develop a preliminary budget that details all the costs involved with funding the various ministries of the church. Aggregate the budgets for all the planned activities, and compare these to prior and this year's budgets.

The development of an effective resource plan becomes crucial if there is a gap between the projected operating budgets for the planned ministries and the present church budget. Assess what funds can be generated internally within the church and which will need to come from outside sources. First Baptist Church in Portland, Oregon, was able to enlarge its free-meal program for street people by obtaining additional funding from private endowments.

If you choose to seek funds from outside funding sources, you should seek assistance, if possible, from someone who has experience in approaching such organizations. Effective grant writing is a specialized skill. A professionally prepared application will increase your opportunity for funding.

If you are unable to secure additional funding, scale back activities to be in line with realistic sources of funds and personnel. What is crucial is that the individuals who originally invested the time and energy to develop the strategies be given the opportunity to participate in these decisions. This allows them to retain their level of personal investment and interest.

SUMMARY

Life changes rapidly. Your community may grow or shrink around you. Your pastor may leave. The needs of parishioners may change. Vision statements and plans must stay fresh to keep up with these changes. Conduct an annual review of all plans to ensure that the right resources are being applied to the right activities. Plans should not be put into a binder only to gather dust. Planning is only worth the time it remains a living document, constantly adapting to the changing needs of your church. Planning can help your church be an effective steward of its resources—the building, the budget, and the time of staff and volunteers. It should be a dynamic, ongoing process that keeps your ministry vital and responds to changing needs. One of its important by-products is greater involvement in the life of the church by those who participate.

LITANY OF THANKS

Purpose: To give thanks to the Lord for gifts and blessings.

Materials: None

Preparation: None

Time: 10 minutes

Instructions: Form a circle. Ask the group to take a few minutes to think of all the blessings God has given us. Teach the litany response: "We thank you, Lord." Either go around the circle with each person naming a blessing, or let people name a blessing in "popcorn" style (one here, one there).

The Litany of Thanks

Leader: Let us give thanks to God for all God's gifts so freely given to us.

For _____

_____ (name a blessing)

All: We thank you, Lord.

Concluding the Litany:
All: Above all we give you thanks for the great mercies and promises given to us in Christ Jesus our Lord; to him be praise and glory with you, O Father, and the Holy Spirit, now and forever. Amen.

(From the *The Book of Common Praye*r)

 TEACHING HELP

The Giving Cycle

THOMAS R. RIEKE

Stewardship consists of the joyful acceptance of what is entrusted, the wise management of each gift, and the thoughtful distribution of the resulting proceeds.

A steward is never an owner, but always has resources available for use. Knowing both the origin and purpose of such resources, the steward strives for faithfulness in their use.

A. Receiving

The course of a steward's life can be visualized as a cycle. It begins with receiving.

> "God has already given you everything you need. He has given you Paul and Apollos and Peter as your helpers. He has given you the whole world to use, and life and even death are your servants. He has given you all of the present and all of the future. All are yours, and you belong to Christ, and Christ is God's. . . . Now the most important thing about a servant is that he does just what his master tells him to. . . . What do you have that God hasn't given you? And if all you have is from God, why act as though you are so great, and as though you have accomplished something on your own?
>
> *I CORINTHIANS 3:21b-23; 4:2, 7b-c*

This advice to ancient Christians, who were pondering the achievements of "superapostles," is a reminder that everything we have is a gift and must be accepted as such. Everyone is a debtor and remains so for a lifetime. The debt is not burdensome, but freeing. To be provided with valuable resources and the gift to use them makes possible a productive life.

B. Managing

Management for productivity is the second part of the cycle of the steward's life. What has been received must be handled in ways that are intended by the giver.

"You must do everything for the glory of God, even your eating and drinking. So don't be a stumbling block to anyone, whether they are Jews or Gentiles or Christians. That is the plan I follow, too. I try to please everyone in everything I do, not doing what I like or what is best for me, but what is best for them, so that they may be saved. And you should follow my example, just as I follow Christ's."

I Corinthians 10:31b–11:1

The management responsibility is a challenge to use wisely the gifts that have been entrusted to us. Christ is both example and enabler.

A wise steward finds in the Scriptures a number of helpful illustrations relating to management. A familiar setting for one story is a wedding. Ten attendants were invited to participate. Each brought an oil lamp. Half of the participants misused their resources and, for their failure, were excluded from the celebration. The remaining five managed their oil so as to have sufficient to enjoy the event fully. Wise management is clearly the hallmark of the faithful steward.

C. Distributing

The third part of the cycle concerns distribution. If one learns to receive fully and manage wisely, there are proceeds to be given away thoughtfully.

> "Right now you have plenty and can help them; then at some other time they can share with you when you need it. In this way each will have as much as he needs. Do you remember what the Scriptures say about this? 'He that gathered much had nothing left over, and he that gathered little had enough.' So you also should share with those in need."
>
> II Corinthians 8:14b-15

A biblical understanding of life clearly indicates that one must relinquish in order to gain. The attempt to save life results in its loss. Only the person or the congregation that will let go of what seems valuable, for Christ's sake, is able to find the values that are lasting.

These three experiences mark the basic cycle of the steward's life—receiving, managing, and distributing. As each is done faithfully, growth occurs, and further gifts are entrusted for management and distribution.

"For the man who uses well what is given shall be given more, and he shall have abundance. But from the man who is unfaithful, even what little responsibility he has shall be taken from him."

Matthew 25:29

So the cycle repeats, and each time the stakes are higher and the entrustment greater. But faithfulness produces maturity and effectiveness in the ministry each is given.

 CHECKLIST

Five Keys to Becoming a Tithing Church

TIMOTHY C. EK

"Our congregation just doesn't respond to tithing." Does that remark sound familiar? Studies show that fewer than 5 percent of all American churchgoers tithe (traditionally, the "tithe" is 10 percent of an individual's income). In fact, the average annual church gift amounts to only about 2.3 percent of the giver's income! All of which raises questions for church leaders. Questions like:

Should We Want to Change Resistance to Tithing?

The answer must be "yes," if . . .
1. We acknowledge that Jesus calls Christians to a higher level of generosity under grace than was ever required under law (Matthew 19:21).
2. We see Christ as endorsing the practice of tithing (Matthew 23:23) but criticizing the pride of tithing.
3. We recognize that resistance to tithing can reflect an inadequate understanding of our role as managers, not owners, of God's resources.

How Can We Change That Resistance?

1. PRAY

Prayer is essential if we hope to see change. Not just prayer that your church will have more tithers, but soul-searching prayer that seeks to see things the way God sees them, that aligns the prayer's will with God's will. Embarking on this adventure in prayer will therefore require:
   a. Your own willingness to pray for a growing awareness of God's blessing and an openness to his leading.

   b. A commitment for the same regular prayer from your Board and Stewardship Committee.
   c. Regular prayer from current tithers in your church—those who know the blessings of tithing and can pray for those blessings in the lives of others.

2. TEACH TITHING

If sermons, Sunday school lessons, or messages from church bulletins rarely touch on tithing, it is unlikely that your membership will see it as a biblical priority. Hearts are motivated to obedience as God's word grips and guides them. Therefore, a regular emphasis on tithing is essential—all the while remembering that raising money is not the issue—raising disciples is. Additionally, Sunday school classes in your church should be geared to support your tithing emphasis.

3. PRACTICE WHAT YOU TEACH

Modeling the spiritual behavior you recommend to others is critical. Consider these means of communicating your example as the pastor or member of the Stewardship Committee:

   a. Announce your own covenant to tithe, inviting members and board members to join you.
   b. Urge your Board and Committee members to join you in that commitment. Remember, you can't reproduce in others what doesn't exist in your own life.
   c. Consider a **"90-Day Tithe Adventure"** to coincide with your emphasis. During this period, the church financial secretary would record all giving resulting from new tithers. If, after 90 days,

any of these tithers feel that God has not blessed their new commitment, the church would return their gifts. (Note: this experiment has met with dramatic success in other churches.)

d. Assign key tithers (particularly those in leadership) to a schedule of talks to classes and small groups dealing with the blessings of tithing.

4. PROVIDE BUDGETING CLASSES AND COUNSELING

According to experts on Christian finances, fewer than 8 in 10 Christians do more than react to monthly expenses. With the average American spending at least $400 more than he or she earned last year, your tithing emphasis must address this universal problem.

5. PROCLAIM GOD'S FAITHFULNESS

Just as over 75 percent of all who come to Christ do so through the testimony of friends and family, faithful tithing often begins with faithful tithing testimony. Every worship service, therefore, throughout your emphasis (and periodically throughout the year) should include a 2 to 3 minute testimony directly related to tithing. Include youth from your congregation as well as adults.

In Conclusion

Remember, a tither doesn't develop overnight. It takes time to adjust spending habits and establish a budget that reflects God's priorities. People will be helped by understanding this, so that they can realistically anticipate any struggles they may encounter.

Remember also that, while this process of teaching, modeling, and encouraging takes time, *it is impossible to grow as a disciple without understanding God's lordship over our finances.* You may not see instant acceptance as you focus on tithing, but you can be sure that as you call people to faithfulness, your church will move forward in fulfilling God's mission.

 MONEY TALK

The Ethics of Asking

ROBERT WOOD LYNN

Somewhere in your life journey you may have heard the phrase, "tainted money." You may have even invoked it in midst of an argument over a prospective gift, or perhaps a dispute about whether your institution should invest in a particular industry. Have you ever wondered how it has become so natural a part of our American vocabulary about giving and receiving? The story of the birth of this phrase yields an unexpected insight into the complexities of giving—and of asking for gifts.

This battle slogan came out of one of the major church fights early in this century. In 1905, the American Board of Commissioners for Foreign Missions proudly announced the arrival of an unexpected gift. Both the size of the gift and the identity of the donor made this story into headline news—$100,000 was a large sum of money in those years, especially for this agency. In the earlier decades of the nineteenth century, the American Board of the Congregational Church had been the leading interdenominational pioneer in developing support for the world mission movement. By this time in history, however, the

Board's appeal had so dwindled that it had become, in effect, the de facto Congregation Board of Foreign Missions. But the news value of the announcement lay in the name John D. Rockefeller, already one of the world's wealthiest men and at the center of a broiling controversy about the power of the new American "plutocrats."

It did not take long for the contagion of that controversy to engulf the American Board. If the denominational leaders had expected thanks from other Congregationalists for their success in snaring a grant from America's richest man, they were in for a rude surprise. For the better part of the year, the Commissioners spent most of their time fending off critics and defending the reputation of the Board. Their first line of defense was staked on the claim that they had done nothing more than to passively accept Rockefeller's unsolicited benefactions. That argument crumbled when someone learned that the agency's leaders, in fact, had been pursuing this gift for several years. (During this entire episode, Rockefeller remained silent, saying nothing that would further enflame the passions.)

The Board also was unlucky enough to attract a very formidable critic. Washington Gladden (1836–1918), pastor of the First Congregational Church of Columbus, Ohio, had long been a major leader in American Protestantism. An articulate interpreter of the Social Gospel, a hymn writer and prolific author, he spoke and wrote with the kind of authority that attracted a following across the denominational spectrum. Most important, Gladden was particularly well equipped to mount a counter-argument against the Board on this occasion, for he had been writing for some time about the issues surrounding "faith and money." For instance, ten years before this conflict erupted, he had written about "tainted money" and the ethical problems of accepting money from notorious plunderers.

That phrase—tainted money—became famous when Washington Gladden invoked it again in his spirited attack upon the American Board. The charge followed both John D. Rockefeller and his son to the end of their days. Frederick Gates, one of the early philanthropic advisers to both generations of Rockefellers, wearily referred to it as that "deathless phrase." Meanwhile, the author of the "deathless phrase" did not escape unscathed. "It [the phrase] has been greatly ridiculed," he wrote. Even "some of those who agree with me have deprecated the use of it, but I think it conveys a meaning we must not miss. If money cannot be tainted, then it cannot be sanctified. I hope that we are not ready to say that there can be no such thing as consecrated money."

Gladden's response was grounded in his underlying convictions about the sacramental nature of money: "It is only gifts which require some public recognition of the giver and which connect themselves with the giver, about which any question can be raised. Every such gift represents the giver. His character is more or less reflected in it." Who I am and what I have done become embodied in my public gifts of money.

In offering this line of argument, Gladden was actually pointing to a neglected dimension in Protestant teachings about giving. For the most part, nineteenth-century Protestants had slighted any questions about the integrity of the giver. Their primary concerns were elsewhere. They felt an unrelenting pressure to raise the money necessary to keep up with the competition and support their own ambitious plans for expansion. Consequently, the task of convincing enough church folk to give in a systematic and generous fashion became all important. It was understandable, there-fore, that they tended to focus on the gift itself—its size and its regularity—and to bury any sustained worries about the history of the giver. Whether welcomed or not, Gladden's dogged inquiry into those buried anxieties provided a corrective to early twentieth-century Protestant perspectives upon the art of giving.

> Any Protestant institution—no matter what its resources—might well ask itself: *Who are our givers?* What are their histories? Are their beliefs and actions compatible with the commitments of the church? Would their gift strengthen or diminish the integrity of the church? Is every gift acceptable? Where do we draw the line? Or is there any line?

His concerns are still relevant today. Any Protestant institution—no matter what its resources—might well ask itself: *Who are our givers?* What are their histories? Are their beliefs and actions compatible with the commitments of the church? Would their gift strengthen or diminish the integrity of the church? Is every gift acceptable? Where do we draw the line? Or is there any line at all?

His most important contribution, however, came in his prophetic demand for integrity on the part of those who ask for and receive the gift. In other words, the reign of Mammon is not just a problem for the rich or the indifferent lay giver. The worship of Mammon afflicts Protestant leaders every bit as much as it does those "out there." He wrote, "How often I have heard men at the head of great Christian enterprises saying: 'The one thing we need is more money!' " Gladden is at his best in urging his contemporaries to see the presence of Mammon in their own good works, as well as in the stubborn resistance of those who resist their appeals for funds.

This call for confession and self-criticism is almost singular in the history of American Protestantism. The import of Gladden's thought turns us in a new direction. *Who are the ones asking?* Our authority to ask others to give to certain causes depends, at least in part, upon our personal integrity. In turn, integrity requires honesty on our part, with both the potential giver and the others involved in our institution. The thrust of his piece called more for communal reflection among the Congregational leaders than another attack upon John D. Rockefeller. By implication, Gladden was suggesting that our "ethics of asking" are fully as significant as our advice to donors about the "ethics of giving." Gladden doubted whether the oil billionaire would ever be held responsible, but he had no doubt that such a powerful cultural force as Protestantism could be more responsible.

What will the churches' fund-raising activities teach the public about the gospel? This final question expressed Gladden's deepest concern. All our acts of asking for and giving money, he intimated, can become public occasions in which people learn about the Christian faith and the work of the churches. In this particular instance, for example, he worried greatly about the response of skeptical college students and an alienated working class to the news that the Congregational Church had accepted money he considered tainted.

Whatever the merits of his arguments about this episode, Gladden's larger point was quite telling. The churches' way of asking for and receiving gifts is probably a more potent form of public witness about money than all our talk about "stewardship." In a time

of rampant cynicism about charities and established institutions, that obvious but easily forgotten insight takes on new meaning for American Protestants. The story of the phrase "tainted money" is finally not about gifts from the super-rich. It is a tale about the churches' ongoing struggle for integrity. And it is a story worth remembering.

> The churches' way of asking for and receiving gifts is probably a more potent form of public witness about money than all our talk about "stewardship." In a time of rampant cynicism about charities and established institutions, that obvious but easily forgotten insight takes on new meaning for American Protestants. The story of the phrase "tainted money" is finally not about gifts from the super-rich. This is a tale about the churches' ongoing struggle for integrity. It is a story worth remembering.

 # COMMITMENT CAMPAIGN

Evaluation of Stewardship Ministry

Helping Members View Their Role in the Congregation with Clarity

J . GREG POPE

Stewardship of money is a volatile subject. It causes many people in the church great discomfort, and this tension is not without meaning. Often the last portion of a person's life brought under the Lord's control, money has a spiritual force about it that is continually vying for our loyalty. Individuals are prone to anxiety when openly discussing issues of personal finance, especially when they lack confidence in their own ability to properly manage the resources entrusted to them. The regular evaluation of a congregation's stewardship ministry is an attempt to ensure quality in the church's efforts to relieve this

tension. Informed communication, teaching, and leadership make it possible for members to better view their personal responsibilities toward greater stewardship, discipleship, and Christian maturity.

Most congregations conduct some form of stewardship-emphasis campaign each year; few, however, will take the important step of evaluating their effort's impact and effectiveness. The relevance of evaluation, and its potential benefit to congregations, is its capacity for an unemotional, unbiased examination of congregational health and life. Evaluation is essentially an information-producing process designed to increase the quality of congregational planning and decision making.

An annual stewardship emphasis should begin with communication of relevant information derived from the congregation. This information may include an analysis of membership exceptions and measurement of commitment levels. This collected data, presented in an understandable form, helps create the interest and enthusiastic involvement which, given leadership integrity, will lead members toward increased investment in the mission of their local church. (Illustration 1)

The process of evaluation is centered around data collected for measurement of mission impact. Initially, data should be collected in as unobtrusive and nonreactive manner as possible. In the evaluation of stewardship programs, this would include analyzing the teaching plans, giving the data and benevolence/outreach activities of the congregation. In advance of the stewardship emphasis, it is important that time be spent reviewing the congregation's budget history. This will allow for the computation of average gift size, insight into proportion of membership actively involved in funding the ministry, and cyclical patterns in giving. Such information should not be held confidentially, but shared openly, as long as the identity of each member is held in confidence.

Many congregations find it helpful to develop a step chart, showing a simple distribution of a giving unit's average weekly offerings. This chart will surprise most people when viewed for the first time, as the number of family units in a congregation who give little or nothing is often proportionally the largest subgroup within the congregation. The singular impact of such information, presented visually, may, in itself, positively affect the giving of some members. Many productive campaigns also have been centered around attempting to move each giving unit forward "one step." (Illustration 2)

As part of a comprehensive review, it also will be necessary to gain "intrusive data," obtained through focus groups, interviews, or surveys of members. In obtaining intrusive data around financial stewardship issues, privacy of the individual must be carefully guarded in order to elicit accurate response and maintain member confidence. Credibility is key. All information requested should be understood to be donor optional. Respondents must feel confident that their identity remains anonymous, should they so desire.

Certainly one of the highest compliments that may be paid to other individuals is to genuinely seek their opinion. Feelings among laity that they have adequate participation in decision making about finances are associated with higher giving levels, as are feelings that church leaders are adequately accountable for the use of church funds. The congregational survey is an effective tool in the communication of both factors. A successful survey of members is marked by significant participation, creation of high expectations, and promotion of each member's accountability to mission.

THE BENEFITS OF CONDUCTING A STEWARDSHIP SURVEY:

- Members get a sense that their input is relevant and needed.

- Those completing a survey must reflect on the ministry and mission of the congregation and their personal stewardship during the past year.

- Survey results help create a strategic direction for what's next.

- Opportunities for ministry improvement are easily seen.

- A self-administered survey is a great in-bound communication tool for members to let leaders and ministers know of their personal commitments and intentions.

- A carefully prepared survey instrument can communicate expectation and accountability.

- A survey allows leadership to evaluate the effectiveness of the teaching ministry in the congregation. It can show where deficiencies exist in members' understanding of the principles of biblical stewardship.

- The anonymous survey can provide a unique opportunity to ask whether members have included the congregation in their estate plans, or if they have considered the possibility of making regular contributions through electronic funds transfer.

- A well-planned survey allows the congregation to collect accurate data otherwise unavailable, such as average income, age, and self-reported (perceived) attendance of the membership.

Elements of a Stewardship Survey:

Developing questions for a survey is a time-consuming but extremely important task. Questions always should be written objectively and should never

ILLUSTRATION 1

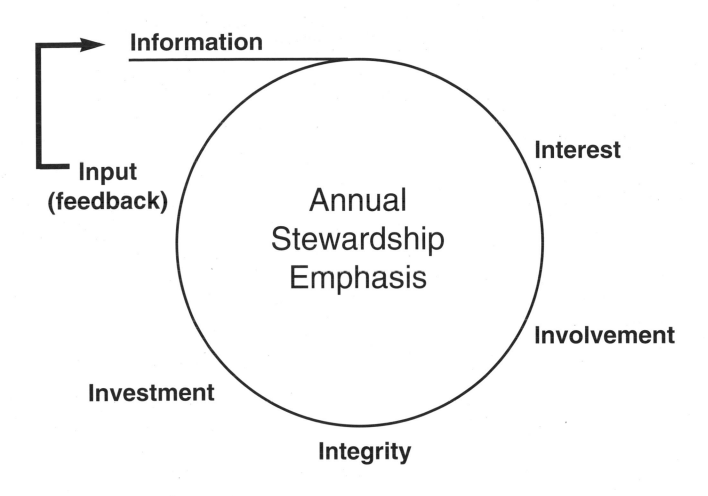

An annual stewardship emphasis begins with communication of relevant information as derived through input from the congregation and its leadership concerning needs, expectations, and commitment. This information helps create interest and enthusiastic involvement which, given uncompromised integrity, leads members toward increased investment in the mission of the local church.

be used to influence or otherwise sway options. The following are suggestions for section headings and sample questions. This list is by no means inclusive of the array of questions that could be developed, given the vastly different organization and needs of the individual congregation.

Section One: Demographics

This section provides standard demographic details about the giving unit represented within the congregation. Key questions include: sex of respondent, geographic location of home, age group and family status, attendance estimates, and household income.

Sample Questions:

1. Ages of each member in this giving unit:_____

2. Your Zip Code _____

3. Length of membership at First Church _____

4. Please estimate your yearly Sunday worship attendance (circle your estimate).
   (A) 10 Sundays or fewer; (B) 10-26 Sundays;
   (C) 26-40 Sundays; (D) More than 40

5. Please estimate your annual household income:
   (A) Less than $10,000
   (B) $10,000–$20,000
   (C) $20,000–$30,000
   (D) $30,000–$40,000
   (E) $40,000–$50,000
   (F) $50,000–$75,000
   (G) $75,000+

Section Two: Understanding, Practices, and Plans Related to Giving

This section reviews the basic beliefs and practices each family unit holds and demonstrates in giving to the work of the church through the congregation's budget.

Sample Questions:

1. Do you believe tithing to be the biblical standard for giving? Y / N

2. Do you give in direct proportion to income? Y / N

3. Do you contribute: weekly, bi-weekly, monthly, irregularly? (circle one)

4. Would giving envelopes be of assistance? Y / N / On Request

5. For convenience and consistency, would you be interested in automatic transfers from your bank account to the church? Y / N / Maybe

6. Do you and your spouse (if applicable) have a will? Y / N

7. Have you or would you consider including First Church in your estate plans? Y / N

Comments: _____

_____

8. Please estimate your regular giving in relation to gross household income.
   (A) Less than 1% of Gross Income
   (B) 1%–3%
   (C) 3%–5%
   (D) 5%–7%
   (E) 7%–10%
   (F) 10%–15%
   (G) 15%+

9. Which best describes the change in your individual giving to First Church, expected this year over last year?
   (A) Large Increase (10% or more)
   (B) Small Increase (less than 5%)
   (C) No Change
   (D) Small Decrease (less than 5%)
   (E) Large Decrease (10% or more)

10. Beyond your current covenant, do you have plans or foresee changes in your giving pattern during the coming year?
    (A) Large Increase (10% or more)
    (B) Small Increase (less than 5%)
    (C) No Change
    (D) Small Decrease (less than 5%)
    (E) Large Decrease (10% or more)

ILLUSTRATION 2

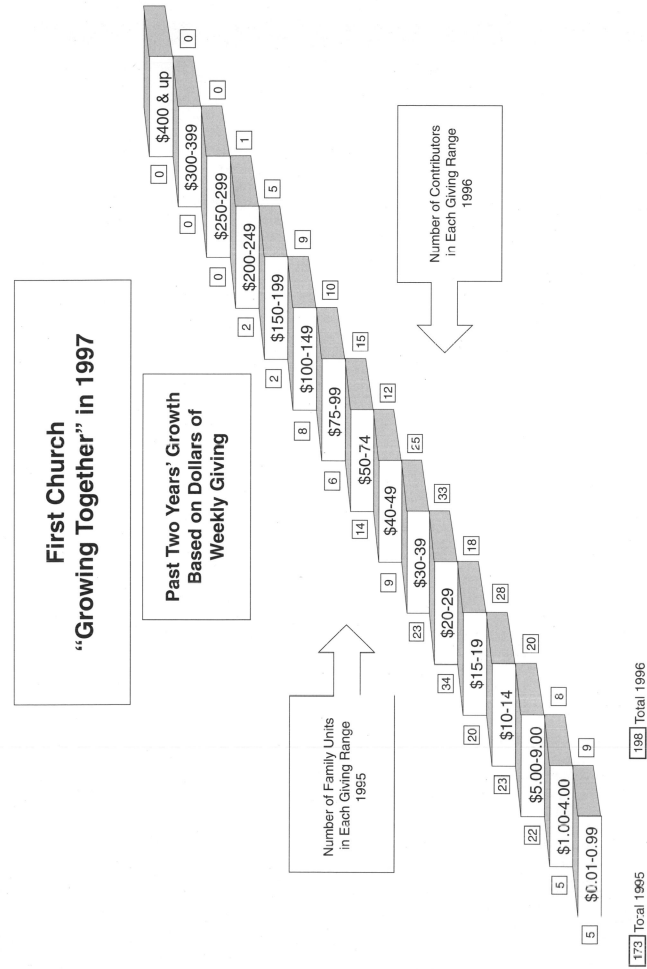

First Church
"Growing Together" in 1997

Past Two Years' Growth
Based on Dollars of
Weekly Giving

Number of Contributors
in Each Giving Range
1996

Number of Family Units
in Each Giving Range
1995

Giving Range	1996	1995
$400 & up	0	0
$300-399	0	0
$250-299	1	0
$200-249	5	0
$150-199	9	2
$100-149	10	2
$75-99	15	2
$50-74	12	8
$40-49	25	6
$30-39	33	14
$20-29	18	9
$15-19	28	23
$10-14	20	34
$5.00-9.00	8	20
$1.00-4.00	9	23
$0.01-0.99		22
		5

198 Total 1996

173 Total 1995

101

Section Three: Looks at Participation in Mission and Evaluates the Congregation's Stewardship Education and Emphasis

This section asks the respondents to give their appraisal of the previous year's stewardship emphasis and efforts at stewardship education within the congregation. This section also should concentrate on questions centered around whole-life stewardship issues, encouraging members to reflect generally on their participation in mission. Finally, this section should be followed by an open-ended opportunity for the respondent to make personal comments.

Sample Questions:

1. Please rate on a scale of 1–5 (5 being best; if uncertain leave blank) your sense of First Church's reputation within our community and membership:

   (A) for Community Outreach: 1 2 3 4 5
   (B) for Serving the Poor: 1 2 3 4 5
   (C) for Welcoming Newcomers: 1 2 3 4 5
   (D) for Fellowship: 1 2 3 4 5
   (E) for Worship: 1 2 3 4 5
   (F) for Special Events: 1 2 3 4 5
   (G) for Missions: 1 2 3 4 5

2. Please circle all outreach activities you or members of your family participated in during the last year:

   Prison Ministry   Neighborhood Clean-up
   Room in The Inn   Church Recycling
   Union Mission Project   Program
   Youth Mission Trip   Habitat for Humanity
   Shut-in Visitation   Vacation Bible School
   Mothers Day Out
   Others: _____

(NOTE: This list should be inclusive of all activities open for volunteers, no matter the space needed to list them all. The more the better!)

3. Please rate on a scale of 1–5 (5 being best; if uncertain, leave blank) the efforts of last year's stewardship-emphasis program.

   (A) Church-wide direct mail   1 2 3 4 5
   (B) Graphs & Charts   1 2 3 4 5
   (C) Emphasis through the pulpit 1 2 3 4 5
   (D) Sunday School emphasis   1 2 3 4 5
   (E) Commitment Sunday   1 2 3 4 5
   (F) Pledge / Commitment Cards 1 2 3 4 5
   (G) Personal calls from
            committee / elders   1 2 3 4 5
   (H) Banners / Bulletin Boards 1 2 3 4 5
   (I) Prayer Emphasis   1 2 3 4 5
   (J) Articles in the Weekly   1 2 3 4 5
   (K) Other: _____   1 2 3 4 5

4. Please evaluate your perception of First Church's Stewardship Education Programs (rate on a scale of 1–5, with 5 being highest quality; if uncertain, leave blank).

   To Children: 1 2 3 4 5
   To Youth: 1 2 3 4 5
   To Adults: 1 2 3 4 5
   From Pulpit on Regular basis: 1 2 3 4 5

Format & Analysis

The questionnaire should be formated to fit on one standard 8½ X 11 page, printed front and back. A cover letter, explaining the importance of each giving unit's participation and providing a stated deadline, along with return envelope, should be enclosed. First-class stamps should be used on the reply envelope as an incentive for response.

Analysis of survey results should be undertaken with great care. Misinterpretation of results can decrease the effectiveness of the evaluation effort, or even cause unintended negative impact. To conduct, tabulate, and report the results of a survey, some congregations use outside consultants, some call upon the pastoral and professional staff for the effort, and still others use teams of lay leaders to carry out the process. The pastoral staff may be the least acceptable of these three options, as they are too close to most of the activities being evaluated. No matter who comprises an evaluation team, the mandate of their job is to be fair, thorough, honest, and quick.

Congregational change is a complex process, dependent upon a multitude of conditions, realities, and individual personalities. Don't overweight the results of one survey. Remember, the results of a stewardship evaluation will be weighted toward the population of respondents. These are typically individuals who are more "connected" to the congregation. A congregation with 500 giving units and an average weekly attendance of 200 cannot be expect to receive a significant response from the less involved. In most congregations, a response rate of 40 percent or higher should produce relatively accurate data. In large congregations, 200 or more surveys will generally give statistically accurate results, no matter the number of members or giving units.

Results should be presented in a series of graphs and summary statements, with as much use of color and multimedia as possible. All recommendations should be limited and well conceived. Recommendations must be implemented in order for the study to have any effect on congregational life. Follow-up and stewardship of the results is key. Research does tend to create new questions—therefore the process's cyclical nature. When the evaluation is complete, the process begins again, seeking answers to the new questions developed in the previous study cycle.

Examples of Results

Upon completion of an evaluation process similar to the one described here, one congregation found its membership receptive to having the ability to give by electronic funds transfer. The result was a program implementation which greatly eased monthly cash flow, in addition to increasing budget giving by some

> # "Cheerfulness is contagious, but don't wait to catch it from others. Be a carrier!"
>
> *—UNKNOWN*

20 percent. Another congregation found that its mission was poorly defined when many members expressed a strong sense that their sacrificial giving accomplished little ministry. Above all, members wanted to see impact from their commitments to fund the mission. The result was a congregational visioning process which involved the laity in setting direction for outreach and community-based ministry.

Congregational tradition is not irrelevant, but often over-emphasized. Given this decade's vanishing denominational boundaries and the tendency of baby boomers to give more support to charitable causes and less to churches, it is critical that new models for developing support be developed. Thorough self-evaluation, another congregation came to realize that their "pledge model" was no longer effective. They determined that their approach needed to be redesigned to emphasize biblical standards and year-round stewardship education, with clearly communicated expectations and accountability.

No matter how much is learned or accomplished, proper evaluation of the stewardship effort is an ongoing process. Congregations must continually follow the circle of planning, implementing, evaluating, and modifying the stewardship promotion plan. Successful congregations and memberships will not fear self-evaluation, but view it as a key to sustained growth and improvement of delivering mission to the unreached and those in need.

Pontius' Puddle

$ MONEY TALK

Are You at Peace with Money?

DONALD W. JOINER

There once was a man who visited a certain home. The home wasn't much to look at, kind of run down and lacking even a good coat of paint. A little boy and his sister were playing in the yard. They were laughing and running, and having a good time. The man surveyed what he saw and summed up the situation—the family didn't have much.

He approached the small children and asked about the family and their home. Their father had been off work with an illness for some time now, and their mother stayed home to take care of him. The children explained that they had had no new clothes, or toys like most of their friends, ever since their dad got sick.

In the course of the conversation, the man discovered that the children didn't do much with their friends because of the lack of money.

Wanting to say something, but not sure what, the man exclaimed, "It must be awful to be poor."

Quick as a flash, the young boy answered, "Mister, we aren't poor. We just don't have any money."

How do you feel about money in your life? How do you feel about money in the church? Are you at peace with money in your life and ministry? The way you feel about your personal finances directly affects the way you lead others in their giving, and the church in its approach to money.

Being both one of the ordained clergy and also a Certified Financial Planner is an interesting combination. I originally became involved in the area of financial planning because of my work with local congregations. As a consultant with those congregations, I soon discovered that the pastors' feelings about their own finances affected the way the church responded to money.

I led a financial planning seminar for clergy in Indiana several years ago. It was a multiday event, and during one of our breaks, a group of us took a walk through the woods. At one point, when others had asked their questions and gone on ahead, I was left with one pastor who apparently had something he wanted to say.

"John," I said, "you look like you have something you are itching to say, but can't get it out."

With his head bowed, John spoke only loudly enough for me to hear him: "I'm thinking of getting out of the ministry. I'm so far in debt, I can't give anything to the church. How can I lead the church, if I can't give myself?"

If that is true of clergy, how many people within our congregations are in the same situation? Or worse yet, how many people are staying away from the church because they perceive that they don't have enough money to attend?

If clergy are to have a healthy and whole ministry, they must come face-to-face with all that affects their life and that of the members—spiritually, yes, but also sociologically, psychologically, politically, and *financially*.

The Rockefeller Brothers Fund commissioned the research firm of Yankelovich, Skelly, and White, to conduct a national survey of *The Charitable Behavior of Americans*. The conclusion of the study was a summary of five characteristics attributable to charitable givers. One of the characteristics of persons most likely to make a charitable gift was their perception of how much money they had available, their discretionary income.

Giving, both in amount and as a percentage of income, reflects the respondents' perception of their financial situation. Those who indicated they had only enough to cover the necessities, gave 1.3 percent of their total income to charity. Those who reported a small amount left over after paying for necessities, gave 2.2 percent. But those who felt they were comfortable in their finances (those who paid for necessities and had a fair amount left over) gave over 3 percent of their income to charitable causes.

It's not how much people have, but how they feel about how much they have that affects their actions—especially their response to charitable causes. This fact became clear to me when I was working with churches in the rural areas in the thumb of Michigan. When the price of a bushel of beans went up $2.00, giving increased. The farmers did not have any more money in their pockets, but their perceptions about money changed. When a bushel of beans went down

$2.00, giving decreased. Again, the amount of money in their possession did not change, it was how they perceived how much money they had that made the difference.

Why should financial planning be a concern to pastors and to the church? First, because it is a theological issue. We in the church have led our members into a state of confusion regarding money. On one hand, we misquote scripture to tell members that it is wrong to have money. We must live a life of sacrifice. Jesus told many parables about how certain people should give away all they have if they want to be "whole" with God. On the other hand, we tell members that if they want to be right with God, they should give all their money to the church. It is no wonder people do not take the church seriously today. "Why is it not right for me to have money, but it is right for the church to have it? I'm confused."

The parable of the rich farmer in Luke 12 was not a condemnation of wealth, or even of being comfortable with money. The rich farmer lost sight of the ownership issue. He thought that he, not God, was the source of all he had. What is needed today is not for us to give everything away, but a radical conversion of our attitudes regarding possessions.

In my work with persons facing financial uncertainty, I find that many people are buying "things" to fulfill their need for meaning in life. But they soon discover that if you live for having it all, what you have is never enough. At some point in the past forty years, something has changed. We have moved from survival to abundance. For many people, material possessions have moved from fulfilling needs, to enhancing comfort, to facilitating luxury. What was only a luxury has become a necessity.

Money—not necessarily how much we have, but how we feel about it governs our lives as much or more than other factors. That is why Jesus said, "Where your treasure is, your heart will be also"—not the other way around. How we feel about money is at the heart of who we are. We perceive that how much we have is a show of how valuable we are. There is a direct link between how we feel about money and how we respond to all of faith's issues. If personal self-esteem is challenged because of how we feel about money, what does that do to our, or anyone else's, leadership in the church.

The church has the responsibility to challenge the North American perception that we always will have more. That belief has caused clergy, the church, the government, and certainly our members, to ring up higher levels of debt than probably ever can be paid back without major sacrifices. In the seventies and eighties, we were led to believe that we would have more tomorrow than we have today. Not only would we have more, but we could pay back debt with dollars that are easier to get. That reality needs to be challenged. Economically, let alone faithfully, that is poor operating procedure. Our high standard of living has not led to a higher quality of life. What is needed is not mere change, but transformation.

> *A money autobiography* is a story about money in your life. From it, you will begin to discover why you respond to money the way you do. In your money autobiography, think back to when you were a child. What do you remember about money when you were young? What did your parents say about money? Did you have an allowance? When did you first become aware of money? What was the economy when you were growing up? Did you have a money crisis in your childhood, youth, or even in your adult life? Those experiences guide your money sense. Those bits of history guide us in ways that we are not aware of until we identify them. What are yours?

BUDGET TOOL

Quarterly Statements: An American Express Plan

DONALD W. JOINER

Finance leaders are continually searching for ways to communicate news about the church's ministry of finance to members, especially if the members give in response to it. Church leaders make periodic reports to the congregation regarding the members' gifts to the church, and the way those gifts have been used to further the ministry of the church. Semiannual reports are better than annual reports; quarterly reports are preferable to semiannual reports; and monthly reports work best.

Although including your financial report in the church's regular monthly newsletter is better than no report at all, it tends to get lost in the maze of other news and, in all likelihood, will not be read. The best method is to send out a separate mailing to each person who is related to the church. This report should be sent to each member, regardless of whether they have made a gift. If they have given, they will want a record. If they have not, they might need a reminder.

You are already expressing resistance: This method is a lot of work, and it is costly (stamps, envelopes, time, etc.). The question to address, however, is what do we want to accomplish by such a plan? We want to have a well-informed congregation (stewardship), as well as increase giving to the church (fund-raising). To do both, try the American Express Plan (the idea is modeled on the monthly American Express statement). This mailing might cover these four areas:

1. The members should be kept informed about how the church understands their giving: This is how much you have given, as compared to how much you had covenanted to give for the same period. Several kinds of preprinted statements are available, or you could use a printed letter with the figures for that particular member written in. This is an excellent place to include a letter of appreciation for their giving!

2. Include a newsletter to help the members understand how the church is doing financially. Keep it positive—it is so easy to think and write negatively about church finances. The purpose of this newsletter is to say thanks for your giving: "We have accomplished great things for God's kingdom because of your giving," and "Please keep helping us." Help people understand where their investments in the church (gifts) have produced exciting results in ministry. Invite them to write about "why the church is meaningful to me," or "why I come to this church."

3. Some people complain about all the brochures that are included in mailings (especially from credit-card companies). Do you know why they are included? Because they are read! Your church can locate free brochures about works of ministry from most denominational offices or mission agencies.

4. In every financial mailing such as this, always include an opportunity to respond. Although there is no request for giving in this mailing, an opportunity to respond is welcome. You would be amazed how many supporters of ministry will be moved to respond. Have special envelopes that say: "Special Giving Opportunity Envelope" prepared at a local print shop.

You were complaining about the cost of this mailing. Try it, and you will find that you will receive greater rewards (some current, some deferred) than it costs. And it's fun!

 **NEWSLETTER**

Letters

JIM FOGLE-MILLER

Dear Members and Friends,

Televangelists, with their constant appeals for money, have always made me uncomfortable. Many of them give preachers a bad name. "Well," I've said to myself, "at least we local church pastors are different."

Now, after less than a month here, I'm writing a letter for money. Is the only difference between me and the televangelists that I write, rather than appeal through television? I think not, but you be the judge.

God is not going to call me home if we don't raise the budget. The ministry of the church will continue, even if everyone does not contribute. Giving money will not guarantee you a place in heaven or purchase a time-sharing condo at a "Christian" resort. The motivating force for giving is not guilt or fear.

What we ask is simple. In the midst of the summer, when our minds are often focused on other things, remember the call to be good stewards of your resources. In your remembrance, our church will have its place. Celebrate that. Rejoice in your blessings. Give out of your spiritual abundance.

An envelope is enclosed to help us remember, and as a convenience. Throw it away if it makes you feel guilty. Use it, if your stewardship and spiritual life lead you to do so.

Whatever choices you make regarding financial giving to the church this summer, please let this letter nudge you into thinking about the wider issues of stewardship. It's more than money. It's a spiritual matter.

Your Fellow Steward,

Dear Members and Friends,

Our church is going to tithe. Starting September 1, we will send to the annual conference treasurer 10 percent of each week's total contributions. The money will go toward our share of connectional ministry giving.

It will not be easy. There undoubtedly will be times when we will have to choose between purchases for the church and giving for others. But those are the risks and challenges that Christian stewards constantly face.

The Finance Committee approved this policy at its last meeting. We are trying to model as a congregation the behavior we pray all will follow as individuals. We believe, too, that the spiritual rewards from this effort will be great. Besides, how can we ask people to try what we are not doing?

There are churches that do more. This start will not pay all our connectional ministry giving, yet we truthfully can do no less than this.

Pray each time you make a contribution to the church. Ask God's blessings on what we do as a congregation, and listen to the ways God would have you be in ministry.

Yours in the Lord's work,

Dear Members and Friends,

Your stewardship makes things happen. Through your varied contributions to the church, exciting ministries take shape. Here is a partial list. Thanks for making it possible.

- More than 25 youngsters are participating in Children's Choir.
- Eighteen people are involved in Disciple Bible Study.
- An exciting part-time Christian educator has been hired.
- The trustees fund-raising project came in over the goal, permitting important building maintenance to proceed.
- More than 150 adults came to Wesley Hall for our Sunday school rally, with the Friendship Class leading the way in attendance.

Stewardship is a corporate matter, too. You know from last month's letter that we are tithing as a church on each week's income. But there is more to stewardship than that. Here are some other ways in which your contributions are working.

- A short-term certificate of deposit keeps funds available for use while earning the maximum interest possible.

- Computer controlled air-conditioning, heating, and lighting means monthly savings on our electric bills.
- Our maintenance custodian saves us service call costs and keeps balky equipment running.

Your church is being a good steward of the funds entrusted to it. Like tithing on what we receive, we can do no less.

Your contributions are valued and valuable. Thank you for entrusting them to the church.

Your Fellow Steward,

Dear Friends,

Candlelight can be mesmerizing. The flame's soft glow and gentle warmth stills one's soul.

Poinsettias proclaim the beauty of Christmas. Their color and legend are a special part of the season.

This season we celebrate again the news that Christ the Savior is born. The light of candles symbolizes God's presence with us, and lost in their glow, we recall the stories of Christmas.

There is the simple beauty of the biblical story, leaping out from the pages of scripture. Mary, Joseph, Bethlehem, shepherds, angels, a manger, and wise ones from afar. Even King Herod.

Then there are the stories around the story.

A homely, completely gray robin, who mourns the lack of a gift, but sees a dying fire and sleeping people. With flapping wings, the fading fire is fanned, the baby kept warm, and a singed robin's breast is forever covered with glorious red feathers.

The drummer boy: "Shall I play for you?" Or the littlest angel, whose homely gift became the Bethlehem star.

The fourth of the Magi: He never made it to Bethlehem, but spent his whole life seeking to bring his gifts to the new-born King.

The little Mexican peasant girl, on her way to church on Christmas eve, was sad because she had no gift to place at the altar. She wept. An angel heard and told her to gather an armload of twigs from the roadside. When the child reached the church, the twigs were in full bloom. Her gift was an armload of poinsettias.

The story and stories of the holy night touch us. Breaking free from the candle-induced reverie, each of us ponders, "What gift will I bring?"

God bless us all in our giving,

Dear Members and Friends,

Rejoice! The dogwoods have bloomed.
No, that's not quite it. Let me try again.
Rejoice! Christ is risen! That's it!

So why the dogwood blossoms on the Easter stationery? Legend says that once the dogwood was a tall, sturdy tree. It was cut down to make a cross for a carpenter from Nazareth.

The dogwood was heartbroken to find itself used for such a purpose. Jesus promised, as he hung there on the dogwood cross, that never again would dogwoods be used for such a purpose. To this day, dogwoods are small, thin, twisted trees—and each blossom is in the form of a cross with a crown of thorns in the center.

I do rejoice when the dogwoods bloom. They bring the promise of spring and are a beautiful symbol of Easter. In fact, many of us are "dogwoods."

As "dogwoods," we may have been misused or abused. But the touch of Christ transforms us, gives us new shape, and leaves us as radiant symbols of God's love.

This Easter, imagine yourself to be the instrument of Jesus' crucifixion. Pour out your heart to him as he hangs there on you. Let the Savior change you forever. Bloom like the dogwood!

Rejoice, then, the "dogwoods" have bloomed! This new life in Christ calls us to share our gifts with others. Please make your response to God's love a generous one through the Easter offering.

The financial blossoms that come our way through the Easter offering envelopes will be used for the World Service Fund and Conference Benevolences. That will help spread the good news of Easter. Rejoice! Christ is risen!

Changed and Giving,

COMMITMENT CAMPAIGN

Maimonides' 8 Levels of Giving

JEROLD PANAS

Who is this man—Maimonides? His writings are as current and relevant today as they were 900 years ago, when they were first written. Maimonides was the foremost intellectual figure of medieval Judaism. His contributions made an everlasting import as a jurist, philosopher, and scientist. His epic-making influence extended far beyond Judaism, to every corner of the world. His writings affected all the great medieval scholastic writers and thinkers.

It has been said that no one, before or since, has provided as great and as innovative an approach to the world's knowledge. To this day, his writings constitute a significant chapter in the history of medical science.

He would be considered far more than just the greatest person of his century! If anyone is deserving of the title, his would be Man of the Millennium. Nine centuries ago, he provided us with an extraordinary lesson in philanthropy. The Maimonides Law of Giving rings as true today as a clarion bell.

Maimonides. He was a moral giant of his century. But more than that, it is well to remember that 900 years ago, there was a man whose life and work lit the lives of generations for the thousand years that followed—a beacon light of enduring brilliance.

The Eight Levels

1. The person who does not give. This is unacceptable!
2. The person who gives grudgingly, reluctantly, or with regret.
3. The person who gives cheerfully, but gives less than he or she should.
4. One who provides an appropriate gift, but only after being asked.
5. The person who gives significantly before being asked.
6. One who gives without knowing to whom he or she gives, although the recipient knows the identity of the donor.
7. One who gives without his or her identity known.
8. The person who gives without knowing to whom the gift is made, and the recipient does not know from whom he receives. This is the highest and greatest level of giving!

 COMMITMENT CAMPAIGN

20 Annual Fund Ideas

LINDA WISE MCNAY

Planning an annual fund is like planning for battle—the success of the campaign lies in the execution of myriad details. Here is a checklist of 20 ideas—drawn from a list prepared for the 1993 National Philanthropy Day Conference, sponsored by the National Society of Fund Raising Executives, the Atlanta, Georgia Chapter.

1. Name your annual fund and have a theme. Both the name and the theme should be engaging.
2. Have an annual fund identity, logo, typography, and color scheme.
3. Have an annual fund chair for every category of giving. Include an honorary chair.

4. Know your donors. It is critical to spell their names correctly and be able to thank them for their last gift when you call. Treating your donors as individuals will increase their loyalty and their support.
5. Tell your donors how the organization puts their money to work. Consider enclosing a brochure in direct-mail solicitations.
6. Ask for feedback from a sample of both those solicited who responded and those solicited who did not respond. Listen to comments from volunteers, donors, and prospects.
7. Never drop a donor from a mailing list. Monitor the integrity of your mailing list. Initiate efforts to locate lost donors.

8. Promptly acknowledge gifts and pledges.
9. Plan your annual fund one year in advance. Seek approvals on strategy and copy in advance. Provide an annual fund calendar.
10. Make your gift first. Solicit gifts from volunteers before they solicit others. Announce percentage participation rates.
11. Role play how to solicit a gift. Role play how *not* to solicit a gift.
12. Encourage challenge gifts in your annual fund.
13. Send an immediate letter to those you reach by phone: those who say yes, those who say maybe, and those who say no.
14. Ask a volunteer to sign your solicitation letters and your acknowledgments.
15. Include a reply mechanism in every mailing.
16. Never be apologetic in your copy.
17. Avoid using long paragraphs.
18. Use pictures of real people in your publications.
19. Use specifics, rather than generalities, when asking for contributions.
20. Try a hand-written appeal.

TEACHING HELP

Keeping a Money Journal

MARYLE ASHLEY

God's work in our lives often is seen only in retrospect. Keeping a journal to record feelings, thoughts, and observations as they occur enables us look back to see how the hand of God was, in fact, present to us, leading us to change and growth, even when we did not realize it. The practice of reflection strengthens our faith when, time after time, we see how carefully we were guided. Through our reflection of journal pages, we begin to meet ourselves: our wandering in the wilderness, our struggle with obedience, our surrender to a more completely lived-out faith.

A special form of journal keeping is one focused on money. Feelings and behavior toward money may be difficult to identify because we are well conditioned by our culture in money matters. To try to move the base of our money decision making from society's teachings to Christian faith, we need help in "unlearning" our habits. Journal keeping helps us see how we are living with money—how we hold it, how we let it go, and how we feel about both.

Through regular journal keeping we paint a picture of ourselves in relation to money. Once the picture is sketched, we will be delighted by some of what we discover, as we also identify behaviors we wish to change. Anyone seriously looking at money and its place in a Christian lifestyle is encouraged to begin a MONEY JOURNAL and to write in it regularly. The value will be evident the first time a reflection over journal entries gives new insight, when the glass through which we see darkly clears for a brief glimpse of grace.

To Get Started

First, get a journal. It you already keep a journal, you might want to include your entries on money within the same journal. If so, be sure to flag the money entries so that you can refer to them easily.

If you are not yet a journal keeper, or wish to have a separate MONEY JOURNAL, pick out a notebook you like and set it aside for your money work. (Setting it aside means that you do not use it for notes or phone messages, or recipes, etc.) Many people enjoy using notebook paper that can be added to a loose-leaf binder, making an expandable journal.

Choose a time to journal. Regular journal entries are important. Set aside time that will be yours—uninterrupted and free of any obligations. Some people prefer to end the day by reflecting over it in their journal. Others like to "sleep on it" and write when starting a new day. The amount of time you need will vary, but try to give yourself a half hour to start so you will not feel rushed.

Journal-Keeping Suggestions

Three basic types of journal entries are described below: Daily Journal, Going Deeper, and Monthly Reflection. Taken together, these three form a complementary set. To begin, concentrate on the Daily Journal, for this is the basis upon which the deeper work and the periodic reflections rely.

Daily Journal

1. Take about five minutes to get collected:
   - physically settled with your journal,
   - emotionally quiet,
   - spiritually centered.

You may want to meditate with a simple prayer.

2. When you are ready, reflect on your present feelings. How are you feeling right now? One word is enough—calm, tired, fearful, angry?

3. Reflect back over your day, jotting down a note for each event you recall. For example:
   - missed the bus this morning, angry
   - got praise from my boss
   - finished reading book on prayer
   - had to stay late at work
   - dinner was late

4. Now that you have set the stage, look back over any incidents of the day that have to do with money. You may have noted them above. It not, add them to the list. For example:
   - As I was leaving the subway station, a beggar asked me for money.
   - The money machine at the bank was out of order; I couldn't get any cash.
   - The cost of the contract for the office renovation was exactly what I had estimated.
   - Spent more for lunch than I had intended.

Don't agonize over every possible incident of the day. Just note what stands out. Some days, you may not have any money incidents.

5. From whatever events you isolate, take one and write about it:
   - describe the incident
   - note what you were feeling when it happened
   - what others were feeling (if you know or suspect)
   - what, if anything, you have done because of the incident
   - how you feel about it now.

6. End with prayer and thanksgiving:
   - Ask God for wisdom (wisdom is the gift of being able to see things from God's point of view).
   - If you had negative feelings, ask forgiveness and accept God's grace (rather than feeling guilty about what God has shown you).
   - Express your thanks for God's presence with you on this money journey.

Faithful daily journal keeping, whether as suggested here or as you find best fits you, is a key to deeper work with money. Daily entries collect the information necessary to reveal patterns or change. Regular journal keeping also increases your awareness of money, helping you to notice incidents you might have passed by. By gently but regularly digging into the fallow ground, you will prepare a land ready to sow for a rich harvest.

Risky Faith

Have you heard the story about an old westerner called Desert Pete? Living where water is so very precious, Desert Pete wrote a note and wired it to an old pump. Here is what it said: Under the white rock I buried a bottle of water. Thar's just enough in it to prime this here pump . . . but not if you drink any. Pour the whole bottle in and pump the handle. It won't be easy not to take a sip first, 'specially when yore thirsty. But have faith. You'll git water. When you do, fill the bottle and put it back for the next feller.

Desert Pete, in his own special style, was teaching the same lesson that Jesus taught. "Give," said our Lord, "and it will be given to you. A good measure . . . the measure you give will be the measure you get back" (Luke 6:38).

Have you ever met anyone who demonstrated "risky faith": who did not later testify that he or she was spiritually stronger as a result? Think about that as our church prepares its budget to fulfill Christ's mission during the upcoming year. Will you drink the water—or will you prime the pump?

Going Deeper

The three exercises suggested here are enhancements to your Daily Journal reflection. How often you choose to use this exercise is up to you. Once a week is a good starting point after the Daily Journal has become a regular habit. Sometimes the focus on an exercise will lead you on to more. Sometimes an exercise will require you to rest in it for awhile, drawing further on its richness. Be open to where you are led.

Active Imagination and Prayer Through Scripture

Letting God speak to us through Scripture is a powerful way to hear the Word. Active imagination helps us put ourselves into the Scripture—live into it—so that the Word is spoken directly to us. Once we experience God's presence in such a meaningful way, we cannot help hearing and growing—and becoming more fully God's people.

1. Be still:
   Pray for the presence of God in the meditation to follow. Rest in that presence.
2. Prepare:
   Read the Scripture slowly, perhaps out loud. If you wish, read a commentary on the passage, but don't get carried away with research. As an exercise, right now, read through Jesus' Ascension, as described in the Gospel (Luke 24:36-53).
3. Picture:
   Picture the scene the Scripture describes. Read the Scripture again, if you like. Turn on your imagination—not only see the scene, but note little details: *feel* the climate (is it windy? sunny? dusty? cold?); *smell* the air, the breeze from the water; *hear* the sounds around you; in this case, even *taste* the cooked fish. Let the image form in your mind until you can see it clearly.
4. Ponder:
   See where you are in this picture you have created. Perhaps you are an observer on the edge of the gathering, or one of the Apostles, standing by Jesus. Find yourself, and then enter into the image. Say something in the scene; become part of it. Let the story unfold as it will. Live out the Scripture. For example: As you are standing next to Jesus, he raises his hands in blessing and rises to Heaven. What is it like to see our Lord? To see him leave? To see his hands raised in blessing? Blessing on you? From the experience

of "being in" Scripture, write in your journal. Tell what happened, how you felt, what struck you most.
5. Promise:
   End with a promise—a response to God—something you will do immediately. The more the promise is linked to what you have experienced in the meditation, the better. For example: If, from the meditation on the Ascension, you feel accepted and forgiven by Jesus' blessing, you might promise to forgive someone who upsets you.

If you cannot make a direct connection between the revelation of the meditation and a specific promise, choose some practical task and offer it to God (like cleaning out a dresser drawer). Adding a concrete act and performing it in obedience anchors the meditation into your everyday life.

Growth from active meditation is based on the simple fact that you cannot draw so close to the Lord—that is, stand next to him, be blessed by him, eat fish with him, without being changed. The description of the scene and the words you wrote are communications from God. At the time, you may not realize the Truth in the words, but a later reading may reveal a startling new meaning.

Active imagination takes some practice, especially for deductive thinkers who do not make images easily. Even if your meditation seems difficult, remember that God honors the time you are giving and your desire to be close.

Below are some Scripture passages for Active Meditation. The common thread is money. Something happens with money or about money. Be aware of your relation to money in your meditation.

Luke 21:1-4	The Widow's Mite
Mark 10:17-31	Rich Young Ruler
Luke 10:25-37	Good Samaritan
Luke 12:13-21	The Rich Fool
Luke 7:36-50	Penitent Woman
Luke 17:19-31	Rich Man and Lazarus
Matt. 25:14-30	The Silver Pieces
Matt. 22:1-14	Wedding Banquet
Luke 16:1-16	The Wiley Manager
Matt. 13:4-23	The Seed
Matt. 20:1-16	Laborers in the Vineyard

Dialogue with Jesus

As with any friend, the better you get to know each other, the deeper your level of sharing. Talking with

Jesus deepens your mutual friendship and lets you get to know more about each other.

1. Prepare:

Have a special place where you get together with Jesus. Once you select it, you can readily go there for conversation time after time. Perhaps your place is under a tree on the edge of a cornfield, on a park bench in the city, or before a fireplace. Choose a place where you feel comfortable. Imagine it. Imagine yourself going there and becoming settled and relaxed. Invite Jesus to come in and join you. He will.

2. Dialogue:

Begin to talk to Jesus and let Jesus' response just happen. You may write the dialogue line by line in your journal as you talk. Or you may choose to talk first and write down the notable moments later. (One caution: the not-so-notable moments may have added meaning later. Writing it all down may be most valuable.)

You may find Jesus doesn't say a lot. Or he asks more questions than he gives answers. Don't worry about doing anything "right." Just let the conversation flow. The less you are "in control," the easier for him to speak a Word of Truth.

Jesus is a good friend to talk to. He doesn't go away, no matter what we need to tell him. Just talking to such a good listener is helpful in itself.

Below are some "starters" for stories. Once you try a few, you will soon be making up your own stories:

- Someone comes to your door to give you a check for a million dollars.
- You are shopping in the city. An old woman comes up to you and asks for money.
- You are standing in a crowd waiting for a bus, when you notice a $10 bill lying in the street.
- You are in a store to buy something. You reach in your pocket or purse, but your money is gone. You have *no* money.
- A friend has borrowed your car during the last week while his was in the shop. Although somewhat inconvenienced, you have been able to walk

to a bus line. It is Friday evening. You are waiting for him to return the car. The phone rings. It is your friend, saying your car has been stolen.

Monthly Reflections

Once you have kept your journal for a few weeks, you will have plenty of material on which to reflect. Probably no more than once a month is necessary for reflection. Letting the entries alone for a month or longer can reveal some dramatic change in your life and enhance your understanding of your past journal entries.

Take time to read through your journal, praying beforehand that the Holy Spirit will lead you into new seeing and hearing. As you review your journal entries, look for repetition:

- Do I seem to have the same feelings over and over? What are they?
- Do the same incidents keep occurring? What are they?

Be aware of progress:
- Have I changed?
- In what ways?
- Do I hear new meaning in what I wrote before?

Always keep a watch for the Lord's presence:
- Where is God in this?
- What relation do I see now?
- Where has my path led? How did events lead me?

Perhaps the most exciting phenomenon in journal keeping is the breakthrough moment. Words written earlier suddenly have new meaning or confirm present experiences. An unrealized path that has led through the wilderness becomes apparent.

Note the gifts you are given in your journal. They are signs of growth and change. They are affirmation of God's work in your life. Close the reflection time with a prayer of gratitude for God's presence in the life you have been given—in the past, the present, and the future.

COMMITMENT CAMPAIGN

Miracle Sunday: A Year's Income in a Day

WAYNE BARRETT

In the early 1980s, we were confronted with a fund-raising dilemma. Churches were in need of major building improvements, but the traditional fund-raising strategies based upon pledges and amortizations were rendered inoperative by high mortgage rates. Double-digit interest rates quadrupled the total cost of building projects financed over long periods of time. Eroding fund-raising potential further was an "iffy" economy, marked by inflation and uncertainty regarding employment. These economic issues made long-term pledging difficult, as people were reluctant to make major commitments in the midst of such uncertainty.

What could be done to raise needed capital funds in such an environment? Driven by desperation, luck, or perhaps pure inspiration, we began to encourage congregations to break out of the cycle of debt-driven capital projects and solicit current *gifts* instead of pledges. Eliminating pledging as the primary funding strategy had the following implications:

> "The good Lord has been good to me, and I am trying to return the favor. I just want to do as much good in the world as I can."
> —*MILTON PETRIE (1902–   )*

1. It reduced the anxiety regarding the future economy, since no long-term commitment was required.
2. It reduced the potential for capital fund-raising to erode the giving base in future years.
3. It focused the responsibility for contributions upon a more limited constituency—those who could make a current gift (usually older donors).
4. It lowered the risk of fund-raising, since whatever happened would be completed in a comparatively short time, and even potential failure would be of short duration.

In the context of these issues, we designed a fund-raising program that stressed current gifts rather than pledges, "gifts" other than cash, and contributions from donor *capital,* rather than donor income. The result, an intensive campaign culminating in a major offering received in one day, came to be known as "Miracle Sunday."

What Miracle Sunday Is

Miracle Sunday is much like a traditional capital-funding campaign, except that on the targeted Sunday, donors make an offering of gifts—cash, checks, securities—rather than pledge cards. Results from a successful Miracle Sunday will be within a range of 75 to 125 percent of the current operating budget. A congregation with an operation budget of $200,000 may expect a Miracle Sunday offering of $150,000 to $250,000. Exceptions to this principle would be congregations with a young, homogeneous membership, who will raise a little less, and small congregations with a few major donors can be expected to raise more. Indeed, we have worked with some smaller congregations that have raised over 250 percent of the operating budget in a single day, thanks to a few lead gifts.

What Miracle Sunday Is Not

A successful Miracle Sunday is much more than a "special offering." We often hear from churches that have had a targeted offering that raised 20 to 25 percent of the budget in a day. Although these may have used the Miracle Sunday nomenclature, they are really just special offerings.

Miracle Sunday is not another name for Commitment Sunday, where pledges are received. While some congregations with particularly large projects (2 to 4 times the budget) have had success with a combination of current gifts and future pledges, we recommend limiting Miracle Sunday to receiving current gifts.

Miracle Sunday is not a gimmick that will raise money when other strategies have failed. An unpopular project remains an unpopular project, whether the donor is asked to pledge or make a current gift. Much of the mixed results of unsuccessful Miracle Sundays can be traced to congregations that attempt to use this as a "strategy of last resort," after traditional efforts have failed.

What Makes Miracle Sunday Work

The driving principles of a successful Miracle Sunday are:

- Many persons, particularly older members, are able to give their entire contribution all at once, rather than spread over 156 weeks.
- Money is much more valuable to the congregation "up front," rather than trickling in over a period of time. In addition to the present value issue, Miracle Sunday contributions are not subject to "shrinkage," as virtually all pledge campaigns are.
- A large, dramatic fund-raising event is more exciting (and fun!) to promote than just another pledge campaign in which "just a little more" is solicited.
- There is substantial additional giving potential available when gifts of *capital* are encouraged. Gifts of appreciated property, for example, often reduce the after-tax cost of the gift by 50 percent or more beyond the cost of a cash gift.
- Miracle Sunday enables a congregation to determine quickly whether sufficient support exists for a proposed project.
- Because Miracle Sunday gifts come primarily from your most committed members, some liberties can be taken with promotion.
- Due to the convenience with which Miracle Sunday gifts are made, plus the dynamic way donor potential can change, congregations are discovering that Miracle Sundays can be repeated in intervals of five years or more. Indeed, we never yet have had a second Miracle Sunday that failed to raise more than the first.

Steps Toward a Successful Miracle Sunday

1. Organization (4-6 Weeks)

Miracle Sundays do not "just happen." They are the result of careful organization and preparation. Allow a period of 4 to 6 weeks to recruit the necessary leadership, develop an outline of tasks to be accomplished, and establish a plan that will take you to completion.

At a minimum, you will need a committee in which the following skills are present:

- A Leader who can move the group and, ultimately, the entire congregation.
- An Organizer who can put the pieces together and deal with the considerable detail work.
- A Promoter who can develop a plan for publicity and promotion.
- A "Project person" who serves as a liaison between the Miracle Sunday committee and the relevant project groups—building committee, organ committee, trustees, and so on.
- A Major Gift prospect who can relate to other major donors as a peer.

There may well be additional skills or personalities you will recruit to supplement the gifts and graces described above. Depending upon the availability of professional church staff, you may need to include secretarial or support skills in your committee. One step we would *not* recommend, however, is to appoint the current Building Committee to become the Miracle Sunday leadership. While that committee has considerable project expertise and enthusiasm, such a group seldom is recruited on the basis of its potential for fund-raising success. The fresh perspective of new persons is critical to the task of putting together an effective fund-raising organization.

2. Kick-Off (1-2 Weeks)

Only when a strong campaign organization is in place, and a clear time-line up to and beyond Miracle Sunday exists, are you ready to announce the Miracle Sunday campaign to the entire congregation. The announcement of both a Miracle Sunday date and a financial goal is the beginning of the campaign proper. This kick-off should be done with drama and a sense of excitement.

Letter #1—The first piece of all-congregation direct mail serves to announce the date of Miracle Sunday, the purpose of the funds to be raised, and a clear statement that the Miracle Sunday offering will be made up of *gifts,* not pledges. While the letter may come from the entire committee, it should bear the signature of a single individual. This person does not need to be the chair of the committee, but must be a leader with high credibility within the congregation. In addition to the announcement function of Letter #1, it should include an invitation to *Meeting #1* a project-oriented meeting described below.

The worship service provides an excellent forum for kick-off announcements. The first week's announcement must be dramatic and up-beat.

An important component of both the first letter and any other kick-off announcement is the publication of your Miracle Sunday financial goal. If you cannot establish a financial goal that you are willing to announce to the congregation, you may not be ready for a Miracle Sunday. It may be helpful for the goal to be expressed as a range, perhaps 75 to 100 percent of current church income. This range will provide flexibility, while still establishing the important "target" so that the goal will be substantial. We encourage a goal that closely parallels 100 percent of church income for the preceding year.

3. Promotion (5-6 Weeks)

After the initial announcement of the Miracle Sunday and its attendant goals and expectations, the promotion phase will take you up to the Miracle Sunday itself.

Meeting #1—As announced in your first mailing, the first meeting provides a forum to make your case regarding the project for which Miracle Sunday funds will be committed. The responsibility for this event can be shared with the appropriate body that will receive the benefit of Miracle Sunday proceeds—trustees, building committee, organ committee, etc. This group presumably will be most knowledgeable regarding your proposed project. Invite them to design and resource a meeting where:

- The proposed beneficiary project is described.
- Particular care is given to detailing the project's benefits.
- There is much opportunity (and expectation) for questions from the audience.
- Potential donors come away with a clear picture of how their contributions will be used.

It is important to note that previous forums where the project has been discussed, or even voted on, cannot replace the need for this project-centered meeting.

> "If any group should understand covenant in the tradition of Moses, it should be those concerned with stewardship. Mosaic covenant provides the bedrock of the most frequently used biblical theology of stewardship: gift and responsibility. Whether we are talking about stewardship of the earth, our financial resources, or the gospel, we remind people of the gifts God has given them and their responsibility to be good stewards."
>
> —*EUGENE F. ROOP*
> *Let The Rivers Run*

The primary reason for this is that a discussion or authorizing meeting has a different context. People have a different interest level, different questions, and a different attitude when the project is about to be funded. (*Note:* Each of the two meetings is important enough to schedule while the maximum potential for participation exists. Strive to have the meetings when you can attract a crowd. "Prime time" for your congregation may be on Sunday, when most of your people are already a church. If your meetings are scheduled in such a way as to require participants to return to church, in the evenings perhaps, you will need to provide an additional draw, such as a meal or dessert.)

Major Gift Development—Perhaps the greatest determinant of success or failure in a Miracle Sunday campaign is the degree of success in receiving lead or major gifts. Such gifts make or break any capital-fund development, including Miracle Sunday. Traditional fund-raising theory suggests that you will rarely raise more than 10 times the largest single gift. A $100,000 goal, for example, will require a $10,000 single gift; $500,000 a $50,000 gift, and so on.

After the announcement of Miracle Sunday and before *Meeting #2* (see below) you will need to contact those donors whose gifts will have the greatest influence on the success of the campaign. In general, the determinants of those included in such major gift contacts are:

1. Those whose potential gift is $10,000 or more.
2. Those whose potential gift is "major" in terms of its impact upon your campaign, though it may be less than $10,000.
3. Your top 10 current donors.

A small Major Gift Task Force should make a personal call on all major gift prospects. I say "call," because this is not a solicitation. You will not need to ask for money at this time. The contact is to clarify the donor prospect's attitude toward the campaign and their likelihood of making a lead gift.

The content of this personal contact may be no more than asking two questions and issuing an invitation.

The first question: "What are you hearing about our Miracle Sunday campaign?"

We express this as "What are you hearing?" because we do not wish to make the prospect defensive. What they tell us may be their *own* opinion, but they do not need to claim it. It is merely something they have "heard." Eliciting this response gives you an opportunity for rumor control. Occasionally a fine project will fail due to misunderstandings and ambiguity. Persons may be confused over cost, project sequence, or the nature of Miracle Sunday itself. Identifying such issues early, among this critical major gift constituency, may allow you to redeem an otherwise lost cause. If the donor prospect merely misunderstands any element of the project, this visit is the ideal time to correct it.

If you reach a time when the reaction to "What are you hearing?" appears positive, you may ask the second question: "And how are *you* feeling about Miracle Sunday?"

No matter what the prospect's response may be—positive, negative, or neutral—it is important to remind them of the importance of their gift to the campaign"s success.

Finally, invite these prospects to *Meeting #2*. Their giving potential is great enough that even incremental increases that might arise from their participation will produce a meaningful return.

Letter #2—This second mailing recaps much of what was in the first letter: announcement of the Miracle Sunday, emphasis that this will be a collection of *gifts* rather than pledges, plus the establishment of a goal. In addition to this repeated information, the second letter should include an invitation to *Meeting #2*, described below. It usually is a good idea for Letter #2 to be signed by someone other than the person who signed Letter #1. This reinforces the fact that Miracle Sunday has wide support, a critical issue in any fundraising effort.

Meeting #2—This meeting is designed to present new giving strategies that have the effect of raising the sights of key donors. It may be helpful to give this meeting an intriguing title, such as "How to Give More at Less Cost." This is your best opportunity to help motivated donors discover the most effective and satisfying ways for them to make their gift. The content you will want to include at Meeting #2:

- Giving out of assets as well as income.
- Identifying assets that can be the source of the donor's gift.
- Tax implications of giving property (special emphasis should be placed on donating appreciated securities and real estate).
- Some suggestions of "idle assets" that can be satisfying gifts—cash-value life insurance, collectibles, etc. (It is important to encourage donors to liquidate these items and bring cash on Miracle Sunday.)
- If your church has access to a gift annuity program through your denominational foundation or its equivalent, this is an excellent way for older donors to replace any income lost through gifts of investments.

The purpose of this "How to Give" meeting is not to hype the Miracle Sunday, nor encourage people to give beyond their true commitment to the program. The purpose, rather, is to present new giving strategies, in the hope that this will pique interest in more substantial giving than traditional "special offerings." Because the goal of Miracle Sunday is so far beyond the usual, new strategies establish the important principle that this will require more than merely writing another check. For this reason, a fairly reliable measure of potential Miracle-Sunday success is the size and responsiveness of the audience at Meeting #2. If the attendance for this meeting is much below 50 percent of worship attendance, committee leaders should view this with alarm. If the majority of your active members will not participate in learning new giving strategies, they have already made up their minds about their Miracle Sunday gift. This situation is deadly, because it means that such persons will give as they usually do—in small amounts not likely to make a miracle happen.

Letter #3 may well be the most critical part of the entire promotional effort. This letter is a *testimonial* from at least one member of the congregation who enjoys respect from the other members. Every congregation has some persons who are admired by the membership and whose opinions are held in highest regard. Such persons must be recruited to write the testimonial letter.

The longer I am involved in fund development in the church, the more convinced I become that today's donors do not give money for institutions or causes. The modern donor gives only to *other people*. The testimonial letter is your best opportunity to place a human face on your project.

There is power in a testimony. This influence is most strongly felt among the ambivalent, those who do not feel strongly one way or another. Often the catalytic effect of a fellow member declaring support for a project is all that is needed to bring others aboard. Work at finding the right spokesperson for this task.

If your congregation is diverse, you may wish to have multiple testimonies drawn from representatives of the key constituencies. While it is good to include newcomers and younger donors, it is critical that at least one of your testimonies be made by an older long-time member. It is the older constituency, after all, from whom you'll get most of your lead gifts.

Letter #4 is the final component of your promotional work. This is the Pastoral letter. The message of the pastor need not say anything more than "I believe in this project." Many older members will not give complete support to any project the pastor is not clearly supporting. The pastor's message is meant to make it clear that all parties, including the clergy, are on board.

4. *Miracle Sunday* (One Week)

The great day has arrived! What should the Miracle Sunday service look like? The dominant theme for the day should be celebration and high expectations. Because this could be the largest offering in your church's history, it should be given special emphasis.

Have the offering early in the service to enable a tabulation to be completed before folks go home. If your tradition is to pass offering plates among the pews, why not have worshipers bring their gifts to the front of the sanctuary? Use a special receptacle, such as a large basket or something graphic (a model of the new building, for example) to receive the gifts. Make available special offering envelopes (No. 10 or larger) that will accommodate the occasional non-cash gifts such as securities or life insurance.

Arrange for counters to tabulate the offering, so that a total can be announced by the end of the service. If your congregation has more than one worship service, you will want to develop a special all-church event following the last service for this total to be announced. Have a meal or a special coffee hour to bring everyone together for the announcement of the Miracle Sunday results.

5. *Follow-Up* (One Week)

Although it is common for a congregation to experience spontaneous receipts in the 7 to 10 days following Miracle Sunday of something approaching 10 percent of what was received on Miracle Sunday itself, you should plan to contact the households you have not heard from yet. Your contacts in this follow-up period can be both extensive and intensive. An *extensive* follow-up method is to send a mailing to each member household, announcing the results of Miracle Sunday, announcing that it is not too late to participate, and including a return envelope for their response.

An *intensive* level of follow-up is to make a face-to-face or phone contact on any prospect whose annual giving places them in the top 50 percent of current contributors. Remember that this contact will be only upon those from whom you have heard nothing. Those who are known to have been present at Miracle Sunday but gave nothing, should be presumed to have responded and should not be contacted again.

Because Miracle Sunday is not intended to be a marathon, strive to complete all follow-up work within one week after your Miracle Sunday offering.

Miracles in the church are exciting. The atmosphere is dramatically charged as morale skyrockets and a powerful "can do" feeling pervades the congregation. If you have a valid project, a motivated congregation, and a firm belief in miracles, you can experience Miracle Sunday at your church.

 DEVOTIONAL

A Litany of Gratitude

DONALD G. STONER

Leader: For this place of worship, where praise and prayer are raised to God,

People: We offer our thanks, O God.

Leader: For the preaching and teaching of the Word and the celebration of the sacrament,

People: We pay tribute to pastors and teachers, past and present.

Leader: For the nurture of families, a sharing community, and outreach to others,

People: We remain indebted to those who have traveled the way of the cross before us.

Leader: For all who have given of themselves and their substnce in ministry to others,

People: We offer thanksgiving and renew our dedication.

Leader: For those who have provided special gifts for the mission to present and future generations,

People: We feel your presence surrounding us still.

All: We give thanks, O God, for this church's rich heritage and faithful stewardship, praying for your continued blessing and guidance for all the days ahead. Amen.

PART FOUR

PLANNED GIVING

Introduction

DON JOINER

One of the major trends in funding ministry today that is dramatically different from that of the past is encouragement to give outside the Sunday morning offering, from funds other than "earned income." People have two pockets: earned income and accumulated assets. In stressing giving through "pledges," we encourage giving from the first pocket. Tim Ek's article points to giving from the other pocket. Financial experts indicate that between $3 and $10 trillion will pass from one estate to another in the next ten to twenty years. Will your church participate in part of that transfer?

William Gray will help you think through the gift possibilities and lead your church to discuss future funding resources.

Most successful funding programs include one-liners on newsletters, bulletins, letterhead, and other mailings. "A Baker's Dozen" and Renard Kolasa's one-liners (see Volumes 1 and 2 for more!) will give you ideas to use throughout the year.

Donner Atwood's message of love to his family is a must-read! When I first saw it in the Foundation newsletter of the Reformed Church of America, I said "WOW!" I wrote to Donner and said all Christians need to hear his thoughts. The article is a powerful examination of not only what to leave the persons who stay behind when we die, but of our theology of death (and resurrection).

 PLANNED GIVING

Giving Beyond the Offering Plate

TIMOTHY C. EK

Most of us think of stewardship as management of the financial resources God has entrusted to us. And it is. It is also more than that. It is our management of *all* the resources over which God has made us stewards. God also gives us time, abilities, and non-cash possessions, which many of us overlook, as part of the way we can respond to Christ's lordship.

1. WHY CONSIDER A NON-CASH GIFT?

While most giving takes the form of cash contributions, we should also consider opportunities to give personal assets. Contributions of this type not only bless the church, but also can result in blessings to the giver, such as favorable tax treatment on the sale

of the assets and tax deductibility of donated assets.

Because these gifts rarely are viewed as cash, they often are neglected. But they actually can be even more significant to the ministry of the local church, sometimes providing facilities, properties, and other items not otherwise available for ministry support.

2. WHAT KINDS OF GIFTS ARE WE TALKING ABOUT?

Non-cash gifts can include things like:
- Stocks and bonds
- Real estate
- Use of a home as a gift
- Life insurance

- Personal property of all types (furniture, autos, etc.)
- Bequests through a will or trust
- Life income gifts
- Gifts of service

3. SOME BENEFITS OF NON-CASH GIVING

Stocks and bonds

Securities can make excellent gifts for those who have held stocks or bonds for a long period of time and want to avoid taxes on appreciation that may be involved when the securities are sold.

Real estate

Real estate is another option you might consider (land, buildings, residences).

Life insurance

Life insurance can be used as a gift—usually in two ways. First, a ministry can be made beneficiary of the policy. Second, the ministry can be named as both the owner and the beneficiary. In this case, you receive an immediate tax deduction, approximately equal to the cash surrender value of the policy—and all premium payments you make following the initial gift are also tax deductible!

Personal property

Personal property might include: art, coins, stamps, cars, furniture, cameras, etc. Gifts valued under $500 require very little documentation for tax purposes. Gifts valued at between $500 and $5,000 require only one additional form to be filed. Gifts valued at over $5,000 (other than publicly held stock) require an appraisal.

Wills or trusts

A ministry can be remembered in your estate plan by designating a gift of assets—even a home. Donors can choose to name a specific amount, a percentage of the estate, or the remainder *after* other bequests have been made. Gifts are usually tax deductible.

Gift annuities and charitable remainder trusts

A gift annuity or charitable remainder trust can provide you income for life, or income for the life of a beneficiary you designate. The remainder goes as a gift to a Christian cause. It spares you the task of managing the money, while it provides a charitable deduction and other tax advantages.

4. WHEN IS A GOOD TIME TO CONSIDER SUCH A GIFT?

Virtually anytime, but especially when you have valuables (property, assets, etc.) you no longer wish to manage. A gift made now can be the source of future ministry, while still providing you with significant financial and tax benefits in the present.

5. WHO APPROVES GIFTS?

While most gifts require no special receiving process, gifts of land and gifts designated for specific local church purposes usually need approval. This is to ensure that the costs of maintaining the gift will not exceed the value of the gift itself, and that it is free of unforeseen liabilities.

6. HOW CAN I EXPLORE THIS FURTHER?

Your denominational foundation or estate planning service can help you look further into non-cash giving. This is particularly advisable, because these gifts sometimes involve tax and legal considerations. Naturally, all inquiries into this type of giving on your part are considered confidential and will not obligate you.

> "We give what we are. The thoughts you think will radiate from you as though you are a transparent vase."
> —*UNKNOWN*

$ MONEY TALK

Once Upon a Time in an Undeveloped Woods, or Planned Giving Can Be Fun!

FREDERICK H. LEASURE, CFRE

Once upon a time, in the deep, dark, undeveloped woods, there lived three bears, two of whom were annual donors to the SPCB (The Society for the Prevention of Cruelty to Bears). There was a papa bear, who owned a great deal of land, but had a marginal income. There was a mama bear, who had not yet been liberated from the traditional role of cook, housekeeper, and mother. And there was a baby bear, who was a great concern of both the papa and mama bear.

One Saturday morning the mama bear got up early, as was her custom, and cooked a large breakfast for papa and baby bear. She had remembered that a lady from the SPCB had called the day before and asked if she could stop by for a visit. She couldn't remember when the lady said she would be by, but was sure it would be later in the day. Papa bear, being concerned about his weight and cholesterol, suggested that they all take a walk in the forest before eating the high-fiber oatmeal mama bear had cooked. So off they went on a stroll through their extensive acreage.

While they were gone, Goldilocks, a new planned-giving officer from the local SPCB chapter, came by to visit. She knocked at the door, and much to her surprise, it swung open. Though she found no one home, she saw the dishes on the breakfast table, and, typical of a planned-giving officer, she did not want to miss a free meal. She decided to go in and wait for the bear family to return.

Time passed. Goldilocks became quite hungry and decided to help herself to some breakfast. She tried to sit in the papa bear's chair, but found that, though probably it was a marketable antique, it was just not very comfortable. Moving on to the mama bear's chair, she found this more comfortable, but the wedgwood place setting didn't hold the heat, and the oatmeal had become cold. She then went over to the baby bear's place and found everything to her liking. She ate all the porridge, downed the orange juice, but left half of the glass of milk, as she didn't want to be perceived as too forward.

Meanwhile, the bears had lost all track of time. They were having a delightful walk through their woods. Mama bear had taken the opportunity to tell papa bear that she wished they could have more income, so they would be able to travel and show baby bear some other part of the world. She also suggested that it would be nice if they could afford to vacation during hunting season, so they would not worry constantly about ending up as a rug on some wealthy donor's floor.

Goldilocks was getting a bit drowsy after eating such a filling country breakfast. She decided to go upstairs and look around. She was sure that the bear family wouldn't mind because they seemed to be so friendly on the phone. She sat on the edge of papa bear's bed—no doubt another antique—to review her notes. However, the light wasn't very good, so she switched to mama bear's bed. As she looked through her folder, she remembered that the donor-research department had told her of the massive property holdings of the bear family. Though she was not sure of the bears' ages, she remembered a Conrad Beitell Seminar she had attended and thought that a charitable remainder unitrust with make-up provisions would be just the thing for this family. Just the thought of the Beitell seminar made her sleepy, and she crashed on junior's bed for what she was sure would be just a brief nap.

Mama bear had reminded the family of the time, and the bears had quickly come back home to eat their healthy breakfast.

As they sat down at the table, papa bear remarked, "Someone's been sitting in my chair, and the cushion is all wrinkled."

Mama bear said, "Someone has been sitting at my place, and my Irish-linen napkin is all rumpled."

Baby bear exclaimed, "Someone has been sitting in my place; they ate all my oatmeal and drank my orange juice, but they were polite enough not to finish all my milk."

The bears became suspicious that someone was in the house. Cautiously, papa bear led the way up the stairs to investigate. He quickly discovered that someone had been sitting on his bed. Mama was sure they had been on hers as well, when she found a planned-giving folder from the SPCB lying on the floor.

Baby bear came running into the room, shouting, "Someone's been in my bed, too, and she is still there."

Goldilocks was startled by the noise of the bears' voices and was embarrassed that she had been found sleeping. She quickly rose to her feet, mumbled a quick word of apology to the bear family, and ran down the steps and out the front door, vowing to stick with annual campaigns and never to work with planned giving again.

 CHECKLIST

A Baker's Dozen

Wills Announcements for Bulletin and Newsletter

These announcements may help those who desire to continue to stimulate members of their congregation to remember the ministries of the church in their estate planning.

A Bequest to the Church—Many in the church are taking a second look at their estate plans as a result of our recent Wills and Estate Planning Seminar. While reviewing dreams and goals for your family, please remember the work of the church as well.

Tithing Your Estate—Tithing your estate is one way to remember the ministry of the church you have so faithfully supported during your lifetime. One-tenth in life—one-tenth in death. It may be an idea you'd like to act on.

Are You a Visionary?—A bequest to the church in your will is a wonderful vision of things to come.

There's a Future in Your Will—Your will is an ideal opportunity to care for the needs of your family and advance the cause of Christ. There is great peace of mind in knowing that both your family and the church are taken care of by the final distribution of your assets.

In the End—Why not name the church the final beneficiary of your will, in the event all your heirs predecease you? In the end, the church will still be here.

Effective Stewardship—Planning ahead is part of effective stewardship. When you make your will, please remember to include the mission and ministry of the church.

Is God's Will in Your Will?—Many people who have completed a will have overlooked one important item—including the church as a beneficiary. If you have lived your life for the Lord, don't forget to include the Lord's work in the final distribution of your assets.

Memorial Gifts for Ministry—Bequests for the ministry of the church can be designated as memorial gifts to honor the memory of friends and loved ones whose lives have added meaning to your own.

Peace of Mind—Enjoy the peace of mind of knowing that the final distribution of your estate includes the ministry of the church.

Every Woman Needs a Will—Like most men, most women don't have a will. Since many women live longer than men, the majority of charitable bequests in this country are made by women who are distributing their own assets and those left to them by the disposition of their husband's estate. Not only is this a great privilege; it is a great responsibility as well.

If you are a woman, your will can make a big difference for your family and the ministry of the church. As you make your plans, remember to consider a bequest for the cause of Christ.

Leaving a Bequest to the Church—In addition to writing a will for the sake of one's family, a Christian will also should benefit the work of the church. If you wish to include the church in your will, a simple amendment is all that is necessary.

Your Personal Testimony—Your will is not just another legal document. It is a way to protect the future of the people you love. It is also the final opportunity to share a personal testimony of your experience of God's goodness and provide a blessing to others, by including a bequest for the ministry of the church.

Gifts for Ministry—Gifts for the mission and ministry of this church can be made in a number of creative ways and often can provide significant tax savings that reduce the actual cost of the gift.

After prayerful consideration, if you wish to consider any of these possibilities, please contact the pastor (or name another person who is responsible for these arrangements).

PLANNED GIVING

Endowments Serve to Enrich

DONALD G. STONER

Among the definitions for the word *endow* is "to enrich." Essentially, the purpose of an endowment is to enrich. Income from endowments translate into the enrichment of both the local and wider mission of the church, presently and into the future. An endowment serves to provide a stable financial base, as well as a means for extending the mission of the church, which is not always available through annual giving.

Extend Mission. In what ways do endowments, when wisely and prudently managed, provide for the enrichment of the church's life and mission? Endowments can enhance and extend the mission outreach of the church, as follows:

- ministries to children and youth in the community through after-school programs
- ministry to seniors through parish-nurse program and grants to community agencies
- increased support of our church's wider mission

Maintain Facilities. Endowment income also can assist in maintaining facilities for worship, nurture, and service:

- funds to maintain especially large, older facilities that may be a drain on annual budgets
- special funds for the ministry of music, including organs and special concerts
- major improvements for facilities that provide for enhanced programs of Christian nurture
- maintain space for community groups and organizations as part of community outreach

Provide Stability. In times of economic and demographic decline, endowments can provide stability and viability, allowing churches to avoid the "survival syndrome," by:

- allowing churches to be as competitive as possible in securing capable leadership
- providing social-outreach programs in the community when there is great need

- funding for evangelism programs to reach new-comers to the community

Sustain Ministries. Endowments enable prophetic ministries to continue during precarious times in the life of the congregation by insuring that the church's witness will be voiced and acted upon:
- taking stands on civil rights issues
- addressing justice and peace issues
- working for better housing and public education
- addressing the prevalence of drugs in the community

Encourage Stewardship. Finally, endowments and planned-giving programs may encourage members to consider the stewardship of their accumulated assets and motivate them to engage in estate planning, by:

- modeling the prudent management of accumulated assets
- providing a regular emphasis on wills and life-income gifts
- illustrating how endowment income enriches the ministry and mission of the church now
- inviting individuals to make gifts to the endowment fund of the church

Endowments can truly serve as a blessing to congregations when properly conceived, understood, and promoted. The ministry of the congregation will be enriched and extended far beyond what is possible by annual giving. Endowments help in fulfilling the dreams and visions of the congregation and its members, both now and in years to come.

 # PLANNED GIVING

Pitfalls and Pratfalls

Murphy's Laws of Charitable Giving

J. WILLIAM GRAY, JR.

The primary reason for making a charitable gift is to support a particular project or cause. Having decided to give, the donor then must choose from a sometimes bewildering array of giving options, each with its own tax and financial and practical consequences. Complexity abounds. The income-tax deduction provision alone—originally a single sentence in the 1917 federal tax act—has grown to occupy 19 pages in a paperback edition of the current Internal Revenue Code. That single provision is now interpreted by over 100 pages of Treasury Regulations, scores of revenue rulings, and countless private-letter rulings and court decisions.

Anyone seeking to guide a donor or a charity through the maze of charitable giving rules must realize the risks involved. As the mythical Murphy said, "If something can go wrong, it will." Slight variations in the gift form may mean the difference between a tax deduction for the full value of the donation, a deduction for only the donor's cost basis, and no deduction at all. Failure to plan and analyze adequately also can result in practical problems for both parties to the transaction. And the chances for Murphy's Law to apply increase dramatically at year-end, when the press of business and impending tax deadlines can prevent the parties from analyzing the transaction as closely as they should.

"All I know is that it's been there since I set up that foundation, and now I'm getting these wings."

This article will not provide a complete list of all problems in all types of charitable gifts. Instead, it will highlight four aspects of most gift transactions—the nature of the gift property, the mechanics of the transaction itself, the tax benefits available, and the continuing donor/charity relationship—and explore some common problems that can develop. By becoming aware of them in this context, we may be better equipped to avoid them in actual practice.

What You See Is Not Always What You Get

Problems with the Gift Property

● *It May Not Be There At All*

When a donor approaches you with a gift proposal, you generally can assume that he or she owns the property in question. Occasionally, however, a closer examination will reveal problems with the property title. A deed may give the seller or an adjoining landowner a right to purchase real estate, if the owner seeks to convey it. A buy-sell agreement or other restriction may limit a business owner's freedom to transfer closely held stock. A spendthrift clause may prohibit a trust beneficiary from assigning income or principal interest. Other types of restrictions, often imposed under different circumstances and long since forgotten, may mean that the donor is not free to use that property for a major gift.

● *Always Look a Gift Horse in the Mouth.*

Before seriously discussing a major gift, consider whether your charity can use the property or its proceeds. Be sure that the donor shares your expectations about whether the property is to be used or sold and, if used, how.

● *Beware of Maharajahs Bearing Gifts.*

A seemingly desirable gift sometimes can become a "white elephant" because of hidden costs. You may anticipate revenue from the property, either in the form of investment income (dividends, interest, rents, royalties, etc.), receipts from using it in your exempt activities, or sale proceeds. Carefully compare those items with the associated costs, including expenses of operating or maintaining the property, specialized management needs, brokers' fees, recording taxes, and other transfer costs. Be sure to factor in the possibility that the property will produce less revenue than expected, take longer to sell than you had projected, or otherwise fail to meet expectations. Such an analysis can identify financial problems before they occur.

● *There May Be a Joker in the Deck.*

Environmental exposure arising from donated real estate is every charity's nightmare. Liability under CERCLA and other federal and state "strict liability" statutes can far exceed the value of donated property, exposing the charity's other assets to claims and potentially jeopardizing its ability to carry on its exempt activities. A pre-gift analysis of potential environmental issues (often including at least a Phase I environmental evaluation) is becoming increasingly common in real-estate gifts. Charities that discover they are to receive real estate through bequests or charitable remainder trusts may consider disclaiming their interests if they suspect environmental problems.

● *Them That Has the Gold Don't Always Make the Rules.*

Certain types of gifts cannot be made, even if the donor and the charity are in complete agreement about them. For example, a donor holding tax-exempt securities cannot contribute them to a pooled income fund, nor can the pooled income fund accept cash or other property, sell it, and reinvest the proceeds in tax-exempt securities. Likewise, a donor who has established a charitable remainder annuity trust and made an initial contribution cannot contribute additional assets to that same trust.

There's Many a Slip 'Twixt Plan and Gift

Problems with the Transfer

● *An Oral Agreement Isn't Worth the Paper It's Written On.*

Documentation is essential in a gift transaction. By setting forth the terms of all agreements and understandings between the donor and the charity, proper documentation will help avoid future misunderstandings between those parties or their successors, including later income beneficiaries and development directors, or other representatives of

"Philanthropy is not a spectator sport."

—*SHEREE PARRIS NUDD*

the charity. Proper documentation also will help assure the donor of the desired tax treatment and will confirm the charity's ownership rights in the gift property.

● *If It Weren't for the Last Minute, Nothing Ever Would Get Done.*

Timing often is critical in a charitable gift. The donor may be trying to obtain a deduction in a particular year, avoid capital gain from an impending sale, lock in a high asset value, or accomplish some other time-sensitive goal. Therefore it is essential to know when the gift has been made. The general rule is that a gift is complete when the donor delivers the property to the charity, either unconditionally or subject to subsequent conditions that are so unlikely to occur that they are treated as negligible.

Exceptions have arisen for certain types of property. A gift by check, for example, is complete when the check is either delivered or mailed, as long as it subsequently clears the donor's account in due course. If the check bears a date later than the delivery date, however, the gift is not complete until that later date. Likewise, a contribution charged to a credit card is deductible when the charge is made, even though the donor may not pay the bank or company that has issued the card until a later date. A contribution of the donor's own promissory note, or an option to acquire the donor's property for a bargain price does not constitute a deductible contribution; rather, the deduction is available only when the donor transfers cash or other property in payment of the note, or when the holder exercises the option.

Particular problems may arise in year-end securities transfers. A stock gift is complete when the donor delivers an endorsed stock certificate (or an unendorsed certificate and a separately executed stock power) to the charity or its agent. If the donor instructs his or her own broker or the transfer agent for the corporation to transfer the stock into the charity's name, the gift generally is not complete until the stock is actually transferred in the corporation's records. The transfer will be effective upon delivery to the broker, however, if the written record clearly shows that the broker is acting as agent for the charity and not the donor.

● *Them That Has the Gold Don't Always Make the Rules II.*

Some gift proposals that comply fully with applicable federal rules may run afoul of various state statutes

that regulate charitable gifts. For example, the Securities and Exchange Commission has issued a no-action letter, confirming that pooled income funds that meet certain criteria will not be subject to federal securities' law-registration requirements. Several states, however, classify pooled income-fund interests as securities, and require either registration or application for an exemption certificate. Gift annuities also are regulated as securities in some states. In an increasing number of other states, they are classed as insurance products, subjecting the issuing charities to many of the same requirements imposed upon commercial insurers. Other types of gift solicitations may expose charities to registration requirements under state and local charitable solicitation statutes. Many solicitation statutes are modeled after a uniform act proposed by the National Association of Attorneys General, but others are unique to their particular jurisdictions.

Law Sufficiently Complex Is Indistinguishable from No Law at All

Problems with Tax Benefits

● *Just Because It Looks, Walks, Quacks, and Lays Eggs Like a Duck, Don't Assume It Is One.*

Gifts to an individual are not tax deductible, regardless of how needy he or she may be. Contributions to a worthy organization likewise are not deductible for income-tax purposes unless the organization is described in Section 170(c) of the Internal Revenue Code; nor are they deductible for estate- and gift-tax purposes, unless the organization is described in Sections 2055(a) and 2522(a), respectively. To complicate matters, the three sections are not coextensive. For example, a contribution to a cooperative cemetery company may be deductible for income-tax purposes, but not for gift-tax purposes. To add further complication, state tax rules on charitable contribution deductions do not always correspond to their federal counterparts.

Even within the federal tax system, it is not safe to assume that an organization automatically can receive deductible contributions because it is tax exempt. The tax-exemption rules apply to trade associations, social welfare organizations, chambers of commerce, social clubs, and many other entities to

> "Giving is the lifeblood of happy living."
> —*TODD PARRISH (1960–)*

which donations are not deductible as charitable contributions. In IRS Publication 78, *Cumulative List of Organizations,* published annually and updated twice each year, there should be a list of all organizations eligible to receive contributions for which donors may claim an income-tax charitable deduction. Prospective donors generally are entitled to rely on that listing, unless the IRS has published a notice to the contrary in its weekly *Internal Revenue Bulletin.*

All eligible donee organizations, however, are not included in the Cumulative List. Religious entities and certain organizations with minimal gross receipts do not need to apply for exemption, and therefore are not in the IRS records. Other organizations that have qualified as tax exempt may have been dropped from the Cumulative List because they have not filed information returns, even if no return was required because their receipts did not exceed the filing threshold. Organizations covered by a group exemption are not listed individually. Administrative errors have caused others to be omitted entirely, or included under incorrect or incomplete names. If an organization is not listed, prospective donors should request a copy of its determination letter or other appropriate documentation.

• It's No Fun to Be Hoisted on Your Own Petard.

Prospective donors sometimes find that their own prior actions have made a gift inadvisable, or less advantageous than expected. Conditions or restrictions placed on the property can make the transfer incomplete. Gifts earmarked for individuals or nonexempt organizations will not be deductible if the donee charity has no discretion to control the gift property and change its intended use. Special tax elections, such as installment-sale treatment for sale proceeds, or S-corporation status for a business, may carry consequences that make that property less useful in charitable giving. Prior sale negotiations may cause a donor to be treated as having sold property and contributed the proceeds to charity, even if the transfer takes place before the sale. A gift of encumbered property may cause the donor to recognize forgiveness-of-indebtedness income. Donating encumbered property to a charitable remainder unitrust can disqualify the trust, and donat-

ing it outright to a charity can make the charity liable for income tax on the unrelated debt-financed income it produces.

• Sometimes the Pot of Gold Lies at the End of a Circle (Or, You Can't Always Get There From Here).

Some kinds of gifts are not deductible, despite their clear economic value to the charitable recipient. A gift of services generates no deduction, even if the donor can show what he or she would have charged the public, or what other providers in the area charge, for similar services. The donor may be able, however, to deduct any out-of-pocket expenses incurred in performing the services. A gift of rent-free office space for a defined period is likewise not deductible, even though the donor can prove the fair rental value; and a term loan yields no deduction, despite readily available measurements of the forgone interest.

Where the property is not held in trust, the tax code generally allows deductions for less than a donor's entire interest in only four instances: (1) a remainder interest in a personal residence or farm; (2) an undivided portion of the donor's entire interest in property; (3) a qualified conservation contribution; and (4) a work of art separate from its copyright (estate and gift-tax deduction only). Other partial interests, such as a life estate or an interest for a term of years, are not deductible unless they constitute the donor's entire interest in the property. No deduction is available for contributions of a remainder interest in tangible personal property, if the donor or a close relative retains the right to use the property in the interim; instead, the deduction is postponed until all such intervening rights have lapsed.

• There's No [Immediate] Reward for Being Too Generous.

Corporate donors generally are subject to an aggregate annual deduction limitation: Their total charitable contribution deductions for a particular tax year may not exceed 10 percent of taxable income for that year, computed without regard to certain technical adjustments. Individual donors, however, may find their income-tax contribution deductions reduced both by annual-percentage limitations on various categories of total contri-

> ## "We'd all like the reputation for generosity, but we'd all like to buy it cheap."
> —MICHAEL GATES (1963–   )

butions, and by reduction rules that affect the deductible value of particular contributions. The limits do not apply to gift or estate taxes.

Individuals generally may not claim charitable contribution deductions totaling more than 50 percent of their adjusted gross income in a single year. Donors who have contributed more during the year can claim the excess as a deduction in any of the five following years, to the extent that their new contributions in those years are less than the 50 percent limit. The general limit applies only to contributions to non-private foundations, private operating foundations, "conduit" foundations, community foundations, and donor-advised funds, all of which are sometimes called "50 percent charities." Most gifts of long-term capital gain property are subject to lower annual percentage limits: 30 percent of adjusted gross income or, if less, the amount of the 50 percent limit remaining after all other contributions to all organizations (whether 50-percent charities or not) are taken into account.

Total annual deductions for private-foundation gifts are even more limited. The total may not exceed 30 percent of adjusted gross income or, if less, the amount of the 50 percent limit remaining after all gifts to 50-percent charities are taken into account. Most gifts of long-term capital gain property to private foundations are limited to the lesser of 20 percent of adjusted gross income, or the amount of the 30 percent aggregate capital-gain property limit remaining after all such gifts to 50-percent charities are taken into account.

Note that the 50 percent and 30 percent limitations apply only to gifts *to* 50-percent charities. Gifts *for the use of* those entities (*e.g.,* a gift that remains in trust, or perhaps an insurance premium paid directly to the insurer to maintain a policy owned by the charity) will be subject to the lower 30 percent/20 percent limit, otherwise applicable only to private-foundation gifts. Likewise, a charitable remainder trust gift intended for a 50-percent charity will be subject to the lower 30 percent/20 percent limits for private-foundation gifts, when private foundations are not excluded as potential beneficiaries. That could occur, for example, if the primary charitable beneficiary loses its tax exemption or its public-charity status, or if the donor exercises a reserved power to redirect part or all of the trust fund to a private foundation. Even the IRS sample forms for charitable-remainder trusts contain this trap.

Donors who are aware of the overall percentage limitations on annual gifts may not have heard of the reduction rules that apply to individual transfers. Although

donors generally may deduct the fair market value of their gifts, the deductible value of any particular gift must be reduced by any gain that would not have been a long-term capital gain, if the donor had sold the property rather than contributing it. Examples include inventory property, investment assets held for one year or less, and property for which the donor previously has claimed accelerated-depreciation deductions or depletion allowances. If the recipient is a private foundation, the donor generally can deduct only cost basis (or fair market value, if less), unless he or she contributes cash or, under pre-1995 rules, certain marketable securities. A donor who gives tangible personal property to any charity will find that his or her deduction is limited to cost basis (or fair market value, if less), unless the charity uses the gift property in its exempt activities.

● *Snakes and Taxes Can Bite You When You Least Expect It.*

Donors often name other individuals as immediate or successor income beneficiaries of charitable remainder trusts, pooled income funds, or charitable gift annuities. The actuarial value of such an individual's interest, of course, does not qualify for an income-tax charitable contribution deduction. Many donors forget, however, that the same interests often do not qualify for deductions from gift tax (for lifetime transfers) or estate tax (for transfers at the donor's death). Even the interest of the surviving spouse, which the marital deduction generally would shelter from gift or estate tax, may be taxable if the interest is in a pooled income fund or gift annuity, or if the surviving spouse is not the only successor beneficiary of the charitable remainder trust. A donor who receives an unexpected transfer tax bill generally will not have fond memories of the giving experience.

Encumbered property and gift annuities can hold unpleasant tax surprises also for the charity. If the charity assumes a debt on contributed property, part of the income it receives from the property or its sale proceeds will be subject to income tax as unrelated debt-financed income. Similar income-tax liability can arise if the charity enters into a gift annuity arrangement, in which the donor receives any other consideration in addition to the annuity, the donor is guaranteed a minimum amount of payments, the annuity amount depends upon the income that the property generates, the annuity is payable for a period other than one or two lives, or the actuarial present value of the annuity is 90 percent or more of the gift property value.

"Look, Mr. Claus, as your tax consultant I'm advising you to go with a foundation this year. No more freelancing!"

● ***Eschew Pompous Prolixity (Or, You Can't Have a Discussion with Someone If You Don't Speak the Language).***

Charitable giving is not rocket science, but it is governed by a complex technical body of laws and regulations at the federal, state, and local levels. Like most other professions and specialties, it also has developed its own jargon, which donors uninitiated into the mysteries of planned giving may find confusing and off-putting. Plain English helps. For example, never use "CRAT," "CRUT," "CRT," or their variations when "remainder trust," "life-income trust," or something equally descriptive will do. Don't sprinkle your conversation with references to "QTIPs," "QDoTs," and other acronyms. And never refer to a "NIMCRUT" or "VACCRUT," unless you are trying to impress another planned-giving professional with your buzzword vocabulary.

● ***A Little Knowledge Is a Dangerous Thing.***

Donors sometimes have unrealistic expectations about the benefits they can derive from charitable gifts. Often their confusion stems from conversations with acquaintances or unsophisticated advisors, or from generalizations in newspaper or magazine articles. Sometimes, though, they are misinformed by trustees, volunteers, or other representatives of the charity who do not understand the charitable-giving rules or the facts of a particular donor's situation. It should be obvious that trustees, volunteers, and employees who contact prospective donors on behalf of a charity must understand the basics of charitable giving and, equally important, must understand when to seek professional assistance from the development staff or outside advisors. In addition, charities should consider "basic training" in planned-gift principles for all trustees, key employees, and key volunteers, in case those individuals are drawn into conversations about planned gifts by acquaintances who know of their affiliation with the charity. No situation is more difficult for a planned-giving officer than having to explain to a potential donor why the charity cannot enter into a gift transaction that another representative of the charity has suggested or encouraged.

● ***More Knowledge Can Be Equally Dangerous.***

Donors don't care about all the intricacies of the charitable-giving rules that planned-giving professionals deal with every day. Assuming that they do can lead us to overload them with information, sometimes jeopardizing the charitable gift. One common form of this donor-information overload involves multiple gift options. Rather than focusing on one appropriate type of gift, we may give the donor a detailed explanation of the pros and cons of several different gift possibilities. Presented with too many choices, the donor may go into option-induced paralysis. Without sophisticated advisors who can explain the options and narrow the range of potential choices, the donor may feel unable to make a meaningful decision, and therefore may postpone the gift plans or abandon them altogether.

Another form of donor-information overload involves giving the donor too much information about even a single gift proposal. Most of us have difficulty passing up an opportunity to display our mastery of a particular charitable-giving technique. Bombarded with references to Internal Revenue Code sections, Treasury Regulations, IRS letter rulings, annual percentage rates, actuarial assumptions, and other arcana, however, a donor might well decide that a particular gift is simply too complicated. Better to concentrate only on the basic operational details that will affect the donor directly.

● ***You're Never Too Old to Die Young.***

The deduction attributable to a life estate, remainder interest, term of years, or other partial-interest gift is based on actuarial assumptions related to the age of the donor or other beneficiary, the applicable interest rate, the chosen payment schedule, and similar factors. The IRS has produced tables of actuarial factors to be used with the applicable interest rate that it publishes each month. Donors are entitled to base their computations on the interest rate for the month of the gift or either of the two preceding months, whichever is most advantageous. Because of the complexity involved, most planned-giving professionals calculate deduction values with commercial software packages. Due to changing interest rates, however, even the best projection may be good for no more than three months. If the gift is not completed within that time, the tax results differ from what the donor has been led to expect.

Problems also can arise when federal and state valuation rules diverge. The Uniform Principal and Income Act or other applicable statute in many states contains a valuation table for life estates, remainders, and term interests. Those state tables, rather than the federal tax tables, may govern for state tax purposes, and will apply for such property-law purposes as determining how sale proceeds are to be divided between a life tenant and a remainderman. The state tables often are based on different mortality figures and interest assumptions than are their federal counterparts, and these differing assumptions can yield dramatically different results. Donors, charities, and their respective advisors must understand which tables apply for particular purposes. In cases where a choice between federal and state tables is available, of course, they should agree on which tables will govern.

● *What the Right Hand Gives, the Left Hand Sometimes Takes Away.*

Donors often use deferred gifts to achieve various tax and financial goals, which frequently include both sheltering ordinary income from tax and avoiding tax on capital gains. A change in interest rates or other parameters can have significant—and surprisingly disparate—effects on these goals. For example, when the applicable federal interest rate increases, the charitable contribution deduction available for a gift annuity contribution will increase. At the same time, however, the capital gain and tax-free portions of each annuity payment will decrease, exposing more of the payment to tax at ordinary income rates, and thereby decreasing its after-tax value. Since charitable donors may choose from as many as three (or in some cases, four) different interest rates, they should consider carefully how each rate will affect the various tax and financial characteristics of the gift. In some instances,

annual percentage limitations or other factors may make a higher contribution deduction less advantageous than a greater tax shelter for the subsequent payments.

● *Worth Is in the Eye of the [Qualified] Beholder.*

An individual, partnership, closely held corporation, personal-service corporation, or S corporation contributing property, other than cash or marketable securities that is valued at more than $5,000 ($10,000 in the case of non-publicly traded stock), must comply with specific appraisal requirements to support an income-tax charitable contribution deduction. Special valuation rules apply for groups of similar items, qualified research contributions, and certain contributions for the care of the ill, the needy, and infants. The appraisal must contain specific information about the property, the contribution, the appraisal method, the appraiser, and the appraisal fee. It must be made as of a date not earlier than 60 days before the contribution, nor later than the due date (including extensions) for the tax return on which the contribution deduction is first claimed. An appraisal summary (IRS Form 8283) must be filed with the return.

To substantiate the donor's deduction, the appraisal must be prepared by a qualified appraiser. Unfortunately, the statutory definition excludes the individuals who often are most familiar with the contributed property and thus could best establish its value. Among the disqualified persons are (1) the donor and his or her employees; (2) the charitable recipient and its employees; (3) a party to the transaction in which the donor originally acquired the property, and any of that party's employees; (4) certain persons (and their spouses) related to individuals in the first three categories; and (5) certain appraisers whom the donor or a party to the acquisition transaction uses regularly. Particularly in transactions involving rare art works or collectibles, where the universe of knowledgeable experts is relatively small, the qualified appraiser exclusions may make it difficult for the donor to substantiate a claimed deduction.

● *There Is No Glory in Being the IRS's Chief Messenger and Tattletale.*

If a charity receives property that is subject to the qualified appraisal rules and consumes or disposes of the property within two years afterward, it generally must file an information return (IRS Form 8282) with the IRS and provide a copy to the donor. The IRS then

Let us begin by admitting the hard fact that we are basically selfish and do not want to share our affluence with others. . . . And let's admit that most of us resist the inspiration of the Holy Spirit which seeks to bring about a change that will make us more generous.

—*KENNETH PRIEBE*

can compare the sale price with the donor's claimed deduction. No report is required, however, if the item is consumed or distributed free of charge, in furtherance of the charity's exempt purposes.

Many donors are not aware of this requirement at all. Others assume incorrectly that a sale at less than the claimed deduction value automatically will reduce their claimed tax deductions. If donated property is likely to be sold, the charity should be sure that the donor understands the scope and nature of its reporting requirements. To avoid an argument that it has not been a proper steward of a gift, the charity also should apprise the donor of factors that might result in a lower sale price—for instance, a change in market conditions or the condition of the property, tax law changes, greater carrying costs than expected, or unexpected immediate cash needs.

New substantiation rules effective for 1994 and later years require a donor to obtain the charity's contemporaneous written acknowledgment of any gift valued at $250 or more. A canceled check no longer will substantiate the contribution deduction. Instead, the charity's receipt must state the amount of cash and describe (but not value) the property contributed, state the contribution date, and include either a statement that the charity furnished no goods or services in return, or a description of the goods and services furnished and an estimate of their value. A series of contributions, each of less than $250 but aggregating $250 or more, is not subject to this requirement, unless the donor's purpose was to avoid the substantiation rule. Numerous uncertainties remain, including how gifts are to be reported when the charity and the donor use different tax-reporting years, and how a donor is to substantiate claimed out-of-pocket expenses of $250 or more.

Also beginning in 1994, federal tax law has codified and expanded the *quid pro quo* rules first enunciated in an IRS ruling in 1967. If a donor receives any goods or ser-

vices in return for a contribution of more than $75, in connection with the solicitation or receipt, the charitable recipient must give the donor a good-faith estimate of their value and notify the donor that only the difference between the value of the contribution and the value of the goods or services received will qualify for an income-tax deduction. Special *de minimis* rules apply when the total value of all benefits furnished to the donor does not exceed 2 percent of the gift value, or if less, $64, or when the donation is at least $32, and the only benefit received is tangible personal property that bears the charity's name or logo and cost the charity $6.40 or less.

- *Any Payment That Can Hold a Surprise, Will.*

Trust taxation, bargain sale, and other tax rules all can hold income-tax surprises for donors. A donor who offers to sell appreciated property to a charity for its cost basis, for example, may assume that no capital gain will be recognized because the sale price is equal to his or her basis in the property. The bargain-sale rules, however, separate the transaction into two components—a partial gift and a partial sale. The donor must allocate a portion of the total cost basis to each component. The result is that he or she must recognize the part of the capital gain attributable to the sale portion of the transaction, even if the total amount received does not exceed the total cost basis.

The annuity-taxation rules also can produce unexpected results. If a donor gives appreciated property in return for a charitable gift annuity, each annuity payment generally has three components for tax purposes: part is ordinary income; part, capital gain; and the rest, tax-free return of basis. That treatment will continue for the donor's actuarial life expectancy, determined at the time of the gift; any subsequent payments will be fully taxable as ordinary income. If someone other than the donor is the annuitant, however, any capital gain from the partial sale portion of the gift annuity transaction cannot be prorated over the life expectancy of the donor or the beneficiary. Instead, the donor must recognize the entire amount of capital gain in the year he or she makes the gift. That tax result, of course, can make a gift annuity considerably less attractive.

Charitable remainder-trust beneficiaries seeking tax-exempt income often are frustrated by the "tier" rules of trust taxation. Knowing that a charitable remainder trust can sell donated property without paying capital-gain tax, the donor may think that the trustee can then reinvest the proceeds in tax-exempt securities and immediately begin paying tax-free income to the donor or other income beneficiary. Under the tier system, however, a trust that does not have taxable income must distribute all of its accumulated capital gain before it can distribute any tax-free income. Any capital gain that the trust realizes when it sells appreciated property remains in the trust and must be carried out to the income beneficiary as part of the annuity or unitrust amount. The beneficiary will receive (and pay tax on) all of the trust's accumulated capital gain before he or she receives any tax-free income from tax-exempt securities in which the trustee invests the sale proceeds.

You May Not Still Love Each Other Tomorrow:

Problems with the Continuing Donor/Charity Relationship

● *Every Meeting of the Minds Requires a Quorum*.

If a charitable-gift agreement contemplates that the donor and the charity each will continue to have rights in and responsibilities toward gift property or its proceeds, the parties should clearly understand their respective rights and duties from the beginning. A donor, for example, might anticipate that the charity or a third-party trustee will sell the gift property and reinvest the proceeds in tax-exempt securities, growth stocks, or other particular investments. The donor generally cannot require that result without risking adverse capital-gain tax consequences. He or she nevertheless should be sure that the contemplated action is within the power of the charity or trustee, and consistent with the terms of the governing instrument and state law. The donor also should confirm that the charity or trustee does not view the action as inconsistent with its exempt purposes or general fiduciary duty.

If property is donated for a particular purpose, the donor and the charity should define the use, its duration, and a procedure by which the charity, either alone or in consultation with the donor, can change the use or dispose of the property, if it determines that such an action is in its best interest. In the latter event, the agreement should specify whether the property is

> "Wealth, like happiness, is never attained when sought after directly. It always comes as a by-product of providing a useful service."
> —HENRY FORD (1863–1947)

to be returned to the donor, transferred to some other charity, converted to another use, or disposed of.

Any agreement relating to a gift that is subject to conditions should specify a procedure to remove them if they become obsolete, impractical, or impossible to fulfill. If the agreement does not address that issue, state statutes, such as the Uniform Management of Institutional Funds Act or common law principles of *cy pres,* or charitable approximation will determine whether, and to what extent, the restrictions can be released.

In some cases, the donor and the charity will be co-owners of property, as life tenant and remainderman, as owners of undivided fractional interests, or in some other relationship. To avoid future disputes and misunderstandings, the parties should be sure that they have agreed on how to divide all rights and duties relating to the property, or that they understand how state law would allocate those rights and duties in the absence of an agreement. Among the key points are responsibility for insurance premiums, taxes and other recurring expenses, ordinary repairs, capital expenditures and improvements, and division of income or sale proceeds, as well as decisions about what expenditures should be made and whether the property should be sold.

● *Nothing Strains a Relationship Like a Recession.* Donor-charity relationships may be severely strained if either party becomes unable to honor promised financial commitments. For example, a donor might stop making premium payments on a donated insurance policy, or stop paying taxes and expenses associated with a donated real-estate interest. The trustee of a charitable remainder trust might find that the charity does not have sufficient liquid assets to make payments to the income beneficiary or pay trust expenses. A charity might find itself unable to make continuing gift-annuity payments. The donor might also blame the charity if, for example, a charitable remainder unitrust payment declines because the underlying asset value has decreased, or if a pooled income fund fails to produce the expected level of income. A donor who is warned of these possibilities during the gift process is less likely to be caught unaware or to hold the charity responsible.

● *Them That Has the Gold Don't Always Make the Rules (III).*

Donors often contribute illiquid property to income-only charitable remainder unitrusts with make-up provisions. When the property is sold and the proceeds are reinvested in income-producing form, the trustee can use the resulting income to make up the shortfall from earlier in the trust term. The amount payable is the trust "income," which the unitrust regulations declare will be determined according to the governing instrument and the applicable local law. If the instrument is silent, as are the IRS model unitrust forms, the income definition will be left entirely to state statutes, such as the Uniform Principal and Income Act and the Revised Uniform Principal and Income Act. Individual state modifications in the various uniform acts, however, mean that the same unitrust provisions may produce significantly different payments for donors in some states than for their counterparts elsewhere. The applicable tax regulations allow a donor to modify the otherwise-applicable state definition of income, unless the modification "departs fundamentally" from local law. Donors and charities should be sure that they understand how state law definitions can affect the allocation of income and principal in unitrusts and should agree on appropriate modifications, if state law would not produce the intended result.

● *Not Everything Works as Well the Second Time Around.*

Occasionally a donor will have been so pleased with a charitable gift that he or she will decide to do it again. Charities are delighted to have repeat donors. In at least two instances, though, the subsequent donation can generate unexpected problems for the donor. The first instance is relatively straightforward: a donor who wants to make a second contribution to a charitable remainder annuity trust cannot use the same trust. He or she can, of course, make the second contribution in a separate, identical trust, but some additional transaction costs and on-going administrative expenses are likely to result.

The second is somewhat less obvious. Sometimes the principal of a charitable remainder annuity trust has grown so that it greatly exceeds the amount necessary to support the income beneficiary's annuity. The remainderman cannot use the excess principal for its charitable activities during the income beneficiary's lifetime, unless the income beneficiary is willing to assign the income interest to the charity; and that assignment terminates the trust under state law. The income beneficiary might decide to assign the interest and claim a contribution deduction for its value. If the beneficiary feels unable to give up that income, however, the charity might suggest that he or she exchange the annuity trust interest for a private annuity, to be paid by the charity. The remainder trust then could be terminated and the principal distributed to the charitable remainderman. Whether the charity is obligated to make the annuity payments from the trust principal it receives, or from its general assets, part or all of the income generated by distributed trust principal will be taxable to the charity as unrelated debt-financed income.

● *Nothing Is Private for a Private Foundation.*

Any donor who establishes a private charitable foundation must cope with a baffling array of special restrictions, designed to ensure that such a foundation will operate to benefit the public, rather than to further the donor's own private agenda. Those restrictions include: (1) additional annual reporting requirements; (2) prohibitions against certain "self-dealing" transactions with insiders, even if those transactions provide a clear financial benefit to the foundation; (3) minimum annual distribution requirements; (4) prohibitions against owning substantial interests in any business entity; (5) a general prohibition against investments that could jeopardize the foundation's ability to accomplish its charitable purposes; and (6) prohibitions against "taxable expenditures," including certain grants to individuals, unless the IRS has approved the grant-making procedure in advance; expenditures for lobbying or electioneering; and grants to other private foundations, unless the grantor foundation continually monitors the grantee's use of the funds. All these provisions are enforceable through a system of penalty taxes imposed on the foundation, and in some cases, the individuals involved in the transaction.

> "There is no charity in a man's leaving money in his will; he has simply got to leave it. The time to administer your trust is while you are still living."
>
> —*WILLIAM GLADSTONE*

These private foundation rules apply also to non-exempt charitable trusts, and many apply to split-interest trusts, such as charitable remainder trusts. For example, the trustee of a charitable remainder trust would violate the self-dealing rules if it allowed the donor or close relatives of the donor to continue living in a residence owned by the trust. If a donor contributed real property to a remainder trust, but continued to be primarily liable on the mortgage, the trustee would violate the self-dealing rules by making mortgage payments from the trust. Those rules also would prohibit the trustee from selling trust property to the donor or close relatives of the donor, even if they were willing to pay full market value or a premium.

The excess-business-holdings rule does not apply to a charitable remainder trust as long as any individual beneficiary is entitled to payments. If the trust is to continue after all noncharitable interests have expired, however, the excess-business-holdings rule may require the trustee to dispose of a profitable business interest that it otherwise would retain as a trust investment for the charitable remainderman's benefit.

> "When you stop giving and offering something to the rest of the world, it's time to turn out the lights."
> —GEORGE BURNS
> (1896–1996)

- ### Congress Can Always Find One More Way to Complicate Your Life.

Congress seems continually to be considering legislation, or proposals for legislation, that would affect tax-exempt organizations in general, or charitable gifts in particular. Last year's legislative session produced the charitable gift substantiation and *quid pro quo* gift rules, the effects of which may not be felt fully until next April 15. The continuing debate over health care could dramatically change the rules governing tax-exempt hospitals and other health-care providers. The separate proposal for intermediate sanctions would allow the IRS to impose penalties on a nonprivate foundation that violates the Section 501(c)(3) rules, without having to revoke its tax-exempt status. Hearings on alleged unfair competition with small businesses may lead to calls for additional restrictions on charities' income-producing activities, including certain forms of fund-raising.

One area of Congressional inaction also could adversely affect certain charities. In 1984, Congress enacted a special rule allowing donors to claim a fair market value deduction for "qualified appreciated

securities" given to private foundations. The reduction rules that governed gifts to private foundations otherwise would have allowed the donor to deduct only his or her cost basis in the stock. That special rule, which provided a significant incentive for foundation gifts, expired at the end of 1994. Although numerous professional groups and individual charities have sought to have the rule extended or made permanent, Congress failed to act in time to preserve the rule.

- ### If It Doesn't, the IRS and the States Surely Will.

The Internal Revenue Service has published sample charitable remainder trust and pooled income fund forms, so that donors and charities will not need to request rulings on whether individual remainder trust and pooled fund gifts qualify as tax deductible. Any donor who uses the forms, however, must realize that they do not contain all the available options for lifetime or testamentary gifts through either a remainder trust or a pooled fund. In addition, the forms necessarily do not address state law issues. The remainder-trust forms also do not require the trust remainderman to be a 50-percent charity, so without adding that provision, the donor will be eligible for only the lower 30/20 percent annual deduction limits, even if the named remainderman is a 50-percent charity.

At the same time the IRS published its sample forms, it announced that it generally will not issue individual rulings on requests related to those gift vehicles. It still will rule on most other issues affecting charitable gifts and exempt organizations, but the individual or entity requesting the ruling must pay user fees, which generally are between $100 and $1,775, and sometimes can exceed $3,000. When a ruling is necessary, therefore, the IRS fees and associated legal and accounting expenses can dramatically increase the cost of a charitable gift.

Both the IRS and state regulatory agencies have sought to increase their charitable oversight activities, in response to allegations that donors, charities, and professional fund-raisers are abusing the system. In one recent revenue ruling, the IRS denied unitrust status to certain high-yielding, short-term trusts that have been marketed as vehicles for capital-gain tax avoidance. In another instance, an eastern state forbade charities to issue gift annuities to its residents without complying with its insurance laws, and ordered them to refund money and property previously received in gift annuity transactions. The IRS and state regulators also have worked on different aspects of the same situation, as when a state attorney general brought enforcement proceedings against a fund-raiser under the state's charitable solicitation statute, while the IRS was trying to revoke the charity's exemption because it alleged the charity had paid excessive compensation to the fund-raiser.

● **We Are Meeting the Enemy, and Sometimes They May Be Some of Us.**

Much of the impetus for increased state and federal regulation of fund-raising comes from a perception that some charities and professional fund-raisers are taking unfair advantage of the existing rules—that they are promoting charitable gifts as investments or get-rich-quick schemes. A few are. Others of us may appear to be, when we concentrate heavily on the tax or other financial benefits available from various gift vehicles. We understand that the primary motive for a charitable gift must be charity—a desire to support a worthy project or cause. We must be sure not to lose sight of that underlying principle in all the technicalities and complexities of a particular gift. And we must remind our colleagues and the public. If we fail to do so, and charitable giving suffers as a result, that will be the ultimate application of Murphy's Law.

 # PLANNED GIVING

Why Local-Church Endowment Programs Fail

JERALD JACKSON

What is a "successful" local-church endowment program? I believe such an endowment program is successful, if:

1. It provides continuing opportunities for individuals to fill a spiritual need to perpetuate their values beyond their own lifetime; and
2. It provides an increasing income stream for those ministries that are essential to the mission of the church. Spiritual fulfillment is the fundamental vocation of the Christian. Being in ministry is the fundamental reason for the church. Why, then, are not more local churches successful in the development of endowment programs that support these goals? In far too many churches, the initial dream fades, and the goals are never realized.

Structural Defects

Hindsight is always twenty-twenty, and it shouldn't be argued that if an endowment program fails, it was poorly planned. Nevertheless, we can identify instances when poor planning has led to failure, and we can avoid these particular problems.

Endowments that don't enhance the life of the congregation have little chance. If we block an expression of love in the very structure of the organization, we will find few interested in its success. The goal of an endowment fund should reflect the sense of mission of the local congregation.

If the Endowment Committee is focused on the wrong task, the endowment will not grow. My recommendation usually is to concentrate on promoting the endowment, farm out the management to professionals, and let the existing program and property agencies spend the money. The shortcoming of most promotional efforts is the failure to realize that promotion must be systematic and ongoing. The object of a promotional effort is simply to provide the environment in which the individual may consider a planned gift or bequest to the church, when other factors have provided the motivation.

Too deep a chasm between the organization of the local church and the Endowment Committee often creates distrust and resistance. Any effort to create endowments should be seen in the context of the living congregation. The endowment organization needs to be carefully harmonized with the existing church structure. When the organization of the endowment is so structured that it competes with the Finance Committee, the trustees, or any other existing entity, it already is doomed. From its inception, the endowment

138

program should be seen as an integral part of an overall fiscal and stewardship policy.

Lack of continuity in leadership destroys "corporate memory." In our effort to "democratize" the decision-making process in the local church, we have adopted leadership rotation policies which, in some cases, have led directly to the failure of endowment programs. Certainly, a three-year term is a minimum, with six or nine years not unreasonable.

Failure of Will and Imagination

Failure to account for the long-term nature of endowment building will hamper growth. The assumption that no budget is required for promotion is commonplace. Many churches that take the narrow view are unprepared for the fact that before an endowment can begin to produce money, it must first be raised. Provisions must be made for the publication and distribution of brochures and other preprinted planned-giving materials. While there usually are initial gifts to endowments, bequests and other planned gifts cannot be counted on to provide income for at least ten years.

"If we have written it down, we've finished the job." Many Endowment Fund documents are gathering dust in the local church archives. This points up the difference in talent and interest between those who create an endowment program and those who promote it. At some point, the personnel of the committee should include people with a flare for promotion.

Many are unwilling to devote the time required to make the program succeed. I often argue that an Endowment Committee should meet monthly. I discover that most meet quarterly, or even less frequently. I do not see how it is possible to deal with all the issues that concern any such committee, if it does not commit to spend a reasonable amount of time together. A committee will be motivated only so far as the members have been captivated by the goals of the program.

Playing fast and loose with the purpose of the endowment. As time goes on and leadership changes, it becomes easier to think of the endowment corpus as just another pot of money. New leadership sometimes justifies invading the corpus by saying, "Well, *we* didn't make the decision not to spend it. Things are different now." Too often the moral issue of using money for something other than the purpose for which it was raised is ignored. In my forty years in ministry, the one thing that has not changed is the temptation to plug the financial dike with whatever is at hand, however inappropriate. It may be important to have spelled out the conditions under which the use of principal is permitted, such as that stated in the sample document in the Planned Giving Handbook prepared by the National Association of United Methodist Foundations. This includes the wording: "Any part of the principal may be withdrawn only in extreme and overwhelming circumstances, bordering on the survival of the (Name) United Methodist Church itself."

The Importance of a Proper Theological Basis

In basing our stewardship on theological principles, we should acknowledge two important presuppositions: People have a spiritual need to give in response to the redeeming grace of God, and the church has the duty to provide people with the opportunity to give, as it calls upon us to support its mission.

We have long understood this in relation to the support of the day-to-day operations of the church and its capital needs, and we have tailored our stewardship programs toward the "ready cash" of our members. Only recently have we begun offering our people the opportunities inherent in the stewardship of accumulated resources. It is in relation to accumulated resources that the importance of the local-church endowment program becomes evident. I am reminded again and again of the missed opportunities because a church simply was not prepared to handle permanent funds, or handled them badly—and potential donors know it! Far too often, bequests simply disappear in the black hole of "emergency repairs" or the like, to the alarm of many potential donors.

The effort to create endowment ministries through planned-giving programs will not succeed in each and every situation. But enough of them do succeed, and they are making such a fundamental difference in the lives of individual Christians and congregations that the effort is well worth our time and energy.

 PLANNING TOOL

Planned Giving One Liners

RENARD KOLASA

1. Retirement funds present new opportunities for giving to the church. You may want to name the church as the beneficiary of your individual retirement account or other retirement funds, in the event that you or other family members die before receiving all the funds.

2. Real estate offers opportunities for giving to your church. Consider the gift of vacant land, condominium, commercial property, home, farm, or other types of real estate. You could be entitled to a Federal income-tax deduction for the fair market value of the property at the time the gift is made.

3. Consider making a gift of your personal residence or farm now, and continuing to live there until your death. An immediate income-tax deduction may be available for this arrangement. Maintenance costs also might be shared. At your death, the property would be available for church use.

4. Trusts allow you to make a gift to the church in the future. You may set up the trust now and keep the income for yourself or other beneficiaries as long as you choose, or for life. The church would receive the property after that. Current income-tax deductions can be available.

5. Charitable Remainder Trusts or Charitable Lead Trusts allow you to make a gift to charity of income or principal, while keeping one or the other for yourself or other beneficiaries. We urge you to investigate these possibilities with your tax advisor.

6. Memorial gifts meet two important needs. They allow you to express your feelings at the loss of a loved one or friend. In addition, the gift to the church helps support its ministry. Appropriate cards are sent to the bereaved family, indicating the fact that your memorial gift was made (but not the amount).

7. Our pastor enthusiastically supports the church's planned-giving program. If you are interested in making any special gifts to the church, feel free to discuss this with our pastor. The pastor will help put you in touch with appropriate advisors.

8. Have you received an inheritance? If so, consider gifting part of the inheritance to the church, in memory of the loved one who remembered you. You can make this gift now or in your estate plan.

9. Consider making an endowment gift to the church for a scholarship fund or other memorial, in the name of your family. In this manner, your family name can live on forever. Feel free to discuss with the pastor any special programs or projects you would like to support.

10. Consider giving the use of your property to your heirs for the duration of their life, but after their death, having the property pass to the church as a memorial. Your surviving beneficiaries will have the use of the property for their lifetime. The property will help support the ministry of the church after their death.

11. Did you know that the state has made a Will for you, if you have none? These laws might not leave your property to the people you wish. They definitely don't leave any property to the church or any other charity. Shouldn't you prepare a Will or Living Trust?

12. How long has it been since you updated your Will? Does it carry out your wishes? Does it leave any gift to the church to carry on its ministry after your death?

13. You can share your faith beyond your lifetime by signing your estate-planning documents now. You will have the joy of knowing that whatever you do not use in this life will continue in ministry after your death.

14. When you make your estate-planning documents, consider naming the church as your final beneficiary.

15. There are many reasons to update your estate-planning documents. One is to include a gift to your church.

16. Have circumstances changed since you last updated your estate plan? Do your current estate-planning documents carry out your commitments to your church? If not, amend your documents now.

17. Did you know that an estimated 70 percent of all people who die do not have a Will or Living Trust? Without proper estate planning, no charity can receive gifts from your estate. Be sure your estate planning is up to date. Do you know who your heirs will be? Is your church a beneficiary of your estate?

18. Proper estate planning can reduce administrative time, expense, and inconvenience. Document your estate planning properly. Consider giving the church the administrative costs you could save.

19. Remember your church in your Will and Living Trust.

20. Who needs estate planning? Every adult who is legally competent, owns anything, and cares about who receives it at the time of their disability or death. In addition, estate planning is necessary for anyone who wants to leave a bequest for the church.

21. Have you moved to another state since signing your estate-planning documents? If so, consider having the documents checked by an attorney in the new state. In addition, consider naming the church as a beneficiary.

22. Your Will is the proper place to name the guardians for your children. Pick your guardians yourself, rather than leaving this decision to the probate courts. In addition, consider naming your church as a beneficiary.

23. Who will receive your property if you and your immediate family are deceased? Consider naming the church as the final beneficiary in your estate plan.

24. Good stewardship requires us to think of the future. Have your estate plan prepared now and include a gift to your church.

25. It requires proper planning to avoid probate and minimize estate taxes at death. When you are doing this planning, consider making a gift to your church.

26. The gifts you make in your estate plan can carry on your charitable support after your death. Consider making a gift to the church in your estate plan.

27. Don't wait to have your estate plan prepared. None of us knows when our life will end. Prepare your estate plan now, and remember that a gift to your church will help others even after your death.

28. Be sure that your estate-planning documents are properly prepared. A homemade Will can result in unnecessary expense and delay. When your documents are prepared, consider naming your church as a beneficiary.

29. A gift to the church is a testimony to your faith and the confidence you have in the ministry of the church.

30. Did you know that owning all your assets jointly may result in paying Federal estate taxes that might be avoided through proper estate planning? Ask your tax advisor, and have your advisor add the church to your estate plans as a beneficiary.

31. The costs of having your estate plan prepared can be a terrific bargain. You may save many times the cost in taxes and administrative expenses to your heirs. Estate planning also can make it possible for you to make a gift to your church.

32. Did you know that you can name the church a beneficiary of your estate in several ways? Consider gifting the church a specific amount, a percentage of your estate, the remainder of the estate after other gifts are made, or gifts whose beneficiaries predecease you.

✏ PLANNING TOOL

"Suggestions Upon My Death": A Final Gift of Love

DONNER B. ATWOOD

My wife, Anne, was driving me home from Cape Cod Hospital, where I had spent the last several anxious days. "If you hadn't survived this heart episode," she said, "I wouldn't know where in the world to start in making your final arrangements." Before I could respond, she added, "I wish you'd make a list of the steps I should take."

Her remark set me thinking. For over forty years as a pastor, I had often sat with families when a loved one had died, helping them through the emotional chaos of making arrangements for a funeral and for the days and weeks afterwards I had witnessed the mental and emotional paralysis of otherwise stable people whose spouse, child, or parent had just expired. Many had not the foggiest notion of what to do, whom to call, how to make appropriate arrangements for a funeral, or the legal and financial aspects of living without their mate. They had no idea of the complexity of questions which an undertaker or lawyer would pose in his or her quest to be helpful to the family.

Suddenly I realized that I had failed to do this for Anne, whom I love. Like the lawyer who is too busy

"Ms. Johnson, I've decided to make a large donation to my favorite charity. Please find out which one that is, and get back to me!"

to make a will, the physician who is too pressed to care for a sick loved one, or the plumber who doesn't have time to repair his kitchen faucet, I had failed as a pastor to execute that final gift of love for my wife and our children.

Anne and I had each prepared a Living Will years ago. Because such instruments are not recognized in Massachusetts, we sought legal counsel to draw up an appropriate Health Care Proxy in its place. The purpose: to designate in advance who is to make vital decisions about our medical treatment when we can no longer responsibly make those decisions ourselves. While a Living Will or the Health Care Proxy designates who will make crucial decisions for us while we are still alive, there is a need for an additional document.

"Suggestions Upon My Death" is a final gift which sets forth what we would like our family to do when we die.

Is it morbid to do this? Absolutely not! For the Christian it is a gift of life and hope in the face of death and termination, as well as in transition. It is an expression of one's spiritual faith, for death is as much a part of life as birth (1 Corinthians 15; John 14; John 5:23, 24). Having practiced that with other families, at my wife's request I immediately set about to prepare my own document for her and our children to use at the time of my death. What does it include?

First, since I do not know the circumstances of my death, I felt it would be wrong to impose on my family rigid, unbreakable guidelines that might be inappropriate at the time of my demise. Therefore I began my document with this initial statement: "While these suggestions are offered, Anne and our children shall have full freedom to alter, amend, or reject any and all of them in accord with their own judgments, desires, feelings, and circumstances at the time." This simple preamble frees them from any sense of guilt should they have to act contrary to my current desires. They are expressions on my part, but they remain guidelines.

Second, I have included some basic information. This information includes my full name, resident address, Social Security number, birth date, and place of birth, along with the names and addresses of my family and siblings. My wife's given, maiden, and married names are set forth. My parents' names and birth places, even though deceased, are listed; these are sought by the state's Department of Vital Statistics.

I have made a duplicate copy of these basic facts for my family to hand-deliver to the undertaker. A second sheet for them to give the undertaker includes additional information for the newspaper obituary, including the names of local and distant papers in which the obituary might appear. This document lists academic and employment history, significant positions held, honors received, religious and civic organizations of which I have been a member, and any unique public services which I have rendered. A suggested format for the gathering of such data may be secured from any undertaker.

Men and women who have been honorably discharged from military service should also indicate on this second document the location of honorable discharge papers, with serial number and rank. As a veteran you have the privilege of being buried in a national cemetery. The federal government provides not only a free grave site, but an external casket liner, a clergy person if desired, a grave marker, and an adjacent grave for your spouse. If you wish, an American flag will also be provided to cover your casket and/or be presented to your family on behalf of a grateful nation for your military service. The undertaker will secure these for you and your family.

A *third section* of my document deals with elements of the burial itself. I have indicated where our cemetery deed is to be found. Experience has taught me that many families know there is an old family plot, but have no idea who has the deed which authorizes it to be opened. The undertaker will temporarily need the deed in order for cemetery personnel to open the grave. If you do not have a family plot, you may search out your own or enlist the help of a mortician who will offer cemetery options for you to investigate.

My preference for cremation has been stated in the paper, too. My wife and I have discussed how we wish our bodies to be disposed of, and this is our choice. In drafting your own document, you should indicate your preference for traditional burial or cremation. If you choose the latter, designate in writing whether you wish your own mortician or a cremation specialist to handle this. There may be a significant difference in the cost and type of services offered.

Since I have chosen cremation, I have also indicated how the disposal of my ashes shall be handled. Normally they may be delivered to your family in a small cardboard box by the undertaker, by mail, or by one of the commercial delivery services. You may wish to have the ashes placed in an urn provided by the mortician or in a columbarium. Are they to be buried in a family plot, scattered on a favorite mountainside, deposited in your garden, or disposed of at another place of your choice? Your decision as to disposal must meet local health codes.

In this same section I have expressed my wish that in lieu of flowers any memorial tributes be sent to one of my favorite charities. To provide guidance to my friends, I have designated two charities, stating the name and address for each. I have also put into writing my wish that Anne and the children might hold—with a small group of immediate family and close friends—a private service in advance of the public one, with an open casket if Anne chooses, for a final personal closure. I have requested no public viewing, and that any public celebration be a memorial service, without the casket present. In addition, I have selected not only the clergy to conduct the religious service, but also the hymns and Scripture readings.

The fourth component of my list of suggestions offers factual data about financial and legal issues. I have indicated the location of the key to our safe deposit box, where the box is located, and who has signed permission to enter it. With this is a sheet listing the contents of the box. (An annual update is necessary.)

I have also indicated the name of our family lawyer, together with his address and telephone num-

> "We are temporary stewards with an obligation to manage the inheritance in such a way that it can be passed along even better and stronger than it was when we received it."
>
> —ROBERT L. PAYTON
> (1926–)

ber. He will help with the settlement of my will and other legal issues. On this sheet are also the names, addresses, and telephone numbers of our accountant and of the financial advisor whom I trust to guide my family in the adjustment period.

This section also has a list of my financial assets and where they are located, including a listing of my insurance policies by company and policy numbers, and a similar listing of properties. I have learned it is crucial that a notation be made of where such papers are kept and who has legal access to them.

Fortunately my pension plan makes provision for income to my wife upon my death, so I have listed the name and address of the office she should immediately contact to verify her continued income from the pension agency.

Since we have lived in four communities during our forty years of ministry, I have set forth the main contact person in each location whom I would want to know of my death when it occurs. I have also suggested that Anne review our annual greeting card list for the names of a few others she may wish to notify.

Finally, I have put into writing what all of us should consider: donating organs to medical agencies to give life to those whose organs are defective. I discovered that one may obtain information and addresses of reputable medical facilities and personnel to help in such matters from our family doctor, library, hospital, or mortician.

I have often seen grief engulf a family at the loss of a loved one. It is overwhelming and frequently paralyzing. Even when families have discussed the key issues, the strain is often such that the surviving spouse "draws a blank."

When my document "Suggestions Upon My Death" was finished, I felt relieved, as did Anne. Both of us sensed that the normal personal grief which will surround my death will have been somewhat eased. It is crucial that an annual update of the document be made, however. In recent years mine has been amended three times. When the most recent revision was completed, Anne and I went over it together, and then she filed it where she knew she could put her hands on it when she will need it. It will be my final gift of love.

PART FIVE

THE CHURCH, TAXES, AND UNCLE SAM

Introduction

THOMAS F. TAYLOR, EDITOR

Legal planning and prevention can save clergy, churches, and denominations tens of thousands, and sometimes even millions of dollars otherwise spent on fees for legal advice or a legal defense, court costs, penalties, and taxes. No minister can know all there is to know about the law as it relates to the church. However, all ministers should include as part of their education about church finance a sensitivity to new developments in the law that might affect them and their churches.

This chapter of *The Abingdon Guide to Funding Ministry* discusses recent developments and innovative ideas in the law that can affect churches and clergy. It does not discuss legal advice for particular legal problems. Only attorneys licensed to practice law in particular states can and should be called upon to offer such advice. Instead, the chapter discusses what ministers should know about certain areas of the law when planning church finances.

Outside of criminal and domestic relations, law is divided into two broad areas: (1) litigation, the process of lawsuits; and (2) transactional law, which usually involves tasks like drafting contracts or determining tax liability. *The Abingdon Guide to Funding Ministry* addresses how significant developments in each of these areas impacts clergy and churches. This edition discusses avoiding undue-influence claims in church fund-raising, redeveloping church-owned lands, and insights on developing a prison ministry in your church.

 LEGAL CLINIC

Giving Tithes and Offerings *Back?*

Undue Influence Claims in Church Fund-Raising

THOMAS F. TAYLOR

Do not take advantage of a widow or an orphan. If you do and they cry out to me, I will certainly hear their cry.　　　　　　　　　　　Exod. 22:22-23

Introduction

Undue influence claims are based on a legal theory designed to attack the validity of gifts from one party to another. These claims result from circumstances in which one person takes unfair and illegal advantage of another, thereby exploiting that person for illegal gain. Historically, most American undue influence lawsuits have involved the contesting of wills. However, courts have acknowledged that such lawsuits also are valid in the context of gifts given during a donor's lifetime.[1]

Undue influence lawsuits sometimes are filed against ministers when someone contests the circumstances under which the minister receives a gift, donation, or bequeath. If the complaining party is successful, the minister or church often is required to disgorge the donation. Probably the most stereotypical scenario regarding undue influence claims against clergy is the minister who gains the confidence of a dying, elderly person. Then when the aged victim no longer has all her sensibilities, he persuades her to bequeath her estate to him or to the church. Such acts are stereotypical of undue influence lawsuits against clergy, because lawsuits involving such facts have happened all too frequently.[2]

People place extraordinary confidence in ministers, especially at times of personal tragedy, stress, or weakness. Thus, ministers often have considerable influence over parishioners.

Because of the confidence that people place in ministers, when ministers or their churches are given gifts—especially large cash gifts—they may be accused of undue influence, if it appears that they obtained the gift by using their ministerial influence to gain an unfair advantage over the donor. The test is whether the minister overpowered the will of a giver through undue influence,[3] or the gift was obtained through improper means.[4]

Defenses

Numerous defenses are available to ministers who are accused of undue influence. Of course, this is not to encourage readers to use coercive or questionable tactics in church fund-raising. But it is to assure ministers who are wrongly accused of undue influence when fund-raising or soliciting gifts for the church, that they have an arsenal of defenses available to them in such cases.

"Now this $1-million contribution I made, was it a sincere gesture or just for tax purposes!"

First, ministers wrongly accused of undue influence may argue that no *indicia* (or factual indications) of undue influence existed, if such is the case. If there was no confidential relationship, if the donor was in a healthy state of mind and body, and if the gift was only a small portion of the donor's total wealth, these facts will go far in convincing a court that the gift in question was not obtained through undue influence. The essence of these defenses is that the gift was made knowingly and willingly, and thus was legally obtained.

Ministers also may argue that their fund-raising efforts are protected by the First Amendment. Where churches can meet the low threshold of demonstrating that they have solicited funds from their members based on a sincerely held religious belief, courts will be more reluctant to question their acts.

Where ministers are wrongly accused of undue influence, they may defend their position by arguing that the plaintiff failed to prove a causal link between the alleged acts of undue influence and the plaintiff's ultimate decision to contribute. This list is not exhaustive; other defenses also may exist.

Preventive Measures

The following preventive measures include many that also may be recommended to avoid legal claims for fraud. This is because fraud and undue influence are similar. Both often involve obtaining money through illegal gain. The main difference is that one committing fraud uses *deceit* as his chief tool, whereas a person engaging in undue influence takes unfair advantage over another's lesser or weakened physical, mental, or emotional condition. Ministers should consider the following issues when soliciting church funds, to avoid undue influence claims.

1. Does a confidential or fiduciary relationship exist? As noted, undue influence is any improper or wrongful persuasion whereby the will of a person is overpowered, and that person is induced to act in a way he or she would not, if left to decide freely. Courts will be more persuaded that undue influence occurred where gifts are disputed, if they find that certain factors, or *indicia,* existed in the circumstance surrounding the undue influence claim. One of the foremost factors is the existence of a "confidential relationship."

A confidential relationship can mean a *fiduciary relationship,* a legal relationship of trust, where one party is required to take special care to look out for the well-being of another. Also, a confidential relationship can be based upon informal relationships, where one person simply relies upon or trusts another.[5] It is generally easier to establish undue influence when a confidential relationship exists between parties, because one party has placed enormous trust in the other.[6]

If a confidential relationship exists between a minister and another party, wherein the minister has an advantageous position over that party in some way, there will be a heightened scrutiny of the acts of the minister. In all dealings where a minister is relating to a sick person, a child, an elderly person, an emotionally distraught person, or the like, the minister should act with circumspect care, disclosing all facts that the other party may want to know about a proposed gift or transaction.

2. Consider the health of parishioners. If a person's health in any way impinges upon their ability to understand a transaction or a gift, that transaction or gift may be more vulnerable to later attacks of claims of undue influence or breach of fiduciary duty.

3. Be attentive to the age of the persons with whom you deal. As in fraud cases, if the plaintiff is older and may lack the sensibilities or awareness of a younger person, or the plaintiff is particularly young and may be naive or unable to understand the gravity of a situation, a court is more likely to determine that undue influence could be the basis of a gift.

4. Don't accept gifts made under unusual circumstances. Gifts made to a minister or church under circumstances wherein the donor was particularly vulnerable to the suggestions of clergy—for example, by a person who is dying or very ill—are more susceptible to later claims of undue influence. Ministers should avoid soliciting gifts under such circumstances. If a parishioner asks that a minister be present while they are dying and wants to make a gift under such circumstances, the minister should be sure that others are present at such a meeting. Gifts that represent most or all of a donor's holdings will be more suspect of undue influence, than if they represent only a small portion of those holdings.

5. Encourage all parties to seek independent and disinterested advice. As with fraud, ministers who encourage the people with whom they deal to seek independent advice—from friends, family members, and attorneys—will help to dispel the appearance of unfair dealings.

6. Be sure that all parties exercise "free will." The essence of undue influence claims is that there was improper or wrongful persuasion, whereby the will of a person was overpowered and the person was induced to act or not act in a way that he or she would not have done, if left to act freely. For this reason, parties must be left to act freely and deliberately in choosing to enter into any business negotiations, transactions, contracts, gifts, or bequeaths. Any conduct used to overpower or unduly influence another may be viewed as undue influence, fraud, duress, or another related claim.

7. Create *indicia of honesty and care.* The above list of preventive considerations is not exhaustive. Church and religious workers can creatively consider other ways in which openness, honesty, free choice, and full disclosure from parties will regulate all transactions and occurrences in their church and ministry to avoid undue influence claims.

Consider, for instance, devising with staff and board members a list of *indicia of honesty.* A church may decide that all staff members who approach parishioners or other potential donors outside the church, agree in advance to divulge their intent to do so.

A church also can creatively devise *indicia of care,* to take added precautions when soliciting gifts or funds for ministry. For example, ministers who approach elderly parishioners for church gifts—especially if they are in nursing homes or seriously ailing—may decide, as a matter of church policy, to ask one of the parishioner's family members to be present when the minister

> "The purpose of life is not to be happy. The purpose of life is to matter, to be productive, to have it make some difference that you lived at all."
>
> —LEO ROSTEN

speaks to the potential donor. Or the church may decide never to accept gifts that represent more than a certain percentage of a parishioner's total assets.

Such considerations can be made part of the church's policy statement and will create a milieu of concern for the well-being of the church's parishioners, over and above the concern to raise money for the church.

Conclusion

Laws against undue influence are ancient. They are as morally based as they are legal. The Old and New Testament communities had numerous specific directives against undue influence, for specific contexts such as family law, real-estate dealings, commerce, employment law, and sexual conduct (see Exod. 22:21-23; Lev. 25:14; 25:17; Deut. 24:14; I Thess. 4:3-6).

First Peter 5:1-3 gives the following directive for church leaders:

> To the elders among you, I appeal as a fellow elder . . . .
> Be shepherds of God's flock that is under your care . . .
> as God wants you to be; not greedy for money, but
> eager to serve; not lording it over those entrusted to
> you, but being examples to the flock.

According to these verses, the essence of being a pastor is caring servanthood. The parishioners of any church should be able to presume that their pastor has their best interest at heart, when he or she asks them to contribute of their lives and finances to the church. Conversely, the essence of undue influence law is self-serving exploitation. Few legal claims could be more antithetical to true Christian ministry.

It would be naive to presume that churches can function without asking for commitments, financial and otherwise, from parishioners. Indeed, numerous biblical references demonstrate that it was common in the Old and New Testaments for church leaders to ask for time, money, effort, and other commitments from their parishioners.[7] In encouraging and asking members for such true commitment, ministers become obedient to the Scriptures. Both the moral and the legal principles, however, require that all be done, not for personal gain, but for the nurture and edification of the Body of Christ.

NOTES

1. *Roberts-Douglas v. Meares*, 624 A.2d 405 (D.C.App. 1992); *O'Hearn v. O'Hearn*, 97 N.E.2d 734 (1951).
2. In a case called *Dovydenas v. The Bible Speaks*, 869 F.2d 628 (1st Cir. 1980), such an action was brought against a minister for fraud. The judge, however, characterized the action as undue influence. The defrauded party in *Dovydenas* was a well-to-do woman, who had contributed over $6 million to the defendant church through three major gifts. The woman's family later caused her to recognize that she had been lied to and had been unduly influenced by the pastor. The pastor had led her to believe that by giving the money, she would influence events such as curing illnesses or cause the release of an imprisoned Romanian minister. The Romanian minister, although real, had already been released. The woman underwent counseling and deprogramming and sued to recover her gifts to the church based upon her claims of undue influence.

    As noted, the above case illustrates perhaps the most typical context for undue influence claims in ministry, namely gift giving to the church or minister. In particular, where a minister cajoles an elderly or sick person in a weakened mental and emotional state to give a large sum to the minister or church, a court may later void that gift because it was obtained inequitably, in circumstances where one person had unfair advantage over the other. The court in *Dovydenas* held in favor of the elderly woman, reasoning that she had been lied to and improperly influenced by the defendant pastor and church.
3. *Beyer v. LeFevre*, 186 U.S. 114, 22 S.Ct. 765, 46 L. Ed. 1080 (1902).
4. *In re Estate of Weir*, 475 F.2d 988 (1973).
5. See e.g., *Roberts-Douglas v. Meares*, 624 A.2d 405 (D.C.App. 1992); *First Christian Church v. McReynolds*, 241 P.2d 135 (1952).
6. *Dovydenas v. The Bible Speaks*, 869 F.2d 628 (1t Cir. 1980)
7. See, e.g., 2 Chron. 31:5-6; Luke 9:62; Rom. 12:1-2; Eph. 4:11-13; Heb. 10:25.

 **LEGAL CLINIC**

If You Build on Them, They Will Come:

Redeveloping Church-Owned Lands

J O H N   A .   S A P O R A ,   E S Q .

For you have been a refuge to the poor, a refuge to the needy in their distress, a shelter from the rainstorm and a shade from the heat. Isaiah 25:4

Introduction

Does your congregation own real estate accumulated through purchase or gift? Is it vacant or under-utilized? Many urban and suburban congregations do own such real estate. Often, these same congregations also are called to respond to the desperate need for affordable housing, but have yet to find a tangible way to make a difference.

These congregations might use their church-owned lands to develop affordable housing and rejuvenate neighborhoods. An Episcopal congregation in Jacksonville, Florida, has done just that. In the process, the church has found a new reason to remain downtown, to act as a catalyst for residential and commercial redevelopment and spiritual renewal.

The 1,200-member Saint John's Episcopal Cathedral has existed for more than 160 years in a downtown neighborhood called the Cathedral Area. The Cathedral Area is also home to several other churches, professional offices, and a supermarket. For decades, St. John's has owned almost 60 percent of a twelve-square-block area surrounding the church, some of which remained vacant land used for parking.

Thirty years ago, the Dean (senior minister) of St. John's resisted the Episcopal Bishop's desire to move St. John's to the booming suburbs. Instead, he felt called to maintain a downtown congregation sensitive to a diverse population and growing neighborhood ills. A few years later, St. John's built three high-rise senior-citizen residences and a nursing home, now

operated by a subsidiary nonprofit corporation. Since then, St. John's made several attempts to develop additional housing on their vacant land, but each attempt fell through due to the difficulty of coordination, the lack of political will in local government, or the perceived lack of interest in living downtown.

In February 1993, however, the new Dean of St. John's appointed a local attorney, a St. John's board member, to chair a new Citizens Committee charged with exploring ways to utilize St. John's land to create a viable downtown neighborhood in the Cathedral Area. The 17-member Committee was comprised of St. John's members, bankers, social-service providers and representatives of governmental agencies knowledgeable about the development process.

The initial task of the committee was to articulate a vision for land development. St. John's hope was to integrate modern design and financing concepts with its focus on housing development. Its vision was to complement its other downtown ministries of housing senior citizens, feeding the hungry, and helping establish the new homeless shelter. The committee then followed three steps to formulate a development proposal.

First, the committee determined what type of housing and neighborhood it wanted to develop. It decided to explore market-rate housing for moderate-income persons, defined as those earning between 80 and 120 percent of local median income. The housing would not be rent-subsidized, but geared toward people who worked full time, but had no down payment to purchase their own residence. The committee and the Dean of the Cathedral also assured neighborhood churches that any housing would coexist with the existing senior residences and social services in the Cathedral Area, to create a livelier, more diverse neighborhood. The com-

> "This may be the day God gives me a great opportunity to serve someone who needs help from me."
>
> *—BILL GROSZ*

149

mittee members agreed that if, at any point in their investigation a housing initiative no longer seemed viable, they would end their investigation.

The second step was critical. Government experts educated committee members on the development process and showed members how government funds could supplement St. John's project. A market study was done by a polling company, paid for by a grant from a local foundation interested in downtown housing. It concluded that a market did exist for downtown housing. This was true, despite no moderate-income housing in the area and the widespread perception that living downtown was unsafe or otherwise undesirable. This market study sparked interest from the local government redevelopment agency. It further fueled a response from private developers to the formal written "Request for Development Proposals" published jointly by the committee and the local redevelopment agency.

Finally, St. John's selected a nationally recognized housing development company and a local architect long interested in downtown rebirth. The developer then worked with the local redevelopment agency to present initial design drawings, a construction budget, and a financing package for Committee approval. The final development proposal had the following characteristics:

1. Renewed Neighborhood Infrastructure and 96 Initial Residential Units. The developer proposed rebuilding the neighborhood infrastructure, in order to draw the critical mass of residents needed for a viable neighborhood. The developer proposed rebuilding all utilities and landscaping the entire 12-square-block Cathedral area in the traditional southern style of Charleston, South Carolina. These infrastructure improvements would eventually support the construction of up to 500 residential units. The developer planned an initial phase of 96 units in condominium and townhouse buildings, on prime vacant land owned mostly by St. John's. The buildings would surround a small park and pool area.

2. An Affordable Lease-Purchase Program. The committee was attracted to the developer's unique lease-purchase housing program, in which persons who never dreamed of owning a residence could put $1,000 down, lease at a market rate for two years, then obtain

a mortgage to purchase their condominium unit. Closing costs, a five-percent mortgage down payment, operating expenses, and construction bond interest charges during the lease period would be funded *entirely* from lease payments! (The key to this program is to finance housing construction with low-interest, tax-exempt bonds issued by the local government, purchased by banks and repaid at the end of the lease period from the sale of units.)

3. Public-Private Financing Package. The committee was informed early in the process that conventional bank financing would not work in this situation, where no moderate-income housing existed, and costly infrastructure improvements were required. Thus, St. John's became a joint-venture partner with the developer and local redevelopment agency to finance and build the improvements. Each party offered something in the deal. St. John's offered its land to construct the 96 units at no initial cost, and would delay compensation for its land value until the developer, city, and all creditors were paid at the end of the two-year lease period. St. John's pledge of land thus helped finance the project and make the unit selling price affordable for more people. The city and its housing agencies were asked to provide a combination of grants, loans, and mortgage guarantees to build the neighborhood infrastructure improvements and issue the tax-exempt bonds to finance the housing construction. The developer covered most predevelopment planning expenses, and constructed and marketed the units.

4. St. John's Protected by Pre-sales Requirement. To attract bank and government financing and to protect St. John's land investment, the developer planned to lease or sell at least half of the 96 housing units before breaking ground on the infrastructure improvements or housing units.

Carrying Out a Redevelopment Ministry

Equipped with a vision for ministry and an unshakable commitment to overcome obstacles, St. John's established a partnership with local government and private businesses to build affordable housing. In the process, St. John's became a catalyst for downtown

> "God likes help when helping people."
> —IRISH PROVERB

redevelopment and provided a tangible and needed ministry.

St. John's story serves as a model for the way congregations can tap their vacant or underutilized land to foster hope and human dignity through housing. Although St. John's focused on moderate income housing, other obvious housing needs exist. The elderly, abused women and children, orphans, families visiting hospitalized children, and people of all ages who are homeless, mentally ill, addicted to drugs or alcohol, or afflicted with HIV/AIDS—all need adequate housing in a caring community. The type of housing and land development is limited only by the imagination of the congregation seeking to serve its community in God's name.

> "What we do during our working hours determines what we have; what we do in our leisure hours determines who we are."
>
> —ABIGAIL VAN BUREN (1918–)

If your congregation owns land and is called to a housing or downtown redevelopment ministry, you should take the following steps:

1. Inventory church-owned lands and obtain an appraisal of value and potential uses.
2. Decide whether your congregation is called to use its land, and formulate a specific vision for housing ministry.
3. Consult with congregation members experienced in real estate, such as brokers, appraisers, developers, or real estate attorneys, and enlist their assistance in further investigation (you may want to form an initial development committee for this task).
4. With a vision for ministry and a small cadre of people willing to investigate, consult the local governmental agency charged with promoting neighborhood or downtown redevelopment to learn how your congregation's land could be used.
5. Establish a diverse committee of persons experienced in development matters and housing ministries. Attempt to include people whose approval and funding decisions will later be required to obtain financing and break ground.

Although complex and time consuming, the ministry of housing and redevelopment is Bible-based, rewarding, and one of the most tangible ministries in which congregations can engage. The key to success is for the congregation to prayerfully integrate a ministry-based vision for housing with the design boards, financing concepts, and political approvals of the development process. With a housing vision responsive to community needs and oriented toward creating places where people can live and serve one another in peace, a congregation can go a long way toward breathing new life into city neighborhoods and witnessing to the incarnate power of God.

 LEGAL CLINIC

Go Directly to Jail: Developing a Prison Ministry at Your Church

FRANK D. MYLAR, JR.

"I was in prison and you visited me." Matt. 25:36

Introduction

You receive a call at 2:30 A.M. from a distressed parishioner, pleading with you to visit her seventeen-year-old son, who was just arrested on drug- and gang-related charges. After rushing off to the local county jail to see the teenager, you are confronted by the jail security officer, who refuses to verify whether the boy is even at the facility. After discussing the matter further, you finally agree to heed the guard's advice and return to the prison during normal visiting hours. When you return the next morning, however, you are told you must submit to a strip-search of your person before visiting this inmate.

Although this may sound like a Kafaesque experience in a totalitarian country, such experiences are not out of the question in America. Moreover, such actions by correctional officers may be perfectly legal in many jurisdictions. This article explains the legal rights of those who want to develop a prison ministry and the rights of the inmates visited.

Prison Limits of Religious Freedom

Although a prison or jail inmate has a general right under the First Amendment of the U. S. Constitution to practice his or her religion, this right may be limited, based upon the safety, security, and management concerns of a penal institution. Under the 1993 Congressional enactment of the Religious Freedom Restoration Act (RFRA), corrections officials must articulate a compelling state interest for a particular policy and show that the restriction on the inmate's religion is the least restrictive means of accomplishing a prison's objectives. Essentially, this means the restriction must be a logical way of furthering a necessary prison objective and not burdening the inmate's religious freedom more than is absolutely necessary. Based upon this legal standard, dangerous maximum-security inmates normally may be prevented from attending group religious services or possessing crosses or other religious objects made of anything more durable than cardboard. A limited amount of religious literature, on the other hand, may generally be possessed by all inmates. Some less secure institutions often allow inmates to have small metal crosses and a small personal library of religious books.

The right of a visitor to see an inmate stems from the inmate's right to exercise his or her religion, not the right of a minister or church volunteer to visit the facility. It is therefore crucial that the inmate wants a visit from the religious leader. In many jails and prisons, ministers must be placed on an inmate's list of approved visitors, or must obtain status as religious volunteers at the correctional facility. As a general rule, visiting is more restrictive at a state prison, where the most dangerous felons are incarcerated for long periods of time, as compared to county jails, which normally house pre-trial inmates or persons convicted of less serious crimes (i.e., misdemeanors). However, even the most dangerous terrorist cannot be indefinitely and totally denied religious materials or visits from ministers. Indeed, the majority of prisons and jail officials welcome religious visitors because they have a positive effect upon inmates. Prison ministers, thus, should not assume that they are being harassed merely because visiting conditions are highly restrictive.

Visitation Recommendations

Whether visiting a maximum-security prison or a minimum-security jail, the following tips will make most pastoral visits more positive experiences.

1. Telephone the correctional facility to arrange pastoral visits. Such calls will avoid unnecessary delays in visitation caused by conflicting meal times, cell searches, or inmate counts. Such calls also provide opportunities to ask questions about the specific visiting procedures and hours. Many prisons require a background check of visitors by the state criminal identification bureau. Such a requirement is constitutional when it applies uniformly to all visitors. However, even the most stringent requirements can generally be waived by wardens or jail commanders, if they can be convinced that visitors are not a security risk, that a situation is urgent, or that a request will not unreasonably inconvenience corrections personnel.

> "Of all the things you do, probably no one of them or all combined are as important as your personal influence."
>
> *WALTER F. MacPEEK*

2. Bring an official picture identification such as a driver's license. Visitors may be asked to leave their licenses with the visiting officer during the duration of the visit.

3. Advise the visiting-room officer that you are a religious visitor. In some institutions, visitors may have greater privileges if they are there for religious purposes. Be prepared to show the officers a church business card or some other church identification.

4. If at all possible, try to keep visits within the required visiting hours. For longer visits, one should obtain prior authorization from a warden or jail commander. Arriving even one minute after posted and assigned visiting times is generally legal cause for denying a visit.

5. Do not bring weapons into the prison. "Preposterous!" you say. "Why would any minister have a weapon in a prison?" While most ministers would presume that many states make it a criminal violation to bring a nonauthorized weapon upon prison land, many would not guess that seemingly innocent items like a letter opener, comb, or ball-point pen can be considered weapons, and thus illegal prison contraband. Personal items—such as a Bible or brief case—will normally be inspected for any such contraband. So prepare to check all such items at the prison gate. Personal property is typically returned when one leaves the facility. Under no circumstances should visitors attempt to circumvent the property policies by giving the inmate forbidden but seemingly innocent items. In one recent criminal death-penalty case, a defense attorney was threatened with sanctions by a judge for giving a maximum-security inmate a hamburger and a candy bar. Such food items, to prison officials, could be a conduit concealing a handcuff key or other contraband.

6. If pastoral visitors are asked to submit to a search of their person or property, they should have the opportunity to leave the facility, rather than submit to the search. However, a cursory search of personal items and your clothing can legally be expected. Such nonintrusive searches are generally constitutional when applied uniformly to all visitors. Correctional officials need "probable cause" in order to demand that any visitor submit to a thorough and intrusive body search. This is the same justification required when a police officer arrests a private citizen on the street. Because of the security requirements of correctional facilities, however, visitors' rights are more limited than those of private citizens visiting a place like the grocery store. Still, visitors possess more rights than the inmate they are attempting to see.

Conclusion

New Testament references to prisoners often show sympathy to those in detention.[1] Assisting prisoners is likened to assisting Jesus himself. Paul recognized the oppression of the entire prison system when he compassionately remained with a terrified and suicidal prison guard in Acts 16:16-33, after an earthquake had rumbled open the prison doors and set Paul and the other prisoners free.

Prisoners in our society represent those with some of the fewest rights and the lowest reputations. Yet we are not called to be respecters of persons, but to be servants to all. Christians who can should strive to make prisons more compassionate and merciful places for those housed there. In this way, we serve not only those in prison, but Christ as well.

NOTE

1. See, e.g., Matthew 25:31-46, where Jesus groups prisoners with the hungry, the thirsty, and the sick.

PLANNING TOOL

Tax Tips

Things Clergy Can Do to Reduce Taxes—Now

DONALD W. JOINER

1. Maximize the use of your housing allowance.

Total all expenditures used in or for the purpose of providing housing, furnished, for this year. If you anticipate going over your prearranged allowance, go back to your Board and negotiate an increase. If you anticipate not expending the full allowance, but plan on purchasing something next year, consider the purchase of that item in this year, and fully utilize your excludable allowance.

"Money should be used to make things happen, so you can enjoy seeing the results."

—JORGEN ROED (1936–   )

2. Save for Retirement

One of the best investments you can make today is in your Tax Deferred Annuity account. Figure your maximum contribution, and do everything in your power to pay that amount before December 31.

3. Save for Retirement 2

You also may qualify for an Individual Retirement Account (IRA) contribution. If you earn less than $50,000 (joint

153

return) or $35,000, you may make a contribution to an IRA. The more you earn, the less the deductible contribution you can make. But you still can make a full contribution of $2,000 or 100 percent of what you earn, although all of it may not be deductible. Remember that the gift of an IRA is in the tax-deferred growth of the account, not just in the deductible contribution.

4. Charitable Contributions

If you do not quite have enough deductions to itemize, consider doubling up on your charitable contributions. Give two years in one. That might allow you to itemize this year, and not next year. But in the year you do not itemize, the IRS will still give you a sizable standard deduction.

5. Medical Deduction

The same is true for your medical deduction. In the year you will itemize your deductions on Schedule A, take a look at your medical expenses for the year. If you can pay ahead for any expenses (especially dental or orthodontics for your family) you could benefit by deducting it on your taxes. Otherwise, most persons do not have enough to itemize their medical expenses.

6. Business Deductions

Check your business acquisition plans. If you plan on any major purchases in the next two years, purchase them now and benefit from the tax deduction this year. Remember, tax laws change. Never plan a deduction for the future. Do it now when it counts. Tomorrow's tax laws will be different!

7. Records

Records that substantiate your deductions are the key to tax savings. Without those records, and if you are ever audited, you have no basis for the deduction. Keep up-to-date and accurate records. When you wait to accumulate those records and receipts, you often miss many tax deductions in the rush.

 PLANNING TOOL

Financial Resolutions

DONALD W. JOINER

Each year as I do my taxes, I think I need to make some changes in my money habits. This year I am thinking of making some financial resolutions. Sometimes I wonder why I make resolutions—I keep some, and I miss some by a wide margin. I also know that if I didn't make any resolutions, I wouldn't get anything done.

So consider making some financial resolutions:

1. Get Out of Debt

The best action, and one of the best investments you can make this year is to reduce (eliminate) consumer debt. The only debt that makes sense is mortgage, investment, and business-related debt that is deductible. With lower than usual (meaning what we have come to expect) investment returns, paying almost any debt interest is excessive. If you cannot eliminate debt this year, resolve to cut it in half by year end.

2. Don't Use Credit Cards

There are only two times when using credit cards makes sense—when you have the money to pay off the debt when it comes due (therefore no interest charge); and in an emergency (then make changes in your spending to pay it off in no longer than three months).

3. Tithe

If you cannot tithe this year, increase giving by 1 percent. It is a great investment, and the return is exciting.

4. Save/Invest

Set aside money from your earnings to save at least 10 percent of your income by year end.

5. Increase Pension Contributions

Any retirement contribution, especially a tax-deferred contribution, is a good investment in today's low-investment return, high-tax environment.

> "O give thanks unto the Lord; for he is good: for his mercy endureth forever."
> —*PSALM 136:1*

6. Get Healthy

Resolve that your financial health will be better at the end of the year than it is now.

7. Pay Less Income Tax (in spite of tax increases)
- Keep better tax records.
- Keep a daily record of business mileage.
- Keep a record of supplies, meals, and other expenses.
- Fully use the housing allowance exclusion.

8. Pay Estimated Tax on Time

Besides a penalty for not paying it, it is easier to pay it in installments than to find a large amount to pay all your taxes at one time.

9. Save on Automobile

If you are planning to purchase a new vehicle this year, keep it one year longer, pay yourself what you would have paid on monthly payments, and make a larger down payment next year.

LEGAL CLINIC

Taxing Church Property: An Imminent Possibility?

JEFFREY WARREN SCOTT

In 1977, the chief counsel of the Baptist Joint Committee on Public Affairs, the late John Baker, warned of a coming crisis for the church over the issue of property taxation. Because a growing population was placing increasing demands on the government for public services, Baker was convinced that government would begin to look for additional sources of revenue and that church property would be a prime target for taxation.

What was clear to Baker in 1977 is even more obvious now. Government obligations and deficits have continued to escalate, pushing the federal debt ceiling higher and higher. The Reagan administration responded to the crisis by trying to shift many social programs down to the state level. The result has been—and will continue to be—an enormous burden on the states' already strained budgets.

The potential impact of this shift on churches becomes apparent when one realizes that the average local government receives 64 percent of its general revenue from property taxes, and churches own a vast amount of untaxed property. In 1976, one study estimated that church property was worth at least $118 billion (see Martin A. Larson and C. Stanley Lowell, *Praise the Lord for Tax Exemption* [New York: Robert B. Luce, 1969]). In

times of budget difficulty, it is only natural that churches will be considered for taxation.

To be sure, state and local government budgets have been strained before with little threat to churches' tax-exempt status. This time, however, courts have made it possible to remove the property-tax exemption currently enjoyed by the churches. To understand the courts' dramatic shift, it is necessary to understand the history of the exemption.

The notion of tax exemption for church property is an old one. Genesis 47:26 records Pharaoh exempting the priests' land from taxation, and Ezra 7:24 indicates that none of the priests, Levites, singers, porters, or ministers of the house of God was to be charged tax, toll, or custom. In the days of Roman Emperor Constantine, church buildings and the land surrounding them were exempt. Centuries later, European countries continued the tradition of exemption, albeit because the church frequently controlled the state.

In the U.S., property tax exemption for churches began in colonial days and continued with the birth of the new nation. In 1802, for instance, the Seventh Congress specifically exempted religious bodies from real-estate taxes. On the state level, specific exemptions from property taxes for churches were established in

> "Societies are renewed . . . by people who believe in something, care about something, and stand for something."
>
> —*JOHN W. GARDNER*

155

Virginia in 1777, in New York in 1799, and in the city of Washington in 1802.

"The exemptions [for churches] have continued uninterrupted to the present day," Justice William J. Brennan has said. "They are in force in all 50 states" (quoted by Leo Pfeffer in "The Special Constitutional Status of Religion," *Taxation and the Free Exercise of Religion,* edited by John Baker [Baptist Joint Committee on Public Affairs, 1978], p. 711).

Despite this long and unbroken history of property-tax exemption for churches in this country, courts recently have paved the way for the destruction of this privilege by setting precedents that easily can be used to end all church property-tax exemption.

The Supreme Court's shift away from the time-honored position of tax exemption first became apparent in 1970, when the court handed down its opinion in *Walz v. Tax Commission of the City of New York.* Walz had sued to enjoin the New York City Tax Commission from granting property-tax exemption to religious organizations for properties used solely for religious worship. He argued that the exemptions indirectly required him to make a contribution to religious bodies, and thereby violated the establishment clause of the First Amendment. In a close 5 to 4 decision, the court held that exempting church property was permissible, but not constitutionally required.

Many church groups filed *amicus curiae* briefs, urging that the court declare a constitutional requirement of property-tax exemption for churches. However, the court sidestepped this question, preferring to focus instead on the establishment clause. The court reasoned that property-tax exemption differed from a tax subsidy—which would not be permissible under the entanglement principle of the free-exercise clause—because: "the government does not transfer part of its revenue to churches but simply abstains from demanding that the church support the state. . . . There is no genuine nexus between tax exemption and establishment of religion."

Had the court ruled that the tax exemption was a subsidy, there is little doubt that the 5 to 4 decision would have been reversed and the exemption declared unconstitutional.

In 1972 the federal courts began making the same shift. In *Christian Echoes National Ministry, Inc. v. U.S.,* the Tenth Circuit Court addressed what the *Walz* decision had sidestepped, holding that "tax exemption is a privilege, a matter of grace rather than a right."

The major shift of the Supreme Court came in 1983 when, in *Regan v. Taxation with Representation,* the court held 8 to 3 that tax exemption was equivalent to a tax subsidy. The question before the court involved tax exemption for nonprofit organizations—religious, charitable, scientific, public-safety oriented, literary, or educational. Justice William H. Rehnquist spoke for the court: "Both tax exemptions and tax deductibility are a form of subsidy that is administered through the tax system. A tax exemption has much the same effect as a cash grant to the organization of the amount of tax it would have to pay on its income."

The significance of this decision often is overlooked. If tax exemption is a form of subsidy, then church property tax exemption is a clear violation of the establishment clause of the First Amendment. All that is necessary to make church property tax exemption a thing of the past is for an irate taxpayer who is tired of high taxes to file suit to force churches to pay their "fair share." With the *Regan v. Taxation* precedent in effect, the court could easily slip from the 5 to 4 *Walz v. Tax Commission* position and rule property tax exemption for religious institutions to be unconstitutional.

Another omen of the impending ill is found in the *Bob Jones University v. U.S.* decision, issued the day after *Regan v. Taxation.* In *Bob Jones,* the court declared that religious schools that are tax-exempt or that receive tax-deductible contributions must comply with government policy or lose their tax-deductible status. Bob Jones University had been following religiously motivated practices that had the effect of discriminating against blacks. The court upheld the decision of the Internal Revenue Service to withdraw the university's

"So then I said to the IRS agent, 'Receipts? What do you mean I need receipts for my charitable gifts?'"

right to receive tax-deductible contributions, because discrimination was contrary to public policy.

The danger of the *Bob Jones* decision is that if the university can be forced to comply with public policy in order to retain its tax status, then all other nonprofit institutions—with churches listed first in the tax regulation—can be forced to do likewise. The logical end of the *Bob Jones* decision would be to take away the tax-exempt status of churches that actively oppose U.S. military involvement in Central America, that speak out against current policy on nuclear weapons, or that provide sanctuary to aliens in violation of Immigration and Naturalization Service policy.

When *Regan v. Taxation* is linked with *Bob Jones,* the court's direction on the question of tax exemption for churches is clear: The foundation has been laid for taxing church property, and perhaps even church income.

As Justice Douglas pointed out in *Walz v. Tax Commission,* the long and unbroken history of tax exemption for religious organizations should not be taken lightly. Nor should the reason for not taxing churches be overlooked.

First, tax exemption for churches has helped a pluralistic society, in which a broad spectrum of religious perspectives—including irreligion—can flourish. Such pluralism safeguards against extremism and should be maintained.

Second, taxing church property and income would destroy the free exercise of religion that the Bill of Rights seeks to protect. The old principle that the power to destroy is still valid. In regard to taxing door-to-door religious solicitation, the court held in *Murdock v. Pennsylvania* in 1943: "The power to tax the exercise of a privilege is the power to control or suppress its enjoyment. . . . Those who can tax the exercise of this religious practice can make its exercise so costly as to deprive it of the resources necessary for its maintenance."

The power to tax religious institutions must be construed as the power to limit the free exercise of religion. Levying property taxes upon churches would have the effect of closing the doors of thousands of small congregations that operate on a shoestring. Many downtown churches would be forced out by the property taxes on their valuable land, and their buildings would be replaced by high-rise office complexes.

A third reason for not taxing church property is the excessive government entanglement that such taxation would bring. What agency would be responsible for assessing the value of the property, and how would the value be calculated? To what extent would the government require inspection of church property and, in the process, its records? These are but a few areas of church-state entanglement that would come with church property taxes. Of course, with government intervention comes government regulation, which could extend into many aspects of church life. Such entanglement must be viewed as unconstitutional.

As the budget deficits of the federal, state, and local governments increase, the possibility of taxing church property also rises—despite the long history of tax exemption. To help avert such an occurrence, religious groups must become alert to court actions on church-state issues, and they must become more vocal in asserting the constitutionality of church property tax exemption.

PART SIX

FAITHFUL LIVING PROCLAIMS THE JOY OF GIVING

Introduction

NORMA WIMBERLY

Someone has said that we can't think our way into right acting; we must act our way into right thinking. Another axiom is: Don't talk the talk if you can't walk the walk. Or, as Lee Domann reminded us in his song in the introduction to THE GUIDE, we may be "The Only Gospel Somebody Will Read."

This part of THE GUIDE provides insight and assistance for leading children, youth, and adults to continually connect their words and actions. Fred Leasure, Dan Dick, and Chris Stockwell-Goering describe specific models to be used at church and at home. Norma Koenig's article gently reminds us to remember and tell the stories—all the time, everywhere.

"Who Am I as a Steward, and How Am I Doing?" by Barbara DeGrote offers a delightful opportunity to check your own GQ—your giving quotient—based on biblical insight. Later, a small group study of Ephesians 1 and Genesis 1 deals specifically with how and why we give.

The Episcopal Statement on Stewardship closes this group of articles by reminding us that faithful stewardship, joyful giving, are our vocation. We are to become who God made—givers like himself.

 TEACHING HELP

Seeking a Faithful Response

Teaching Stewardship as a Way of Living

NORMA WIMBERLY

Theodore Horvath, a stewardship educator with the United Church of Christ, once wrote: "Stewardship deals with the why of our existence, our identity as to who we are, whose we are, and why on earth we are here—our calling as stewards in every area of our existence." Education about stewardship, then, has to do with identification, with motivation, with propulsion that moves us into action. It is not a program, but a practice.

You and I can be seekers. We can learn to live with the questions, rather than become obsessed with knowing the answers. As teachers, we can help others to realize or remember what they already may know.

Many of us need to let go of our preconceived notions of what stewardship is. How can we suspend our current and inherited reality and become teachable with those we are called to teach?

The story of Gideon could be our story. Judges, chapters six through eight, provides some remarkable images of responding to God in the midst of fear, doubt, and limited resources. The scenario of Gideon grinding grain in a winepress reminds us that often, we are doing necessary work while in hiding from very real or very imaginary adversaries. God calls us from that winepress. Grinding grain was important for Gideon, but God had other work for him. As teachers, we may have chosen to hide in the winepress, or we may have been placed there by others. However we got there, God is calling us to seek a fuller, more faithful response. The task may seem impossible. We may perceive inadequate resources, but God is in charge and will not fail us.

Some definitions of faithful stewardship that may nudge us out of the winepress are:

1. Living in the spirit of the Lord. (This was Pharoah's description of Joseph, one of the most effective stewards of Scripture.)
2. A spiritual understanding of the practical and economic aspects of all of life.
3. A model of faithful and creative living.
4. A way of being in the world as God's people.
5. Paying attention to God, to self, to others, and to all creation.
6. Answering the questions: Who am I? Whose am I? What on earth am I doing here?

Many of the issues, elements, and concepts of stewardship are visible in every day of living. Consider: the earth; food; hunger; nutrition; our bodies; gifts; talents; abilities; time; relationships; money; possessions; peace; justice; decision making; choices; hope; the gospel; responsibility; mission.

Teachers are everywhere, doing many things that teach a more faithful response to God. Look at your own life. Consider the stewardship and giving stories that are evident in the activities of your days.

The teacher, the parent, the pastor best teach by showing others a more faithful response to God. We can show an awareness of the issues, of the variety of responses, of responsibility, and of being a channel for God's resources. We can show affirmation of the various gifts each person has and nurture each person in order to better discover, develop, and use those gifts. We can show action. We don't just sit there. We do

> ## "Life is an attitude. Have a good one."
> —ERIC L. LUNDGAARD
> (1952–   )

something! We show that we, too, are seeking a faithful response to God's generosity.

Gather a group or team of others who want to seek a more faithful response to God. Design a teaching session or church event that will clearly highlight one or more of the issues of stewardship of daily living. How could your congregation deal with that issue from a perspective of stewardship and joyful generosity?

If you are designing a teaching session, you may want to consider this outline:

- Select an issue that will motivate your class or congregation.
  - Select one or more Scripture passages that illustrate that aspect of stewardship.
  - Collect a variety of stories in the life of the church, home, and community that illustrate the issue and the Scripture.
  - Invite the members to add their own stories and illustrations.
- Determine one way that you will try to live differently, because you are more aware of God's calling us "out of the winepress."

If you want to plan a larger church event, you could utilize a similar process on a broader scale. Include ways for all ages to become involved in the event, in the learning and in the doing. Your church's stewardship shows! Help the people of your congregation to see that. Individuals are teachers, models, and so are communities. Use the combined imaginations of the entire community of faith—as seekers and as teachers. All of us are answering the questions of who and whose we are, of what we are doing here. May God give us grace to answer them more faithfully.

Pontius' Puddle

 PLANNING TOOL

Stewardship: Promise and Responsibility

CHRIS GOERING

John H. Westerhoff III defined stewardship as "what we do after we say we believe." Taking this definition as a starting point, Christian stewardship education can reinforce, and be reinforced by, many elements of the church's ministry. Younger stewards—children and young people—should have encouragement and opportunity to learn and grow by:

A. experiencing and participating in worship;
B. sharing the good news;
C. being part of a Christian fellowship;
D. gaining knowledge about the faith; and
E. becoming advocates for and serving others.

Learning about covenant is essential in the teaching of Christian stewardship. Planting and nurturing an understanding of the promises God made in the covenant, as told in the story of Sarah and Abraham, can be very helpful. Too often we emphasize only the components of gift and responsibility, as in God's covenant with Moses. God's promise of "I SHALL" is swept aside to address our responsibility, "YOU SHALL." Cultivating the child's sense of joy, awe, and wonder, and affirming that we are not alone calls for planting the seeds of both the promissory and the responsibility dimensions of covenant.

The church can faithfully communicate both the promissory and gift-responsibility dimensions of covenant. Children can learn that they need not struggle alone. They can hear the promise and be open to change. They can live in covenant with others and with God.

To be effective at planting seeds and nurturing younger stewards, we need to be clear about:

● what Christian Stewardship is;
● who we are as stewards; and
● the importance of denominational identity for particular age groups.

Much stewardship education, some good and some not so good, takes place in a congregation and church school. An intentional program helps to identify issues and educate the congregation, as well as evaluate strengths and weaknesses.

Parents and church leaders have an important role in stewardship education. Church leaders and parents should work together and support one another in the process. Few parents will ever say they don't want their child taught about Christian stewardship.

Create a structure that is specific about Christian stewardship education of younger children, being sure to recognize and plan for differing abilities and interests. One possible approach is "Five LOVES," below.

FIVE LOVES

A. Love of GOD
   ◆ Relationships are witnessed through covenant stories: God is always there for me/us. We love God because we are first loved by God. God is the promise maker and the promise keeper.
   ◆ We can respond to God: we can share our gifts and possessions. We can say "Thank You" to God when we worship and at other times.

B. Love of SELF
   ◆ Celebrate uniqueness: "Who am I?"
   ◆ I can care for myself: I need to take good care of my body and feelings.
   ◆ I have been promised a lot by God. "What can I be?"

C. Love of OTHERS
   ◆ Sharing and giving of possessions is symbolic. The meaning of an item or act for the giver and the recipient determines its value. The financial value of a gift is not the ultimate value.
   ◆ Acts of mercy and kindness are needed. Children have special gifts to offer the world
   ◆ All people are valuable children of God.

D. Love of CHURCH
   ◆ I am named at home and at church by my baptism.

◆ I remember and am remembered at church. Children of God are blessed, and set apart.

E. Love of EARTH
◆ We are partners in God's creation. Be aware of the interconnectedness of creation.

STRATEGIES

Interweaving the "Five LOVES" and the five areas of ministry suggests these strategies:

WORSHIP

The offering is a vital part of congregational worship and church school.

◆ Church School Offering Envelopes. Design your own with No. 6 envelopes in five different colors, to be used in a regular cycle throughout the year. Choose five simple and easily illustrated uses of the offering, and print them on the envelope. Examples:

— "Today's Church School Offering helps us have a place to worship God." (Picture of the church)

— "Today's Church School Offering helps to feed hungry persons in (town)." (Picture of a loaf of bread and carton of milk)

— "Today's Church School Offering helps our church send missionaries to many countries." (Picture of a globe)

— "Today's Church School Offering helps us visit the sick and lonely." (Picture of hospital bed; single older person in rocking chair)

— "Today's Church School Offering helps us share the Good News." (Use several languages)

Envelopes are not numbered, and individual amounts are not recorded. They are distributed every five weeks in the same sequence.

◆ Offertory Pattern. Establish a regular pattern of receiving church school offerings (envelopes, foodstuffs).

FELLOWSHIP

Invite children to participate in the baptismal services of other children. Ask them to come forward so they can see what's happening. Have the children present a gift (made by them) to the newly baptized as a sign of including that person in the covenant community. Sing a welcome song. Help older children make a baptismal stole or garment.

SERVICE

Acts of mercy are often the easiest to do, but sometimes the most poorly explained.

◆ (Love of Others) Make cards for shut-ins and distribute them when visiting. Bake cookies for a shelter/soup kitchen and deliver them. Collect and deliver canned goods for a food pantry. The act of delivering, passing it on, is as significant as the act of creating or bringing. This makes concrete the connection between the gift in God's name and the mission of the people of God. Try doing these things year-round, not just on holidays. Remember that personal contact is the most valuable gift your students can give.

◆ (Love of Earth) Be involved in recycling and environmental projects. Clean up the classroom or churchyard; collect cans or newspaper as a way of conserving resources.

KNOWLEDGE (CLASS PROJECT)

◆ (Love of Church) Compile your own booklet. These can include mission moments, described by adults and illustrated by children. Use the "Five LOVES" plan to balance the examples.

◆ (Love of Others) A giving calendar can be a month-long activity of giving money to help others. It is helpful to do this in conjunction with a church-wide special offering. Create a calendar with an explanation of the purpose and where additional information can be found. The gift can be placed in a designated container each day. The calendar can include dates and gift information. Sample:

— May 1 — Give up one snack today. Donate $.05.

— May 2 — Give $.05 for each after-school activity you attended last week

May 3 — Give $.25 if you have never eaten spinach.

— Continue

Learning Christian stewardship as promise and responsibility can be filled with nurture, love, and hope. Have fun learning, or relearning, with the children you love!

TEACHING HELP

Story Time!
THE REVEREND NORMA E. KOENIG

Tell me a story!—that has been the cry of children from the beginning of time. Even in the most primitive cultures, and long before the advent of the written word, the storyteller was the respected one—the bearer of the great traditions from one generation to the next. It was the storyteller who preserved the ancient biblical heritage.

Children absorb the thoughts and feelings presented in a story at a deep inner level. Parents and teachers who turn over the task of storytelling to the television relinquish the opportunity to be the ones who set the mood, convey feelings, and build relationships. So let us become good storytellers. Let us share our thoughts and feelings, our hopes, and our faith with children through stories.

An adult need not be a master storyteller to do this. Any tired parent or grandparent can snuggle down with a child in a big chair and create a story out of the day's experiences, or out of wishes, hopes, and imagination. With the very young child, it can be a simple story:

The fairies came from the great big moon—
And brought you an apple to chew, chew!

That simple story thought is enough to open a whole world of imagination. Two- or three-year-old children cannot absorb a series of events because the cause/effect sequence has little meaning for them. But the happening of the moment is important. They feel their way into a story: the warm sun; picking the flowers; petting the puppy dog. So we build teaching stories for them around their daily experiences.

Two-year-old Christopher had trouble playing with his friend Amy. Amy wanted all the toys. Christopher wanted all the toys. At rest time, the teacher told them a story about Christopher's brand new stuffed elephant. And you know what! Christopher shared his elephant with Amy because it is more fun to ride on the elephant together. In the story, Amy also shares her crackers with Christopher. The teacher storyteller and the children jump up and down with joy. Everyone is happy! The story helps them feel their way into the joy of sharing, the joy of loving and being loved.

By the age of four, children can begin to grasp a sequence of events. They are beginning to ask the causal question: "Why?" and they want to know, "Then what happened?" Fives and sixes can recall a story and repeat the events in order. But they do not yet have a sense of history. History is simply something that happened before now. They will not have a sense of history until well into the junior years.

■ What Makes a Good Story?

Children in the early elementary years like stories about children their own age. They like to be able to identify with the characters. The world is often a scary place, and it's good to discover that other children have found solutions to problems like their own. These children also have a clear sense of the authority of adults, and they count on adults to keep their world in order. So they like stories about friendly adults who interact with children.

Children have active imaginations. They know a big world is out there, but since they have had so little experience in it, they sometimes fill that world with dangerous animals and monsters, with ghosts and other strange creatures. They like the scariness of meeting such creatures in their stories, especially if the story line is about a caretaking adult who makes things turn out all right.

These children like action and excitement in their stories. They like stories that present big problems and solve them. They lose interest if too much time is spent presenting setting and mood. These elements need to be tucked in as the story moves along.

■ What About Object Lessons?

Sometimes adult storytellers try to catch children's attention with an interesting object—a ball, a piece of clay, a rubber band. This technique can be a good entrance into a story, but sometimes the object so catches the attention that the children do not hear the story at all. An adult knows that candlelight represents a vision or a bit of wisdom, the light of the truth. A rubber band represents flexibility. A rainbow represents hope. But children cannot grasp these meanings. Dozens of studies have demonstrated that children cannot make the leap to abstract meaning until at least the age of ten or twelve. Objects can be used as reminders of story events, but they do not carry abstract meaning for children.

■ Give Them Heroes

Older children and youth like hero stories. They like stories about the past, when heroes walked the earth and did great deeds. They are beginning to know something about today's world and its problems, and they like hearing about people who have accomplished something to make the world a better place. Because they understand about time and distance, they respond eagerly to stories of need, whether far away or at home. They want to be active participants in the work the church is doing to help those in need.

■ Any Place, Any Time, Can Be Story Time

Stories are appropriate for any time or place where the church is gathered. Stewardship committees need to look for those special moments and be ready with stories. Special stewardship stories can be used in the church school or youth group, or they can be sent home to stimulate interest in special projects. Stories can be used in the Sunday morning worship service for people of all ages. Special stories can be prepared for camps and retreats, and for Lenten programs and resources.

■ Stewardship Stories in the Bible

In our efforts to teach good stewardship, we should also look to the Scriptures. The Bible has a wealth of stories that can be appropriately used or adapted for stewardship themes.

There is the classic story of Joseph and the storage of grain for the years of famine in Egypt. There is Elijah and the widow's cruse of oil, and Ruth gathering the sheaves of Boaz. There is that delightful story of Nehemiah's concern for the impoverished families who were working to rebuild Jerusalem's wall.

The New Testament is a rich resource: The parables of the talents, the widow's mite, Lazarus and the rich man, and many others. There are the incidents in Acts where the people in the early church shared their possessions, and where Paul collected an offering for the widows and orphans in Jerusalem.

■ A Story for Younger Children

"I learned a new prayer in church school," Mollie announced one morning, as she scrambled up to the breakfast table.

"That's wonderful," her mother responded. "Would you like to offer that prayer this morning for all of us?"

So they folded their hands, and Mollie prayed: "Thank you, God, for a good night's rest. You care for me, and you know what's best. Please keep me safe all through the day in all my work and all my play. Amen."

"That's a good prayer," Father said. "It's good to know that God will be with you and care for you all day long."

"Hustle along, now," said Mother, "or you'll be late for kindergarten."

So Mollie pulled on her coat, grabbed her school bag, and ran out the door. But Mother came running after her.

"Wait," she called. "Here are your crackers. You are the snack girl today, you know."

"I forgot," Mollie said, and gave her mother a hug.

Mollie had a wonderful day at school. She built a whole new block city with her friends, and the teacher read two of her favorite stories. Of course, on the playground, Mollie skinned her knee on the sliding board, but the nurse washed it and put on a Band Aid. At snack time, Mollie spilled her milk, but the teacher helped clean it up and gave her a fresh carton.

Mollie ran home from school to tell her mother all about it. She was in such a hurry that she stumbled on the curb, but the neighbor boy got off his bike and helped her pick up her papers.

Total Body Response

Your hands have lifted this to your eyes . . . your optic nerve is transforming these words into impulses . . . your brain is processing that energy into thought. All the parts of your body are working in harmony to do your will in reading this. If one part fails to respond, you may not be able to finish this message.

God tells us that Christ's Body, the church, must operate the same way. His will is accomplished through the harmonious response of each member to the task.

"Now you are the body of Christ, and each one of you is a part of it."

—I CORINTHIANS 12:27

That night at supper, Mollie was very thoughtful.

"I don't think I'll need my new prayer anymore," she told her family.

Everyone was surprised!

"Well, when I forgot my snack, Mother remembered. When I hurt my knee and spilled my milk, the nurse and the teacher took care of me; and when I fell down on the way home from school, Bobby Thompson helped me up. All day long, there were people around to help when I needed them. So I don't think I'll need God's help anymore."

"Oh, my!" Mollie's father responded. "I think you're a little bit mixed up. God loves and cares for us in many ways—wherever we go and whatever we do. But one of the most important ways God cares for us is through people—by helping people care for one another. Maybe you need to add one more line to your prayer. Maybe you need to ask God to let you be one of those helpers."

So the whole family folded their hands and prayed with Mollie:

> "Thank you, God for a good night's rest.
> You care for me, and know what's best.
> Please keep me safe all through the day
> In all my work and all my play . . ."

Then they added one more line:

> "And let me help someone for you today."
> (Based on a story line by Margaret Holmes)

■ A Story for Older Children

The Bible tells us about a young man who came to Jesus for advice about what he should do with his life. He had tried hard to obey God's commandments, and now he wanted to know what more God wanted him to do.

Jesus told him to give what he had to help the poor. Then the man turned away from Jesus sadly, because he had a lot of things, and he wanted to keep them.

We know how he felt, don't we!

* * * * *

Jimmy heard the shriek of the sirens and ran out to see where they were going. The fire engines stopped halfway down the block.

"Where's the fire?" he called to one of the neighbors.

Then he stood stock still. It was the Hendersons' house, and Teddy Henderson was his very best friend.

Jimmy stood beside his friend and watched while the firefighters worked with their ladders and hoses. But the fire was a bad one. Teddy lost all his clothes and all his books and toys in the fire.

The next day Jimmy helped his father pack a big box of food to take to Teddy's family. But Jimmy wanted to do more. He asked his father what he could do that would be special.

"Well," his father answered, "What do you think Teddy needs? What do you have that would make Teddy happy?"

"Trucks!" Jimmy answered. "That's it," he thought. "I'll give Teddy one of my trucks."

When he got home, he looked at his trucks and Transformers. He was not so sure he wanted to give them up. Then he found one with a broken headlight. It still made a pretty good truck. That was it! Teddy would be glad to have that one, if he didn't have any toys at all. Jimmy started downstairs. Then he stopped. His father's voice echoed in his mind: "What do you have that would make Teddy happy?"

Slowly Jimmy climbed the stairs again. He looked at all his trucks, and he found the one he liked the very best—the one Teddy most liked to play with when he visited. That was it! He knew he had found the right one. If Teddy would have only one truck, that was the one he should have!

Jimmy ran downstairs to tell his father!

$ MONEY TALK

Walk the Talk: Helping Young People Live the Joy of Giving

DAN R. DICK

There is a wonderful song, "Here on Earth," in the 1991 album of the Crash Test Dummies. The premise of the song is an unashamed resolve to live life to the fullest, taking advantage of every good thing that this world has to offer. There is a simple joy and a blessed hopefulness to the lyric of this song. The more I listen to it, the more I think it captures the idea that God originally had in mind—that we would receive the fullness of this life with gratitude and joy, and live each day to the very best of our ability. Not only will we take everything that life has to give, but we also will give all that we have to life. This concept of receiving and giving is at the heart of Christian stewardship.

Young people can benefit from hearing this message of receiving and giving. Culturally, children and young adults hear a "gospel of gimme," where the emphasis is placed fully upon what goodies we can acquire, accumulate, and amass. Television, the most influential persuader in our culture, does little to promote giving, but it does an incredible job of promoting consumption. In addition, television has helped to undermine basic appreciation for the goodies we do receive by emphasizing a need for more, for better, and for newer. No child can be content with this year's model when the bigger, better, faster, flashier model is coming soon. Columnist Leslie Savan has published a wonderful book called *The Sponsored Life,* which illuminates all the ways our values and desires have been shaped by television. Even people who don't watch television are none the less affected. In a nationwide test, Brassard-Bass marketing found that when shown a series of thirty pictures of past U.S. presidents, the average teenager can identify 7. When shown a series of thirty pictures of states, the average teenager can identify 18. When shown the logo of thirty prominent companies, the average teenager can identify 27. The only age group that can identify more of each category is 70 and over!

Even when a young person can escape the influence of television, the emphasis is on getting, rather than giving. In school, the stress is placed upon performance, and this performance is often measured against other students. Class rank, grading on a curve, no talking during assignments, honor roles and honor societies—all set students on a quest for more, for better, for personal gain. Even on occasions where schools offer opportunities for community service, mixed messages are sent. One elementary school collected blankets and food for the homeless. As an incentive, the class that contributed most in each category would receive a pizza party. The chance to give

and do for others became nothing more than a means to an end!

Where can young people learn the art and joy of unselfish giving in our world today? A generation ago, the answer was the church. The *Handbook of Christian Stewardship,* published in 1947, claimed that tithing was taught in over 75 percent of all mainline Christian churches to primary-school children.[1] A survey of churches in 1989 found that less than 3 percent of mainline churches teach tithing to elementary-age children.[2] In many areas, the Christian church has abdicated its responsibility to inform and educate young people into the ways of giving and faithful stewardship. The sad irony is that children and youth tend to be most willing to give and share, and it takes very little to inspire liberal giving.

As vital as it is to begin educating Christians in formation while they are children, it is imperative that we help turn learning into living with our youth. As teenagers begin to flex their wings and exercise their independence, as they begin to receive and generate more discretionary income (12–19-year-olds in the United States spent $93 billion of their own money in 1992[3]), there is no better time to offer opportunities to put faith into action. A common goal of today's youth is to make a difference in the world, and similarly, to have their life mean something. Young people are tired of sitting and talking about their faith. They want to shift focus from faith as a noun, to explore what it means to be faithful. Often, it takes nothing more than a single opportunity to give to turn them around. Three stories can illustrate.

Morgan Davey is a fourteen-year-old girl from Los Angeles, California. When she was seven, her house burned, and her family lost all its treasures. Morgan has grown up in fear of another fire. Not only does she fear the physical injury that could result; she also remembers the former trauma of losing everything that had been valuable to her.

Two years ago, as fires swept through Southern California, Morgan's church both took an offering for families who had been burned out, and formed rescue help teams to assist firefighters throughout the area. Morgan volunteered to help work to combat the fires.

> "The richest man in the world is the one to whom people owe the greatest number of debts of kindness."
>
> —UNKNOWN

A California Youth Brigade formed to assist the fire department in whatever ways it could. Literally hundreds of area youth took turns contributing to the effort. At her church, Morgan appealed to her congregation to support the fund for fire relief, to collect clothing and supplies, and to find places to stay for people who had been burned out of their homes. Morgan gave half of her savings and half of her college fund to help those in need. By her example and inspiration, the entire church rallied to offer assistance to twenty families. Morgan now travels to other churches to talk to youth groups about giving of their money and time, so they can make a difference when crises hit. She encourages each youth group to find something that is important to them, and then do something about it. Morgan attributes her commitment to her church, which included the youth group when it made its appeal for help. In her own words, "The church gave me the idea."

A New Jersey youth pastor has a vision that youth should be in mission. With just twelve young people, a shared vision began to be created. This group of a dozen teenagers wanted to do more than just "come to church." They wanted to be in ministry. Feeling underappreciated by the congregation, they decided that they would design their own ministry to area people in need. Since they didn't feel that the church had a place for them in its official structure, they created an unofficial structure. The young people affirmed a mission statement for themselves: "Our faith has meaning only so far as it extends beyond ourselves to touch the lives and needs of others; therefore, we commit our time, energy, and commitment to serving the needs of others in the name and service of Jesus Christ."

As discussion ensued, someone asked, "How are we going to pay for what we want to do?" By mutual agreement, the group determined that if the service was really important to them, they would have to pay their own way. A covenant was drawn up in which each member of the group committed to give a tithe of their income, to raise at least $500 each through fund-raisers, and to be actively involved in physical service during the year. By this simple agreement, a youth group of twelve members, with a single leader, put together a mission and service budget of $10,000. Another component of the covenant was that the older members would take responsibility for explaining the covenant to incoming younger members. No one was forced to take part, but for nine years, the covenant

has received 100 percent endorsement. Also in that nine-year span, on only one occasion has the group failed to raise at least $15,000.

> ## "Reputation is what men and women think of us. Character is what God and the angels know of us."
> —THOMAS PAINE (1737–1809)

Young people are often accused of not having their priorities straight. If that is true, then a youth fellowship in Alabama proved the exception to the rule. Harmony Hill Baptist Church youth fellowship was raising money to redo their newly acquired youth lounge (formerly a storage area). They wanted to paint, furnish, and decorate. They also had their sights set on a stereo system and a large-screen TV. They wanted to raise $7,500. Over a period of eighteen months, they were able to raise just over $5,000. Then the floods hit the Midwest. The church held a program on the floods, and Phoebe and Phil Barnes, twins, who were members of the youth group, attended. Moved by the call for help, they took the appeal to the youth group. The fellowship began raising money for flood relief. They held dinners, a talent show, a candy sale, a rocking-chair marathon. They baby-sat, mowed yards, and did cleaning jobs. They went door to door to collect cans and glass for recycling. In just over six weeks, they raised another $5,000. In a unanimous decision, the Harmony Hill youth fellowship voted to give the full $10,000 to flood relief. What makes this story all the more remarkable is that the church served mostly lower-income families. Most of the adults thought it was a miracle that the kids had raised so much for their youth lounge. It was even more amazing when they doubled it and gave it away!

We wait too long to begin teaching Christian charity! Adults are already claimed by the power of the culture. The demands on income are so great that giving seems beyond the reach of many. Young people haven't fallen into that trap yet.

One young woman said, "The reason I spend so much money on myself is that I don't have anything else to spend it on. I'm not trying to be selfish." Her words may be more representative than we realize. Children and youth are natural givers. They are also natural takers. The nature that will win out is up for grabs. Our culture does everything in its power to nurture the taker side. Our church needs to begin coaxing the giving side out into the open. We often wonder how we can begin to reeducate adults into the path of sacrificial giving. Perhaps the biblical reminder that "a little child [or young adult] will lead them" needs to be lifted up.

Churches that are intentional in their messages about giving can have the greatest impact. It would be wrong to say that churches have not taught children and youth anything about giving in the past few decades. We must question, however, what exactly has been taught. When churches take Sunday school offerings and throw them into the general fund of the church, they implicitly communicate that what the money is used for isn't as important as the act of giving. Young people see the world in concrete terms. They are taught by cause-and-effect realities. Children develop understanding through "if I do this, that will happen." It is important that our children and youth understand what happens to their offering after it leaves their hands. When Sunday school offerings are received in support of something concrete and meaningful, it helps them to understand that their giving makes a difference. This is a sound foundation upon which to build later concepts of joyful giving in response to the goodness of God.

Likewise, youth groups that are funded through uni-fied church budgets may come to think that the church provides a free ride, that it is there to serve personal needs, and there is no reason to give anything back. Youth leaders go to the "bargaining table" of many Administrative Boards to lobby for funds for youth ministry, when the more expedient path might be to inspire the kids to raise their own funds and make their own contributions. Most youth groups have a much healthier approach to budgeting than do the churches they are a part of. Youth tends to look first at what needs to get done, then they count the cost, assess their ability to cover the cost, and then they raise the funds to turn vision into reality. Young people tend to work very hard for what they believe in.

There are, in fact, many things the elder generations could learn from our children and youth. Inasmuch as our young people need to be taught the disciplines of giving, we all need to learn together the joyful spirit of giving. It is too easy to become inwardly focused. Until we toss away the institutional nets of talking around the tables, and get out into the world where the gospel needs to be seen and heard, things aren't likely to change. The key is to walk the talk; to put faith into action. Youth groups that are doers of the Word, and not hearers only, appear to have a life and vitality that most churches need to tap into.

> "When you know you're making someone happy by helping them out—that's what counts."
>
> —*PEARL KLING*

NOTES

1. Cleon Johnson, ed., *Handbook of Christian Stewardship* (New York: Newbury Press, 1947), p. 44.
2. "Survey of American Churches," *National Institute on Christian Education Summary Report* (Houston: National Institute on Christian Education, 1989), p. 3.
3. William Dunn, *The Baby Bust* (Ithaca, N.Y.: Demographics, 1993), p. 34.

$ MONEY TALK

What Have You Said to Your Kids About Money?

FREDERICK H. LEASURE

Many a frustrated parent has lamented that children simply do not understand the value of money. Whether it is a preschooler who wants a major item in a toy store, or the teenager who thinks a personal car should be provided, the problem is the same. We have taught our children far more by our example than we have by specific discussions on the topic of money. It should not be surprising that children who see us driving up to the automatic-teller machine and getting "free" money think that this commodity is in endless supply.

At an early age, a false equation is developed in children: "I love you, therefore I buy for you." Though this may have some basis in truth, the counterpart to the equation, "If I do not buy for you, I do not love you," is not true. In fact, I actually may be loving you more! When we consistently reward children with things, we develop an attitude of covetousness for which there may be no effective cure in adulthood.

Educating children about money begins about the same time they are introduced to television. It is at this point that you will be in direct competition with the fantasy world of advertising. Even young children understand how to make choices that have economic consequences. A beginning point may be to help children share in spending decisions.

Before entering the grocery store, agree on the number of boxes of cereal or snacks to be purchased. Accept whatever decision your child makes. A box of cereal that is far less tasty than the TV ads provides a good lesson. As children get older, try giving them an amount of money and letting them decide what to buy. Let them pay the clerk for their own items, so they can more fully understand the exchange process. Other helpful activities may include "playing store" some rainy afternoon, or using coins to play counting games.

Perhaps the most helpful way to teach concepts of money is with an allowance. As one who never received an allowance, it was difficult for me to understand how valuable this opportunity is as an educational experience. My parents felt that since no one "gave" you money in the real world, they should

> ## "Giving is an investment in pleasure."
> —*CECIL H. GREEN (1901–)*

not perpetuate this myth with an allowance. They were very generous, and I did not want for anything I needed. Now as a parent, I believe many signals give children false information about money. I need to be far more pragmatic in educating them. How can I expect my children to discover how to be responsible with money if I do not help them get direct experience?

The amount of the allowance should be age appropriate. Increases in an allowance should be discussed, never simply to match what a peer is receiving. I also believe that there are certain activities in the household—making one's bed, brushing one's teeth, taking out the garbage—that are simply part of being in a family. These responsibilities should not be tied to the allowance. However, other chores may be a part of their weekly "pay."

Allowances not only teach about spending, but about saving and giving as well. In an age of "instant everything," deferred gratification can be taught as admirable through saving. Whether it is a piggy bank or a formal savings account, we can help children discover the goal of not spending at a rate equal to, or in excess of, our earnings. For older children, the discovery of compound interest is a fascinating adventure!

Giving is a lesson to be learned as well. When my preschool son began to sit with me during morning worship, he asked, "Dad, why doesn't the choir have to pay?" A perceptive observation for a five-year-old that may help us rethink how we deal with money in worship! Should the pastor be observed placing an offering envelope in the plate every week? Should children be given offering envelopes of their own? In the children's time, should we begin to talk about dollars, rather than pennies? You probably already have guessed my answer is "yes" to all of the above.

Sharing and giving are not easy concepts to foster in children. A tremendous amount of intentional and consistent practice is necessary. Set an example. Explain why you give what you give. Help them to discover what happens because people give to charitable causes. Remember, children learn more easily from concrete examples than from abstract concepts. One exercise that may be helpful is to obtain literature on several projects that are sponsored by the church. Help your child decide which one they want to support, and what can happen when they share.

One of the most valuable lessons we can learn ourselves and teach our children is the difference between "wanting" and "needing." It is okay to "want" things and to understand how wants can be fulfilled. Many times this means saving, sacrificing, and being very disciplined. "Needing" should not be confused with wanting. Many adults have allowed themselves to become addicted to shopping because they have never identified the difference between the two concepts. Discover a teaching moment to help your children learn the difference.

My children are very fond of the fast-food "kid meals." They are packaged in brightly colored boxes and contain a trinket that lasts for about 8 to 10 miles beyond the restaurant. On one vacation trip, when they began to lament on the quality of the "prize," we spent some time talking about how they *needed* to eat, but *wanted* the "kid meal." The happy result of this experiment was an agreement to add the money saved by just buying the food, then going to a toy store to buy something special. It was not long before they realized that they did not need the "kid meal."

Much of what we say to our children about money is reflective of what we actually do with our own money. As we become more intentional about the economic education of our children, we may discover that it has changed our own habits as well.

 # TEACHING HELP

Who Am I as a Steward, and How Am I Doing?

BARBARA DEGROTE

The trouble with working with kids is that they are so honest. They see right through you. Young people in high school and beyond have the potential for a certain "gift" for sensing whether adults are being truthful. That's why they sometimes are so difficult to teach. It could be that they know when we are being less than fully honest.

All teachers, no matter how gifted, have moments when we teach above ourselves, moments when what we teach—especially in areas of faith—doesn't match "real life." In matters of faith, it's hard to tell the kids, "Do as I say, not as I do," and still feel good about the whole thing.

Does that mean we quit trying? Absolutely not. But it means that we quit fooling ourselves and our kids, and admit that we don't have all the answers. It means that we share our weaknesses as well as our strengths. It means that we "fess up" once in a while and ask forgiveness from our God and those we teach, knowing that the One who "began a good work in us will bring it to completion" (Phil. 1:6). And we keep teaching. Some call that "being faithful."

So what does all that have to do with stewardship?

It never hurts, once in awhile, to look in the mirror. Really look—not just a hurried glance to straighten out a few fly-away hairs—but a close-up inspection! How are we really doing?

How much of what we say we believe is actually reflected in some aspect of our lives?

Does our being a Christian affect anyone else?

Flip the mirror over to the magnified side. Don't feel alone if you cringe at this point. A good close inspection helps us to see who we are and where we are going. That's not all bad.

Let's focus the mirror on our "gifts"—all of God's abundance poured down upon God's children. How do we respond? How do we teach stewardship without first observing our own meager attempts? They'll see right through us. They always do. This is too important a topic to fake, teacher. So let's pull out those mirrors, flip them over, and have a good, honest look at the whole thing. And as usual, at moments like these, it's probably good to start with prayer:

> Lord God, I confess right now that I'm not up to this. Part of me would rather leave this topic to other teachers. But in the end, I can't avoid it; it's too important. Help me, Lord, to "come clean," confess my shortcomings and insecurities, and open myself up to whatever you have in mind. Teach me, Lord, to trust you. Amen.

At My Mother's Knee

We all have built-in responses, automatic actions that come from someplace in our childhood, learned more or less at our mother's knee.

You may have heard the story of the woman whose daughter asked her why she always cut her Christmas ham in two before cooking it.

"I'm not sure," she responded. "I guess because my mother always did it that way." Curious, the mother asked her mother the same question.

The grandmother laughed and explained, "I cut the ham in two pieces because I didn't have a pan big enough to cook the whole thing."

Where do our daily, sometimes automatic responses to God's gifts come from?

What generates either an affirming and warm "yes" or an arctic blast "no" from a person when they hear words like *giving, money,* or *sharing* your gifts?

From whom have we learned to say "please" and "thank you"?

Why do some have "worldly eyes" and others have "eyes for the world"?

"From generation to generation . . . I am God." What an amazing thought, that the God our great-great-grandmothers worshiped is the same God we now call Lord. Perhaps our ability to give thanks at all is not our own ability, but a gentle legacy passed down parent-to-child, parent-to-child, parent-to-child, again and again.

On the other hand, we need to acknowledge that many of us are still "cutting the ham in half," even though we have several pans big enough to hold the whole thing. In other words, isn't it possible that we are repeating spiritual habits mindlessly, just because someone else followed God a certain way? And if the good gifts can be passed down through the generations, can't we also assume that the bad habits—the "sins of the parents"—have now reached our generation? Affluence, or rather the need for affluence, has become addicting. Many of us toil to the point of exhaustion for the right to say, "It's mine!" We own possessions our grandparents never even dreamed of. Many luxuries of the past have become "needs" for the modern family. But how much do we really need? How much is really mine? Doesn't everything belong to God?

Barbara Remembers

My dad would sit down at the kitchen table on Saturday evenings. Writing a check. Putting it in the envelope. Setting it on the corner of the kitchen counter next to his car keys. That's it. He never said anything to my brother and me about stewardship, about giving to God, about the importance of sharing. He just did it. He never missed. He still does it. Every Saturday night. It's a powerful memory, and it goes on. I did not inherit my dad's organizational skills nor, more honestly, his faithfulness. I have been known to search my purse for a pen while the ushers were coming down the aisle, or to fill out my check for the offering while the pastor was recapping the Gospel lesson. If by some chance the plate went by before I finished—more times than I care to admit—that week's offering never made it anywhere.

But I still remember that envelope sitting by the car keys. And some weeks, I lay my own witness on the kitchen counter for my kids to see. I might even write a bigger check to "catch up." It's not a have-to. It's a want-to—something from my past that allows me to be faithful.

Images and Memories

Somewhere in your past are images and memories that encourage, in some small way, a need to respond to God's great goodness. Take a minute. Close your eyes. Breathe deeply several times. Remember yourself as a young child.

Watch yourself play. See how easily you enjoy the small things. Flowers. A pet. The feel of grass on bare feet. Enjoy them again.

Give thanks. Hear yourself singing. What are the words?

Bring to mind a specific scene. A teacher. Parent. Adult friend—someone whom your wise and discerning childlike spirit says is "real," "authentic," "trustworthy." To earn the trust of a child: That is success. Give thanks for this person. Notice them again. Their smile. What are they doing? Saying? Where do you think of them being? At church, home, school, outside somewhere? What specific thing reminds you of them? Zero in on it. Circle it with your childhood presence. It is their gift to you. A strong memory. Full of grace.

So what really makes us tick?

"See, this alone I found, that God made human beings straightforward, but they have devised many schemes" (Ecclesiastes 7:29).

It's a long trip to adulthood. We come into this world with nothing, and the first thing we need is a diaper bag to hold our stuff. Soon comes the overnight bag for trips to Grandma's, and before you know it, the full set of luggage as a graduation present. Then the first move. Remember? The small trailer that hooked on to the car's bumper? We moved last year, and it took their largest truck, and we still had to go back twice with smaller trailers. It there a pattern here? Where does it say that we are supposed to keep on accumulating?

We've seen a bumper sticker that says something like, "The one who dies with the most stuff wins." It's a bit funny and a lot sad. We all know better. Stuff does not make us happy. Jesus did not have a lot of stuff. Somewhere along the way from childhood to adulthood, somebody has told us that stuff is good. And the more stuff, the better.

What they didn't tell us is that all that stuff is in danger of keeping us from remembering our real purpose here: "Fear God, and keep his commandments" (Ecclesiastes 12:13). An excess of "stuff" takes time and energy away from the things that really matter to us: friend, family, faith. "Stuff" sets up a secret and unspoken agenda for us, in which we judge friendships by "Do they have as much stuff as we do?" or "Do they have more stuff than we do?" or "Are they into stuff at all?" Is this the "stuff" we are made of?

Jesus Clears the Air

Jesus really clears the air on the accumulation of wealth and possessions. Take a few minutes and read several of the passages listed below:

"Therefore I tell you, do not worry about your life, what you will eat or what you will drink, or about your body, what you will wear. Is not life more than food,

> "If you love only those who love you. . . . If you help only those who help you, what merit is that to you?"
>
> —LUKE 6:32, 33

and the body more than clothing? Look at the birds of the air; they neither sow nor reap nor gather into barns, and yet your heavenly Father feeds them. Are you not of more value than they?" (Matthew 6:25-26).

"[Jesus] called the crowd with his disciples, and said to them, 'If any want to become my followers, let them deny themselves and take up their cross and follow me'" (Mark 8:34).

"And the crowds asked him, 'What then should we do?' In reply he said to them, 'Whoever has two coats must share with anyone who has none; and whoever has food must do likewise'" (Luke 3:10-11).

"The Spirit of the Lord is upon me, because he has anointed me to bring good news to the poor. He has sent me to proclaim release to the captives and recovering of sight to the blind, to let the oppressed go free, to proclaim the year of the Lord's favor" (Luke 4:18-19).

Other passages you could look up are these from Matthew. Stop and listen. Do you sense a prompting? Allow the Spirit to speak Christ's will. If we say we follow Christ, doesn't it make sense to follow his teachings, too?

- ◆ Matthew 25:35-36
- ◆ Matthew 25:40
- ◆ Matthew 10:39-40
- ◆ Matthew 11:28-30

You may be tempted to pull the mirror away right now. We have, at times. We've tried to pretend Jesus wasn't really saying what he was saying. But inside we knew better. This is our Father's world. Not ours. We're just borrowing it. None of this "stuff" is ours. It's all a gift. And you know God; God has no favorite children. Why would God give one child more than another? God wouldn't, anymore than we would favor one child over another, putting one to sleep in a canopy bed, while another sleeps on the floor.

You know what we are being asked to do? We are being asked to share. We tell our kids to do it all the time. Are their toys or candy any more or less precious to them than our "stuff" is to us? Sharing—it's not just for kids anymore.

Activity: "Declutter"

Find ways to get rid of your excess "stuff" at home. "How much and what is the excess?" Good, you're thinking. You figure it out. Try to get your excess to others who don't have enough. You may be tempted to keep something by using the excuse, "But I may find a use for it sometime." Be honest. If you haven't used something in the past year or two, you probably won't use it in the future. (Donate quality goods—not junk—to the Salvation Army; recycle; have a thrift sale; and so forth. All are ways to make items available to people who can't necessarily afford the items new.) Before acquiring new things, clear out some room in your home (and in your heart) by "decluttering."

Coming Full Circle

"I do not understand my own actions. For I do not do what I want, but I do the very thing I hate" (Romans 7:15).

And so we teach above our ability to live. How can I teach sharing when my own ability to share so often falls short? The good news is just that, the good news! Turn those mirrors away from yourself now and direct them toward the face of Jesus. When a man was sick, his friends brought him to Jesus. When a daughter died, they went to get Jesus. Paul—in all his earlier ego-centered ways—was healed by an encounter with the living Lord. It still works today.

Faced with the humbling task of teaching stewardship to children, we do the best we can. We bring them to Jesus and let him take it from there.

Activities

The following activities can be done simultaneously after hearing the following story. The first suggests drawing illustrations for the story; the second offers questions to stimulate discussion while drawing.

1. Pass out paper and markers and have children of all ages help illustrate "The Eighth Day of Creation." Share your pictures in small groups. Mix ages as much as possible.

2. Ahead of time, prepare slips of paper for each table with the following questions. Ask participants to discuss them while they are drawing.
   a. Is God always serious?
   b. Why is "fun" an important part of stewardship?
   c. Does our church give its members an opportunity to respond to God's gifts through laughter? Is laughter an appropriate response?
   d. How do our church members express their enjoyment of each other?
   e. Do people think of our church as a "fun" place to come?
   f. Does our church know when to be "hard working and responsible" and when to have "fun"?
   g. When can good things like hard work and responsibility become a problem?

The Eighth Day of Creation
A STORY BY BARBARA DEGROTE

It was the eighth day of creation. God was feeling well-rested and satisfied with the newest project as it stood shimmering in its newborn freshness. Everything seemed to be in place. It was peaceful enough . . . and yet God gave pause. Something was amiss in the garden.

It was hard to pinpoint the problem exactly. God watched Adam and Eve going about their business—tending the animals and plants. They seemed happy enough, even content. God laughed for a moment, reminded that God tended to be a bit of a perfectionist. And then God knew.

What was missing in the garden was . . . laughter, something in which God took much pleasure. Those whom God created should find pleasure in creation. God enjoyed nothing more than to hear God's creation laugh and sing and clap their hands at the wonder of it all. This man and woman were so hardworking and responsible—good—but where was their sense of wonder? Where was the sound of laughter in the garden?

No matter. This could be fixed, for what good was creation without that fleck of imagination, that bit of humor, that loud laugh for which God would be famous?

And so God winked at a nearby brook, and the brook begin to giggle. Just a trickle of a giggle, mind you, but enough for both Adam and Eve to stop and scowl (for they hated to be interrupted in their work). And then God winked again, and the brook no longer could contain itself; tears of joy spilling out over its banks, it laughed incessantly.

Adam and Eve, noticing the unusual behavior, ran alongside the little river, trying to get it under control. But to no avail, for the river waters soon turned from a giggle to a chuckle, and then to a full-out roar of pleasure. And Adam and Eve could only watch as the now roaring river rushed forward and catapulted itself over a cliff, landing on the floor of an unsuspecting canyon, holding its sides as it roared uncontrollably in delight.

Adam and Eve stood quite mute at first, a little awed at the actions of one of their most reserved little brooks.

And then Adam clapped his hand over his mouth in surprise, as a hiccup of sorts escaped—not really recognizing his first efforts at a laugh, and not really sure he approved of such things anyway. But one had only to look at the little brook still smiling in the sunlight and be swept along too. You know how contagious laughter can be.

And Eve, swayed by Adam's influence, began her chuckle of sorts, and the man and the woman soon joined this laughter which the comedy of nature played out before them. There was joy, now uncontrollable as they watched the waters of the river rush toward the ocean, and the mountains broke forth into singing, and all the trees of the fields clapped their hands in joy.

"Now that's more like it," God said. "Now that's good. Very good."

So it was on the eighth day of creation that God made laughter, and once in a while, we still can catch some of those first joy-filled moments. The moments God first set into motion, those overtones that are awakened in us each time we hear a child at play, take time to come together in happy worship, or hold hands with those we love.

Activities

These activities can follow the story about the wife of Zacchaeus and can be done by different groups at the same time—a skit on the following story to be prepared by the younger children, questions for older children and adults to discuss, and a bulletin insert to be created.

1. Create a booklet with the responses of members to this unfinished question: "If Jesus came to my house I would _____." Print enough copies to hand out with bulletins. Have children illustrate their responses.

2. Have the younger children go to a separate area and prepare a skit of the Zacchaeus story. Use costuming and props. Present the skit to others in the group.

3. Discussion questions for older children and adults:
   a. What does the story of "The Wife of Zacchaeus" have to do with giving money to the ministry of the church?
   b. What is the difference between using our money and having our money use us?
   c. When we are loved, we realize that the purpose of life is not getting, but rather giving. Explain how this was true for Zacchaeus. How is it true for us?
   d. Jesus says, "I want to stay at your home today!" Why else would you part with your money to minister in his name?

The Wife of Zacchaeus

A STORY BY KEITH FORRESTER

We were young when we married. He was 17 and I was 15. Our parents had arranged our marriage. I wouldn't have chosen him, if it had been up to me. He came from a poor family and the prospects for his future looked pretty grim. He had no land. No money. No trade from which to make a living. He was a small man; manual labor wouldn't suit him. He wasn't the best prospective husband by any means. But I wasn't such a great catch either.

I came from a poor family, too. My parents had little for my dowry, and I wasn't particularly beautiful. I'm sure my parents worried that they might not be able to find any husband for me at all. They told me that Zacchaeus would be better than no husband. How's that for encouragement? They said I should be thankful that his parents had consented to the match. I think his parents probably told him the same thing. So we were married; two people whom no one else really wanted, joined together for life.

"The happiest people I know are those who have learned to live beyond their own special interests by discovering the rewards that come from giving of themselves."

—WINFIELD C. DUNN (1927–)

On the night of our wedding, Zacchaeus said to me, "I know that you didn't particularly want me for your husband, but I want you to know that I'm going to do everything I can to be a good husband to you. Nobody thinks we are going to amount to much, but somehow we're going to prove them wrong, and someday, Golda, you're going to be proud of me."

I began to love Zacchaeus that night, and I've loved him ever since, because he kept that promise. I've never known a man who worked so hard to take care of his wife. He'd take any job, no matter how hard it was, to keep a roof over our heads and food on the table. I'd get to feeling sorry for him, but he wouldn't feel sorry for himself. He'd say, "It's a dirty job, but someone's got to do it." And then he'd tell me, "Don't worry, Golda. We won't always be like this. Someday my break is going to come, and I'll be ready."

Life went on like that for a few years, and we struggled along as best we could. And then one day Zacchaeus came home all excited and said, "This is it, Golda! Finally, I've got a chance to make some real money."

I tried to talk him out of taking the job. It's true that a person could make a lot of money collecting taxes for the Romans, but everyone hated the tax collectors. They hated the Romans who ruled us, and they hated the Jews who helped the Romans. And everyone knew that a tax collector made his money by keeping what was left over after he had paid the Romans the amount they demanded that he collect. I didn't want Zacchaeus mixed up in something like that, but he said that our neighbors had always looked down on us anyway, so who cared what they thought? And he couldn't bear watching me always having to stretch to make ends meet. He said that it was high time he made enough money so that I could have life easier, and have some of the things I deserved.

So Zacchaeus became a tax collector, and he was good at it. Soon the Roman governor made him the chief tax collector for all of Jericho. And for the first time in our lives, we had some money. Zacchaeus loved to surprise me with presents: A new shawl, a gold bracelet. He even bought me a donkey to carry our water and firewood.

Our neighbors wouldn't talk to us anymore. Zacchaeus said they were jealous, and I shouldn't mind them. We were barred from the synagogue. We were told that a person couldn't consort with the Romans and be a good Jew. Zacchaeus told me we could pray at home. He wasn't going to let those hypocrites coerce him back into poverty.

We kept getting more and more prosperous. I have to admit that I liked not being poor anymore, but I worried about Zacchaeus. It seemed as if the more we got, the more he wanted. He said, "Nobody's going to look down on us ever again because we are poor." He had achieved what he had been working so hard for, and yet he wasn't a happy man.

And then one day everything changed. I was fixing lunch, and Zacchaeus came running in the door. He said, "Golda! Throw another potato in the pot. We've got company for dinner!" I'd never seen him so excited. I wondered who this guest could be? None of our neighbors would have anything to do with us, let alone eat at our table.

Zacchaeus brought a man into our kitchen and introduced us: "Golda! This is Jesus from Nazareth. Jesus, this is Golda, my wife." Zacchaeus stood there grinning as if he were entertaining royalty. I told the man that he was welcome, and got some water so that he could wash up for dinner. I took Zacchaeus aside and asked him who this man was. And he said that he was a preacher who had been doing all kinds of amazing things. And some people said that he was the new king of the Jews whom God had promised to send, and others said that he was a phony and a con man.

He said, "I wanted to see him for myself, and I heard he was traveling down the Jericho road, so I went out to see him, but there were so many people that I climbed up in a tree so I could get a look at him. He saw me in the tree, and he walked over and said, 'Zacchaeus, get down out of that tree, because I want to stay at your house today.' So, here he is!"

I asked, "Why did he want to come to our house?" and Zacchaeus answered, "I don't know. I guess he just likes us." Which didn't make any sense, seeing that he didn't know us, but I got the food, and we ate

> "I slept and dreamed that life was happiness. I awoke and saw that life was service. I served and found that in service happiness is found."
>
> *RABINDRANATH TAGORE
> (1861–1941)*

together, and visited, and I understood what Zacchaeus meant; Jesus just seemed to like us.

And then Zacchaeus did something I never thought I'd ever see him do. He stood up and he said, "Lord, I'm so happy that you came to visit us that I'm going to give half of all that I own to the poor, and if I've cheated anyone, I'll pay him back four times as much." Well, you could have knocked me down with a feather!

And then Jesus said, "Salvation has come to this house today. This man is a true son of Abraham. The Son of Man came to seek and to save the lost."

Our lives changed that day. We didn't have as much money anymore, but life was richer. I suppose you could say we learned that the purpose of life is not to get, but to give, and learning that changed us, which is true. But it was more than that. I asked Zacchaeus how he could part with all that money, and he said it was because he found something more important to him than money. A few weeks later, we heard that Jesus had been killed in Jerusalem. He was nailed to a cross and died asking God to forgive those who murdered him. Zacchaeus said that not even death could destroy love like that! They say that he rose from the dead. I didn't see him, but I don't doubt it. I don't doubt it a bit. I know that he gave Zacchaeus and me new life that day he came to our house and liked us. No, that's not strong enough; he *loved* us.

More Activities

1. Create a video. Pass out five videotapes to willing members and have them tape members "doing stewardship" throughout the week at their jobs, at home, at school, and throughout the community. Use your theme song, logo, and theme verse to tie it all together. Have a premier night and serve popcorn.

2. Do "A Day in the life of _____ Church." Have members take photographs of what is happening in their lives at a certain time on a certain date. Compile the best of these photographs into a booklet or video to be presented during the annual meeting or some other group gathering.

3. Call your local recycling center and ask them to arrive in front of the church at a specific time. Members would be waiting with their "Offering of Recyclables" to put in the "plate" (or truck in this case). If you do not have a recycling center that picks up, find someone who is willing to provide a truck to transport the items to the recycling center.

4. Have an "Alternative Travel" Sunday, when members come to worship by bus, bike, walking, by in-line skates, or ride-sharing. Help increase the awareness of the effect of travel on energy consumption by researching some statistics. You might use *Fifty Simple Things Kids Can Do to Save the Earth,* from The Earth Works Group (New York: Scholastic Inc., 1990).

5. Create a cookbook. Have an "Eat as the World Eats" Sunday. Each dish should demonstrate an example of an alternative protein source. Hold a potluck. Create a cookbook out of the different recipes shared.

6. Hold a "Haves and Have Nots" dinner. Feed only half of the group. The other half eats only if the first half shares.

7. Provide offering envelopes. If your congregation does not provide offering envelopes for children to use in Sunday school, consider doing so. Using envelopes will help children get into the habit of regular giving. A box of envelopes can be a child's reminder to take his or her offering to Sunday school.

8. Encourage alternative gift giving. Many of us struggle each year to find the perfect gift for the "person who has everything." Often we give and receive gifts that we do not need. Why not consider alternative gift giving at Christmas, and also at other times of the year when gifts are given? Sponsor an "Alternative Gift Giving Sunday" during Advent. Offer at least two different opportunities.
    a. Designate a number of agencies and charitable organizations that people can support financially. Make a gift card that says "A gift of money has been given in your name to _____ (name of organization or agency.)" Leave a space for the giver to sign the card.
    b. Along with this giving opportunity, consider having a sale of crafts made by people in

developing countries. Handmade items such as jewelry, toys, baskets, greeting cards, linens, and clothing are often offered for sale. Money from the sale of these items goes directly to the persons who make them. You may have an organization in your area that will send you a supply of these items on consignment. There also may be sheltered workshops in your area where persons with disabilities make items for sale. Check your public library to locate organizations in your area that provide items for sale.

9. Create a teacher resource file. Look around your church's educational building. Find leftover pieces of curriculum such as sticker sheets, student activity sheets and leaflets, audiocassettes. Find a place for these items and find a use for them. You may want to use old sticker sheets to make greeting cards. File posters and Bible story pictures by subject, and let teachers know that they can use these in their teaching. Record over old audiocassettes.

10. Recycle items for crafts. When doing crafts in educational classes, preschool, or day camps, consider using things that are donated. Stores may give you old wallpaper-sample books. Your local newspaper may donate end rolls of newsprint for use in your church. Have members save such things as egg cartons, plastic containers, milk cartons, and other items to use in making a variety of crafts. Have a box located at each entrance for donated items. Organize donated items in a closet that is easily accessible to teachers. Remind the members regularly of your need for donated items. Be good stewards of creation by reusing and recycling everything you can!

REASONS CHRISTIANS GIVE

BIBLE PASSAGE	*REASONS TO GIVE*
1 Corinthians 6:19-20	
2 Corinthians 8:8 and 8:24	
2 Corinthians 8:13	

2 Corinthians 9:8-11

_____

2 Corinthians 9:12

_____

Hebrews 13:15-16

_____

 TEACHING HELP

Generous People for Children

PHYLLIS HAIL AND TONYA KENNER

(Can be used as part of a Financial Commitment program.)

THE MAIN IDEA:

Generous people discover and invite all persons into the Christian fellowship.

Objectives

Children will

- recognize that God loves all people;
- invite persons to join them in church activities (S.S., worship, choir, etc.);
- feel included and help others feel included in the Christian fellowship.

Scripture

Luke 14:15-24 "The Great Banquet"

Theme Bible Verse

"Welcome one another, therefore, as Christ has welcomed you for the glory of God" (Romans 15:7).

Preparing to Teach

Read and study the Scripture: Jesus told this parable to show that God loves all people. It was hard for some people to believe that Gentiles and sinners would be included in the "big party" (La Fiesta Grande) given by God. People in Jesus' time were looking for an invitation to God's great feast—God's kingdom. However, when the invitation came, they turned it down! Being included in God's kingdom and the great banquet is the happiest thing that can happen to us! The Christian life should be colorful, filled with joy to appreciate the many different kinds of friends and activities. Help make this experience for the children a bright and meaningful time in their lives.

As you visualize the children who will be in your class and the space you have for working with them, adapt the session to meet your needs. Additional ideas at the end of the session may replace or expand your sessions. Be flexible and creative.

177

Supplies/Resources

Mobile supplies
Worship center supplies
Bibles
Invitations of various types
Pictures of people at gatherings
Name tags if needed
Streamers—party decorations
Party snacks (trail mix made of cereal,
  chips, nuts, candy, raisins, etc.)
Postcards and lists of inactive and potential members
Copies of the take-home sheets
Empty soda cans to cover
Contact or construction paper for covering cans

The Session Plan

Introducing the Session (10-15 Minutes)

1. Prepare the room: Place invitations of various kinds (birthday, wedding, cookout, etc.) and/or pictures (magazine, newspaper, etc.) gathered together around the room.

2. As the children arrive: Greet them by name (make name tags if needed). Encourage children to look at pictures and invitations, and decide what kind of invitation it is, what type of activities will take place.

3. Have children prepare offering cans by covering with contact or construction paper and adding label from take-home sheet. Set aside until closing.

4. Plan a Party: Divide into groups to plan a party— decorations, activities, food. (Party plans probably need to be limited to simple decorations, a game, and simple refreshments.)

Exploring the Bible Message (10-15 minutes)

1. Let the children know that we will be hearing stories and parables told by Jesus.

2. Sharing the Bible Story: Introduce the Bible lesson that tells of a party. Be familiar enough with the Scripture so that you can tell the story with the Bible in your hand. Ask children to listen for the different ways people responded to the party invitation.

3. After telling the story, introduce this simple song/chant/rap:

"We're having a party, won't you come? There'll be food and games and lots of fun! The only gift to bring is you. Plan to come! That's all you need to do!"

Ask children to remember the excuses in the Bible story. A child could lead into an excuse by saying, "I cannot come because . . . " Then as a group, chant the above "We're having a party . . . " Continue until all the Bible excuses are remembered. If children had been invited to the great feast, what excuses might they have given? Use chant and response, "I cannot come . . . " Then talk about the people who came and why they might have responded to the invitation. Use chant and "I will come because . . . . " Remember that the people who came were outcasts. They may have been sick, homeless, or hungry. They may have been considered bad people. They may have been lonely. Maybe they felt that nobody loved them!

Responding to the Bible Message (20-30 minutes)
"Making a Difference"

1. Make a list of people to invite to next session and practice how to invite them. (Teacher will need to provide a prospective list, with children adding others. Practice "You are invited . . . . " one on one.

2. Add the word "invite" to the mobile. (On reverse side, add a symbol of inviting—an invitation card or letter). Draw attention to how that would make a difference in the way the mobile looks, just as the invitations will make a difference to other people.

3. Offering: One way we can celebrate is through an offering of money. Challenge them to bring to the next session a penny for every pair of socks they have. Encourage them to invite their families to join in this offering. Share with them how the offering will be used.

4. Experience a party as time is available.

5. Remind children to take home "making a difference" offering can.

Additional Ideas

1. Plan a party for a time beyond the classroom. Invitations can be handmade. The party could be planned for those children not present, a younger children's class, or an older adult group.

2. Make invitations to remind children to invite others. Wording could be: You are invited to be a follower of Jesus. God loves you—you are invited to love others. Have glitter, markers, crayons, lots of "stuff" for decorations. Sturdy cardboard or tagboard could be used.

3. Invite a pastor to talk about communion and baptism in regard to invitation.

4. Send postcards to absent class members to invite to next session.

5. Bring in youth or rehearse with children to act out this session's Scripture.

6. Your ideas . . . .

TEACHING HELP

Generous People in Action: Youth Making a Difference

KEVIN BROWN

(Can be used as part of a Financial Commitment program)

WHERE'S IT AT?
ON A ROAD TRIP!

Preparation

Communications: The week before the event, send a letter to all your youth, informing them about the stewardship lessons and the importance of attending Sunday school. Let them know that if they do not attend Sunday school, they will be "kidnapped" by other members of the youth group!

Transportation: Estimate the number of absent youth for Sunday school next Sunday. Line up enough drivers to take youth on their "kidnapping" ventures.

Decorations: Prepare your youth room for a party atmosphere. Include streamers, balloons, and party favors for every youth you have on your youth roll.

Coordination: Communicate with the pastor and other stewardship leaders about coordinating youth plans with other stewardship plans.

Setting

Begin in youth classroom; move to "youth-nap" absent youth members; end in a space decorated for a party (this could be the location designated for the Celebration Sunday dinner, such as your fellowship hall).

WHAT'S THE WORD?
PARTIES, KIDNAPPINGS, AND BIG BUCKS

Scripture

Luke 14:15-24—The Great Banquet (Also known as the Big Party); Luke 15:1-10 and Matthew 18—The Parables of the Lost Sheep and the Lost Coin.

Key Points in Scripture

1. The father has a wedding party to which all kinds of people are invited. God is like a good shepherd. God is also like a poor woman.
2. The party celebrates the Son.
3. Many people, especially religious people, do not recognize the significance of the wedding banquet for the Son, and so go about their business as usual when invited to celebrate.
4. The father wants a great celebration/party so much that people are literally "dragged off the street" in order to fill the house! The good shepherd and the woman search persistently to find the important things they have lost.
5. In order for people to enter the party and enjoy the celebration with the Son, they must be prepared—they must be "wearing the right garment."

WHAT'S THE SCOOP?
EVERYBODY'S INVITED TO PARTY!

What is the Scripture saying to us today?

1. God wants to celebrate life with us. That celebration is made possible through the Son—Jesus Christ.

2. God loves us so much that God gave us Jesus Christ. God did not want to remain some far-off, aloof God, living up in the clouds, never to interact with us poor mortals.

3. We humans often assume that God is "way out there." And we try to reach God by working hard to gain acceptance and approval from God. Sometimes we do that through religious works. Often we judge ourselves by how well we do our religious works. Sometimes we judge ourselves by comparing ourselves to other people who are different from us, thinking that we are better than they. In the meantime, we may lose sight of the reason we do "religious work," which is to enjoy life with God and all the rest of creation. When given the opportunity to "party with God," we miss it altogether, because we are too busy with other less important activities in our life.

4. God is not choosy about who is invited to celebrate. As a matter of fact, anyone and everyone is invited to come.

5. Also, God acts persistently, almost to the point of desperation. Jesus the Son acts like a good shepherd, goes after the lost sheep, and doesn't stop until he finds him. The lost coin is so valuable to the woman that she searches high and low, leaving no stone unturned until it is found. That is how sincerely God wants everyone to be included in the party!

6. People need to be prepared for God's kind of party if they want to enter. They need to come with the right kind of spirit! God does not want party crashers! They must first be prepared to celebrate God's presence in the Son. They must recognize that religious practices are not the "ticket" to heaven, or to God. They must understand that no one is better than anyone else in God's eyes. And they must be prepared to celebrate with everyone else who attends God's party!

JUST DO IT!
THERE'S GONNA BE A PARTY!

Activity

Begin planning a big party to celebrate all the gifts God has given you.

Say, what now? Plan a party and get everyone there that you possibly can!

That's right. Plan a party celebrating God's gifts to us and invite everyone to attend. (You may want to have the party coincide with a celebration Sunday for the church's financial program.)

JUST DO IT!
KIDNAP YOUR YOUTH!

Activity

Before you make party plans, you don't want to leave out anybody in your youth group! From the very beginning, include everyone, because remember—everyone can make the difference!

How do you do that? Remember what happened at the Great Banquet? The servants were asked to go out and literally drag people into the party. That's what you need to do today!

Take the roll of everyone who is enrolled in your Sunday school class. Go now and kidnap (youth-nap) anyone who is absent today! That's right! Each of the youth should have received a note in the mail encouraging them to attend Sunday school class this morning. It also warned that if absent, a brigade of other youth would show up at the doorstep to drag them off to church. We want to keep our promises!

🐸 Pontius' Puddle

I WISH I HAD BACK ALL THE MONEY I EVER WASTED ON DUMB STUFF.

SO YOU COULD INVEST FOR THE FUTURE, SHARE WITH THE NEEDY?

NO, SO I COULD BUY ME SOME BRAND NEW DUMB STUFF!

SIGH, THE GRASS WITHERS, THE FLOWER FADES, BUT STUPIDITY AND SELFISHNESS JUST GO ON AND ON!

© Joel Kauffmann

How do you "youth-nap"? Very Carefully!

Determine how many youth are absent. Divide up into groups (preferably of two youth) with an adult driving for each group. Each of the groups will first call the absent youth, reminding him/her of the promise to youth-nap, and letting the youth know that a group is coming over to pick her/him up.

Special notes: You really don't want to embarrass or humiliate the "napped youth." The purpose is to let the youth know, first of all, that the church and the youth group are planning a big party. The youth need to know that they are missed and needed. The "napping" just underscores how much they are needed and that the party plans cannot proceed without them. When your group arrives for the "napping," remember that the parents also should have been aware of the "napping," so they know their youth will be in safe hands. Your "napped" youth simply may have forgotten about the promise in the note they received, or they may not have taken it seriously. At any rate, they may not be "ready." Emphasize that they don't need to be dressed up (just decent). Also be prepared to give them a ride home of they need one.

What if no one answers the phone when you call, and you know of no reason for them not to be at home? Go to their house anyway. Take with you something on which you can write a note telling of your visit, that you will phone them next Sunday if they are absent, and that they will continue to receive information in the mail about the upcoming party and other youth events. You also might want to take along some inexpensive gift symbolizing the upcoming party—a balloon, a festive card, or a candy bar.

JUST DO IT!
PLAN TO PARTY!

Activity

Plan the party. What will happen at this party?

Some of it will be left up to you and your youth leaders. But your church may be planning to have a big celebration. They will call it Celebration Sunday.

In worship, you will focus on celebrating all of God's gifts to us—including all the different kinds of talents that people have. And most important, you will celebrate the gift of Jesus Christ—that God came down from heaven and spoke to us very clearly through Jesus, to show us how to celebrate life! What a fantastic idea God had!

Everybody will be encouraged to think about their commitment to the church and to pray about growing in how they use their gifts and talents for others. After all, the best parties are those that involve a lot of different kinds of people with a variety of talents.

And of course you can't have a big bash without lots of tasty food. Your church will have a big dinner after the worship service and continue to celebrate the gifts that people bring to the church. You also will discover how much your church members plan to grow in their giving for the next year. You will be amazed!

So, what can the youth do? Lots!

Much of the planning for the church-wide celebration will be done through your stewardship leaders and your pastor. You will want to work with them to make sure that youth are involved in the process. But you also may want to plan a party sometime that same day, just for the youth group and your guests. Some ideas for youth party options include:

- Lock-in the night before Celebration Sunday. You might hold brief devotional and prayer times periodically through the night. Ask your pastor to give you information about the offices of prayer in the tradition of the church! Work with your choir director concerning music that might be appropriate for your prayer services.
- Have a pancake breakfast the morning of Celebration Sunday.
- Serve a separate luncheon menu for youth (like pizza, burgers, spaghetti, etc.).
- Continue the party afterward with various youth activities.
- Don't limit your fun to fellowship. Take the party spirit outside the church to others with some sort of afternoon service. Deliver some memento of the party—balloons, flowers, dessert, cookies, to:
  ◆ church members—Visit shut-ins, the sick.
  ◆ nonchurch members—Visit the nursing home, the hospital, the Salvation Army.

Activity

Plan to have the youth organize a "Design an Ad" contest.

What better way to get the word out about church activities than to advertise in your local paper! And what better way to involve your youth than to have a friendly competition!

Work with your pastor, the stewardship committee, and your communications committee to make sure you have the money to purchase the advertising space, have a coordinated plan to select your theme, and choose impartial people (perhaps the ad department from your local newspaper) to select your "winners."

You may publish as many ads as your church budget will allow you. One way to save money is to pool your resources with other local churches. They will be encouraged to utilize the same stewardship materials. You may wish to coordinate your ads with your theme for the week.

 # SMALL GROUP STUDY

Generous People: Adult Bible Study for Small Groups

DR. CHARLES G. TURKINGTON AND DR. RAY E. WEBSTER II

(Can be used as part of a Financial Commitment program)

The following material is one suggestion for a series of small-group Bible studies. You may use the Bible studies in the order presented here, or in the order that best suits the congregation or the particular group with which you are working.

These are only suggestions. They are prayerfully offered in the hope that they will be enriching to the spiritual growth of both the parish and the individuals who are part of the Bible study. It is hoped they will increase an understanding of God's love and our response to that love.

Lesson 1: How Are Christians to Give?

Materials:
—Bibles
—Newsprint
—Markers

Instructions:

On newsprint, draw a center line down the page: Head one side SCRIPTURE and the other side HOW CHRISTIANS GIVE. List the Scripture passages that appear below. Ask for a volunteer to read the first passage from Scripture; then have the group discuss why Christians give. List on the newsprint the reasons given. Continue for each Scripture according to the time allowed. As facilitator, you are responsible for keeping the group on track and keeping the discussion moving forward.

SCRIPTURE	*HOW CHRISTIANS GIVE* (Possible Answers:)
Deut. 16:10 and 1 Cor. 16:2	Give proportionately as God gives

Exodus 22:30	Give the first and best we have
Matthew 6:1-4	Give humbly and in secret
Matthew 6:33	Give first priority to the reign of God
Matthew 25:31-46	Give when there is a need or spontaneously
Luke 21:3-4	Give sacrificially
1 Corinthians 13:3	Give in love
1 Corinthians 16:2	Give systematically
2 Corinthians 8:2	Give generously
2 Corinthians 8:5-7	Give of yourself before giving your possessions
2 Corinthians 9:5-7	Give voluntarily and gladly

Lesson 2: Reasons Christians Give

Materials:
—Bibles
—Newsprint
—Markers

Instructions:

On newsprint, draw a center line down the page: Head one side SCRIPTURE and the other side WHY CHRISTIANS GIVE. List the scripture passages that appear below. Follow the same instructions as in Lesson 1. Again, some reasons the group may come up with are listed as possible answers.

SCRIPTURE	*WHY CHRISTIANS GIVE* (Possible Answers:)
1 Corinthians 6:19	God died for us; we belong to God

2 Corinthians 8:8
and 8:24   Proof of our love
2 Corinthians 8:13   Response to God's grace and gifts
2 Corinthians 9:12   Thanksgiving to God
Hebrews 13:15-16   Sacrifice to God

Questions:

1. What was Paul's life like before he met Christ?
2. Why is Paul thankful?
3. How did a relationship with Christ change Paul's life?
4. Why do you think Paul is writing this to Timothy?
5. When has your faith been shaken? What did you learn from your experience?
6. How is thankfulness important in a Christian sense?
7. What would you say to someone who is seeking God's mercy and patience?

Lesson 3: Ephesians 1:3-14

Materials:

—Bibles
—Newsprint
—Markers

Instructions:

On newsprint, make two columns titled: BLESS-INGS and PAUL'S RESPONSE. Ask the group to name the blessings that Paul identifies in this passage and Paul's response to those blessings.

Then, on another sheet of newsprint, divide the paper into four columns and titles: 1. VERSE; 2. GOD THE FATHER; 3. JESUS CHRIST; 4. HOLY SPIRIT. Go verse by verse, and write the words that describe the work or activity of each person of the Trinity. There may be verses that describe only one or two persons of the Trinity.

Questions:

1. What does this say about God?
2. What does this say about God's relationship with us?
3. What does this say about what God wants us to do, or about our goals?

Read the following, and ask the group to reflect this week on their special God-given gifts, and how they are to be used to God's glory:

Each of us is special. Each of us has a different and wonderful blending of talents, skills, and traits that makes us unique. Creativity, leadership, compassion, care, motivation, intelligence and insight—qualities such as these set us apart and define who we are.

These are the intangible gifts in our lives, and they are given to us by God. Because we are God's children, we are free to use these gifts and to enjoy them. We have the ability to make choices in our lives about what we create, how we live, how we care for the world around us, and how we relate to others.

The most important of God's gifts to us is the gift of God's love. God invites us into a closer relationship. As we give ourselves to God, God opens our eyes to see more clearly what we are created to be. As we recognize God's special gifts to us, we also discover our own individual and unique role in God's world. We begin to understand God's purpose for us.

As well as our intangible gifts from God, we are blessed by our individual talents. Over our lifetime, we discover the skills, abilities, and traits that make us unique. All of us are different from one another, yet each of us is special in God's eyes. Using our God-given talent for God's service is an outward and visible response to God's love for us.

Lesson 4: Genesis 1:1–2:1

Materials:

—Bibles
—One NRSV or RSV Study Bible

Instructions:

Read the background to the Pentateuch and Genesis in the study Bible. Read Genesis 1:1–2:1 aloud, with a new reader for each new day.
Questions:

What is happening in this passage?

Instructions:

Reread verses 26-31

Questions:

1. What responsibilities has God given humankind?
2. What are some ways we can fulfill these responsibilities?

3. What grade would you give the human race in this area? Why?
4. How can you make a habit of fulfilling these responsibilities as stewards for the Lord? What can you do on a daily basis?

Read the following for closure:

Think back. Can you remember clutching a new toy or a birthday present, or holding for the first time your new kitten or puppy?

Do you hear in your memory a parent's voice saying, "That's a special gift. You'll have to take very good care of it?" That admonishment applies to much in our adult lives as well. We are entrusted with so much more, and therefore are responsible for so much.

Psalm 24 reminds us: The earth is the Lord's and all that is in it. We have been given the special gift of our earth and all that God created on it. We can see God's hand in the pure, crisp air that sustains our very lives; the crystal clear water that refreshes us; the rich soil that produces our nourishment. We marvel at the abundance of God-made creatures sharing this home with us.

Are we living in harmony and balance with our physical environment? As we hurry through our modern, high-tech lives, we must pause to remember that all things on and of this earth belong to God. We are simply the stewards of the gifts that God has entrusted to our care.

Let us reflect and ask ourselves if we are being good stewards of the earth and its gifts entrusted to us.

 # MEDITATION

The Statement on Stewardship of The Episcopal Church

Our vocation to be stewards is at the heart of the biblical revelation which acknowledges God as the gracious giver of all things. One task of the church, then, is to become as fully as it can actually be what God has already made us to be—namely, givers like himself. This is one of the most profound truths about ourselves. It is not something that we could have learned by sitting down and figuring it out. The truth itself is a gift from God.

It is the faith of the people of God that God had made us, the world, and all that is in it. The world and our very lives are gifts of God. This faith calls us, then, to be stewards of ourselves, of our brothers and our sisters, of all that we have received, and of the world itself.

That we are accountable for our use of the gifts of God is no grim truth at all. It is rather a great joy; for to be held accountable is to be treated as being of great worth. We are, then, stewards of the worth which God has conferred upon us. The stewardship of our lives and of our deaths embraces the joy we find in our own worth.

We are stewards of the mysteries of God, as we are stewards of the gospel of God. We are also the brothers and sisters of all God's children. The hungry, the naked, the prisoner, the dispossessed, the tormented, the thirsty: All have been placed within our stewardship. Being stewards requires us to find the strategy and a means for giving ourselves to the needs of all of our brothers and sisters. To do the work of evangelists, it is not enough to proclaim God and God's gifts. Stewards give gifts. They give their resources. That means that the steward gives his or her life. To give one's life is to give one's time, one's hours and days; it is to give one's capacities of whatever human strength he or she may possess; and it means one's money. One cannot be a steward if one does not also give whatever it may be by which one measures wealth.

> "Only to a very limited degree do we strengthen values by talking about them. Values live or die in everyday action."
>
> —*JOHN W. GARDNER (1912–)*

PART SEVEN

BIBLIOGRAPHY AND BIOGRAPHY OF WRITERS

For the Church Library or Resource Center

Introduction

NORMA WIMBERLY

Today, worshiping communities are blessed with a wealth of books and other resources to support the funding of ministry. None of us could possibly read, reflect upon, and use all of them.

The editors asked each of the contributing writers to *The Abingdon Guide to Funding Ministry* to name one or two books they believe are "classics"—books that had a major impact on their lives and ministries. The bibliography provided here is intended for support as you continue to grow into the joy, of giving. Some of the entries also appeared in the first two volumes of the *Guide*. Good news bears repeating!

The resources listed include material for financial commitment programs to be used by local congregations. This list is provided for information and does not imply an endorsement or recommendation.

Don and I pray that your adventure in funding ministry is exciting, satisfying, and filled with spiritual wonder. The apostle Paul reminds us that stewards are required to be trustworthy (I Cor. 4:2), rather than successful. We hope you will be trustworthy, keep the faith, and believe that success is possible, in God's way, and in God's time.

Books and Resource Reviews
(Vol. 3)

Barrett, Wayne C. *The Church Finance Idea Book.* Nashville: Discipleship Resources, 1989, pb. 157 pp. ISBN 0-88177-065-5.

Explains ten strategies for commitment campaigns, yet the author offers hundreds of other techniques and methods. Addresses financial administration, fund-raising, capital projects, and planned giving.

—————. *More Money, New Money, Big Money.* Nashville: Discipleship Resources, 1992. pb. 159 pp. ISBN 0-88177-120-1.

In this follow-up to *The Church Finance Idea Book*, Barrett shows that every congregation has significant sources of new and untapped income. More money: increasing results from current sources; new money: discovering new and untapped sources; big money: learning to cultivate major gifts and bequests.

Bauknight, Brian K. *Right on the Money.* Nashville: Discipleship Resources, 1993. pb. 102 pp. ISBN 0-88177-122-8.

This preacher and leader offers sixteen messages for preaching, grouped in four areas that reconnect stewardship with the candor, humor, and biblical depth of Christian spiritual formation: Basic Christian Formation, Toward Tithing, Capital Campaigns, and Words of Encouragement.

Block, Peter. *Stewardship: Choosing Service Over Self-interest.* San Francisco: Berrett-Koehler Publishers. pb. 264 pp. ISBN 0-881052-28-1.

While this book was written for application to business and industry, the church leader will quickly see that the church's word has been used more faithfully than the church uses it. Throughout, one can see biblical stewardship principles (without calling them that) put to work within the setting of everyday life in business and industry. An eye-opener!

Grimm, Eugene. *Generous People: How to Encourage Vital Stewardship.* Nashville: Abingdon Press, 1992. pb. 153 pp. ISBN 0-687-14045-5.

Grimm closes his book with "A Checklist for Vital Stewardship," questions for congregations to ask about the presence and effectiveness of their financial stewardship programs. The author's narrative stresses the importance of biblical foundations, clear definitions, planning, the individual's need to give, a variety of approaches to commitment, and pastoral leadership.

Hall, Douglas John. *The Steward: A Biblical Symbol Come of Age.* rev. ed. Grand Rapids: Wm. B. Eerdmans, 1990. pb. 145 pp. ISBN 0-8028-0472-1.

In this stewardship classic, Dr. Hall explores the biblical symbol of the steward through the ages and calls upon the church in North America to reappropriate this important theological concept.

——————. *Imaging God: Dominion as Stewardship.* Grand Rapids: Wm. B. Eerdmans/New York: Friendship Press, 1986. pb. 248 pp.
ISBN (Eerdmans) 0-8028-0244-3.

This scholarly book argues that our current ecological crisis forces us to reexamine the relationship between humanity and God. What does it mean to be created in the image of God?

Joiner, Donald W. *Christians and Money: A Guide to Personal Finance.* Nashville: Discipleship Resources, 1991. pb. 128 pp. ISBN 0-88177-096-5.

In a world of market pessimism on the one hand, and get-rich-quick schemes on the other, we need a clear sense of the Christian principles for sound financial planning and freedom. In practical terms, Joiner explores these and other issues that concern Christians and their money. Each chapter includes focus questions and exercises. This resource can also be used as a group study.

Joiner, Donald W. and Wimberly, Norma. *The Abingdon Guide to Funding Ministry, Vol. 1.* Nashville: Abingdon Press, 1995. pb. 159 pp. ISBN 0-687-00477-2.

A source book for pastors and church leaders, this volume focuses on developing a perspective on giving. It is designed to assist leaders of the congregation in soliciting, managing, and utilizing gifts and other revenue effectively and appropriately. Compiling materials from experts in a number of denominations, Joiner and Wimberly offer motivation for giving, scriptural understanding, the latest legal information, suggestions for better accountability, worship helps, and stewardship education designs. A plan for a financial commitment campaign is included.

——————. *The Abingdon Guide to Funding Ministry, Volume 2.* Nashville: Abingdon Press, 1996. pb. 158 pp. ISBN 0-687-01989-3.

Like Volume 1, this "almanac for good stewards," contains numerous features to produce a positive attitude toward giving. The theme of Volume 2 is teaching the joy of giving. It contains more than 250 items, organized by function, including: Money Talks; Devotionals; Newsletter Copy; Sermon Helps; Calendar Worksheets; Small Group Studies; Dramas; Planning Tools, and more.

Lawson, Douglas M. *Give to Live: How Giving Can Change Your Life.* La Jolla, Calif.: ALTI Publishing, 1991. pb. 195 pp. ISBN 0-9625399-9-6.

Lawson's book addresses the spiritual malaise of North America, explores the spiritual, emotional, and physical benefits of giving, and offers ways to get involved—with both time and money. The author's "Giving Path" is outlined to cover giving as a vital part of living all of life, from early childhood through the several stages of adulthood.

Meeks, M. Douglas. *God, The Economist.* Minneapolis: Fortress, 1989. pb. 257 pp. ISBN 0-8006-2329-0.

The author assesses our current situation through theological critique and offers the lens of God's "law of the household." Economics, politics, and theology march hand in hand as Meeks centers his argument on a social conception of the Trinity.

Messer, Donald E. *A Conspiracy of Goodness: Contemporary Images of Christian Mission.* Nashville: Abingdon Press, 1992.
pb. 176 pp. ISBN 0-687-09484-4.

Roop, Eugene F. *Let the Rivers Run: Stewardship and the Biblical Story.* Grand Rapids: Wm. B. Eerdmans, 1991. pb. 108 pp. ISBN 0-8028-0609-0.

Roop offers a highly readable book that includes questions for group study. He uses stories and symbols from Genesis and Exodus to focus on biblically grounded stewardship.

Wimberly, Norma. *Putting God First: The Tithe.* Nashville: Discipleship Resources, 1988.
pb. 56 pp. ISBN 0-88177-058-2.

Usually we give only our leftovers to God, because we forget that all creation belongs to God. The author helps individuals and small groups learn about tithing in Old Testament times, and what Jesus has to say about giving with a joyous heart. One section offers testimonies from persons in all walks of life concerning their adventure with the tithing principle.

Biography of Contributors

Edsel A. Ammons was elected Bishop of the United Methodist Church in 1976. He served as Bishop of the Michigan Area from 1976 to 1984, when he was reassigned to the Ohio West Area. He served as Bishop in Ohio until his retirement in 1992. Previously he served on the faculty of Garrett-Evangelical Theological Seminary, and as a parish pastor.

Donner B. Atwood is a retired Reformed Church of America minister. He and his wife Anne live in their retirement home on Cape Cod.

Wayne C. Barrett is Executive Director of The United Methodist Foundation of the West Michigan Conference. He is the editor of the *Clergy Finance Letter* and the author of several best-selling books on church finance.

Brian K. Bauknight, pastor of Christ United Methodist Church in Bethel Park, Pennsylvania, is also a noted lecturer, author, and stewardship presenter.

Bradley G. Call is pastor of Roscoe United Methodist Church in Coshocton, Ohio. He has been chairperson of the East Ohio Conference Stewardship Committee since 1992. Call is currently completing work toward a Doctor of Ministry degree in Christian Stewardship from Garrett-Evangelical Theological Seminary.

Dan R. Dick is Director of Stewardship Ministries and Congregational Leadership for The United Methodist General Board of Discipleship in Nashville, Tennessee. The author of *Choices and Challenges: Stewardship Strategies for Youth,* he is currently working on resources and programs related to pastoral leadership in stewardship, a stewardship theology, and a holistic year-round stewardship program.

Lee Domann, an ordained United Methodist minister, is a singer, songwriter, and storyteller. He and his wife, Norma Wimberly, own *The East Row Group,* a music publishing, consulting, and editing service based in Nashville, Tennessee.

Timothy C. Ek is Vice President of The Evangelical Covenant Church, which includes the position of Director of the Covenant's Department of Stewardship. Dr. Ek serves on the Board of Directors of the Ecumenical Center for Stewardship Studies.

J. William Gray, Jr. is a partner in the law firm of Hunton & Williams located in Richmond, Virginia. Hunton & Williams also has offices in New York, Washington, D.C., North Carolina, Tennessee, Georgia, Belgium, Poland, and Hong Kong. Mr. Gray specializes in Estate and Tax Law.

Sharon Hueckel is the Director of Development for the Roman Catholic Diocese of Lafayette-in-Indiana. She serves on the board of directors for the National Catholic Stewardship Council.

Donald W. Joiner is Director of Stewardship in The United Methodist Church. He is the author of several books on finance, with more than 20 years of financial consulting experience with many denominations.

Norma E. Koenig is a well-known author of books and articles for parents, teachers, and children. For many years, she was editor of *Jed Share* magazine published by United Church Press. She has published work with eight different denominational presses, and is currently adjunct faculty at Lancaster Theological Seminary.

Glenna and Roy Kruger have coauthored a variety of articles on leadership. Glenna is a Human Resource Development Manager for a Fortune 500 Corporation. Roy is a research and program evaluator for a nonprofit educational research organization.

Donald E. Messer, President of The Iliff School of Theology, Denver, Colorado, has been a member of the World Methodist Council since 1986. Dr. Messer is the author of seven books and a variety of articles.

Frank D. Mylar, Jr., is General Counsel for the Utah Department of Corrections and Assistant Utah Attorney General. He is also a Research Fellow for the Institute for Ministry, Law, and Ethics.

John A. Sapora is an Institute Fellow for the Institute for Ministry, Law and Ethics and currently practices real estate and land-use law in Jacksonville, Florida. He is an ordained elder in the Presbyterian Church (USA).

Betsy Schwarzentraub, a clergy member from California, served as a pastor for sixteen years. She is now a church consultant to denominational leaders and individual congregations.

Chris Stockwell-Goering serves congregations of the United Church of Christ in the United States as Steward for Personal Stewardship of the Stewardship Council. He is responsible for working with all the conferences in the Western Region.

Thomas F. Taylor is the author of *Seven Deadly Lawsuits: How Ministers Can Avoid Litigation and Regulation*, by Abingdon Press. He is a litigation attorney and an ordained minister in the Presbyterian Church (USA).

Patricia Wilson-Kastner is rector of the Church of St. Ann and the Holy Trinity, Brooklyn. The Rev. Dr. Wilson-Kastner is the Dean of St. Mark's Deanery of the Brooklyn Archdeaconry of the Diocese of Long Island, and Vice-President of the founding board of the George Mercer Memorial School of Theology.

Norma Wimberly is a teacher, writer, and editor. She and her husband, the Reverend Lee Domann, own The East Row Group, based in Nashville, Tennessee.